Philosophies
of
Art and Beauty

Philosophies
of
Art and Beauty

Introducing Aesthetics

Hugh Bredin and
Liberato Santoro-Brienza

EDINBURGH
University Press

© Hugh Bredin and Liberato Santoro-Brienza, 2000

Edinburgh University Press Ltd
22 George Square, Edinburgh

Typeset in Sempel Garamond by
Pioneer Associates, Perthshire, and
printed and bound in Great Britain by
The University Press, Cambridge

A CIP Record for this book is available
from the British Library

ISBN 0 7486 1191 6 (paperback)

The right of Hugh Bredin and Liberato Santoro-Brienza
to be identified as authors of this work
has been asserted in accordance with
the Copyright, Designs and Patents Act 1988

Contents

Preface   vii

Foreword   *Brian Fallon*   ix

1   Introduction and Definitions   1

2   From Altamira to Athens: The Ancient World   14

3   From Byzantium to Chartres: The Middle Ages   45

4   From the Renaissance to Idealism: The Modern Era   67

5   From Hegel to Semiotics: Art and Crisis   86

6   The Arts   105

7   The Art of Literature   116

8   The Dramatic Arts   138

9   Music   163

10   The Visual and Plastic Arts   189

Bibliography   210

Index   221

Preface

Two of the presuppositions of this book are of particular importance. One is that the philosophy, poetics, history, criticism, semiotics and practice of the arts belong together. Methodologically and actually they may be separate, but beneath their differences they flow together to constitute a single, seamless expression of the human spirit. The second presupposition is that this seamless expression remains seamless across the centuries. The art of the past is as available to us as the art of the present. So also are the reflections on art of past generations, whether philosophical, poetical, historical or critical, or indeed of any other kind. The authors do not accept the cultural imperialism of the present over the past. The past is other than, and an alternative to, the present, but, in the case of the arts and of philosophical reflection, it is not superseded by the present. The thoughts of Aristotle, Plotinus, Aquinas, Hegel or Hanslick about the arts are just as 'relevant' to us as books coming hot off the academic presses. The ways in which the arts were experienced by our ancestors are constantly available to us, both intellectually and imaginatively, and they have the priceless value of revealing to us the limitations of our own.

The idea for this book originated after the completion by Liberato Santoro-Brienza of an undergraduate's introduction to Aesthetics, produced in 1996 for the National Distance Education Centre of Dublin City University. We are grateful to the Centre for allowing us to retain, in this book, ideas and formal elements present in the notes written for its students.

The book is a collaborative enterprise that marks the fruition of many years of personal and intellectual friendship and a profound community of interests. Our thanks go to Jane Feore and, in particular, Carol Duncan of Edinburgh University Press. We also thank the Arts Faculty of University College Dublin, for a small financial subsidy to assist in the preparation of this work. So far as intellectual debts are concerned, there are so many that they cannot all be listed. But we would like to mention in particular Rosario Assunto, Luigi Pareyson (both now deceased) and, above all, Umberto Eco, who is marvellously alive and well and a continual inspiration to both of the authors.

For the translations of quoted text, where possible we have used standard English translations (as listed in the Bibliography); all other translations are by Liberato Santoro-Brienza. We also thank Isabel Bredin for translations from the Pre-Socratic *Dialexeis*.

The authors wish to thank their wives, not only for their beauty and intelligence, but also for their support while this book was gestating and coming into the light of day. We are happy, now, to dedicate it to both of them.

Hugh Bredin and Liberato Santoro-Brienza

Foreword

Brian Fallon

Art and philosophy have often been unhappy bedfellows, so much so in fact that a possible divorce seems periodically to have threatened their relationship, or at least a separation *a mensa et thoro*. The philosopher and the artist appear to stand too far apart from one another to allow for genuine, sustained understanding and mutual sympathy, yet much too close to permit mere indifference or neutrality. This intermittent hostility can be found as early as the early, pre-Platonic Greek philosophers, with whom it mainly shows itself in the form of gibes at Homer and at poets in general. And who does not know that Plato in his *Republic* excluded most artists and poets from his ideal community? Yet Plato was also a gifted poet in his own right, and in other – and better – Dialogues he discourses as eloquently on the arts as anyone in history has ever done.

This curious duality is a recurrent feature among thinkers, including – as this book shows – Kierkegaard, who himself was a considerable literary artist. As that fine writer and musician, Cecil Gray, wrote seventy years ago in his (badly neglected) *History of Music*:

> It certainly could not for a moment be denied, even by their most fervent admirers, that the vast majority of those who are by universal consent regarded as the greatest thinkers of all time cut a very sorry figure indeed when they attempt to explain or define the nature and *raison d'être* of art. Aesthetics, indeed, is perhaps of all possible fields of philosophic enquiry the one in which most nonsense has been talked and written. There must, one feels, be something about art which completely upsets philosophic equilibrium. However much at his ease the sage may be with those plain and homely sisters, the Good and the True, he is completely *bouleversé* when he is suddenly confronted with that fascinating and enigmatic third sister, the Beautiful. In fact he seems to lose his head, and to behave in much the same way as when he encounters her in real life, in concrete female form. It is almost pathetic to see the way in which he becomes either fatuously ecstatic or puritanically disapproving,

according to his temperament; he either falls at her feet in adoration, like Schelling or Bergson, or, more often, calls her a slut and turns her out of the house like Plato or Tolstoy.

In many cases this antipathy of the sages and wise men appears to arise out of their difficulty in fitting art securely into any overall, balanced moral system, or even into any system of ultimate values. The almost automatic hostility of Puritans and utilitarians may be taken for granted, more or less, since from their respective viewpoints art is either a corrupting influence which endangers man's moral behaviour, or a frivolous diversion from the tough realities of existence. The hostile stance of so many fine thinkers over the centuries, however, has a much deeper psychological and spiritual root and has also been stated in far more considered terms. Yet against this, who has written better and more illuminatingly about aesthetic matters than such thinkers as Schopenhauer, Nietzsche, Leon Shestov, Ortega Y Gasset, Heidegger, Croce, to mention only a select few?

This book for which I have been asked to contribute a Foreword is a bold, erudite, insightful and witty attempt to fill a void in English writing. Why English thinkers as a whole (there are exceptions) have fought so shy of the matter, at least in recent centuries, is something which is rather too complex to discuss here. But the separation of theory from practice seems to me a thoroughly wrongheaded and even dangerous heresy, since ultimately the one cannot exist without the other. To state what is fairly obvious, without a theory of architecture there could be no architecture beyond mud cabins, and without a theory of government no state could be governed effectively for any reasonable period of time. Engineering and virtually all fields of science similarly depend on theory and its application. In most fields of human activity, in fact, thought has preceded action, or at least played a decisive role in it. Our modern system of democracy, for instance, existed in theory before it was ever applied in practice and was discussed, written about and argued over for many years before it became established fact.

People who despise theory, or affect to despise it, are merely acting according to the theories of others who have done their thinking for them, though they rarely realise this and usually are very reluctant to admit it. They not only register themselves as intellectual philistines, they also reveal a crippling lack of self-knowledge. Virtually all pragmatic knowledge is the fruit of previous theorising; civilisation is not built on pure instinct. With the arts, the position is similar. Great periods of art and literature were almost always great periods of thought and criticism as well – and criticism is simply aesthetic theory, or theories, applied *in concreto* to individual works of art. Sometimes the best and most trenchant criticism is produced by the writers and artists themselves, as in the cases of Racine and Boileau during France's *grand siècle*, or by Pope and Dryden in England. In art as in life, very little of real value is achieved without hard, precise thinking.

Speaking as someone who was a practising art critic for thirty-five years, I can only wish that I had had the guidance of a book such as this. To write criticism without a definite intellectual setting and background, or basis of thought, is too much like flying blind, as I recognise now and (though only intermittently) recognised then. But what applies to the critic applies much more forcibly, and on a higher level, to the artist or writer. Fortunately, a number of them have risen to the challenge, most notably Delacroix whose *Journals* are not only a literary masterpiece but a considered attempt to establish or codify a whole philosophy for painters, both practical and theoretic. There is no equivalent in English – Haydon's *Journals* do not measure up to it either as literature or philosophy, and in any case Haydon was too marginal a figure.

Coleridge had all the necessary qualifications to produce a definitive work on poetics, but he diffused his energies in heterogeneous writings or else spent them in continual talk. Keats's letters and certain essays by Shelley, such as his *Defence of Poetry*, contain many splendid insights, but not a coherent system of aesthetics. Among all of the early English Romantics, perhaps the most complete and satisfying writings in this field are contained in Landor's *Imaginary Conversations*. Unlike many or most of his fellow-countrymen, Landor took ideas seriously and the dialogue form he uses allows for the thrust and counter-thrust of constructive debate. Certain of Hazlitt's essays, too, in spite of their short timespan contain genuine efforts to come to terms with first principles in art and literature.

The present book, I assume, is largely addressed to students of aesthetics, but that does not exclude a more general readership – in fact anyone who cares about the history of ideas and the eternal relevance of art in our lives can profit by it. It ranges over classical times, with Plato and Aristotle prominent (and of course Plotinus too). It deals learnedly and wittily with the intellectual stances and theories of medieval and Renaissance times. Then it progresses to the modern age which may conveniently be said to start with Hegel. Or perhaps it really started with Kant, as no less a man than Goethe (a mighty thinker in his own right as well as a great poet) realised in retrospect. In a letter to his composer-friend Zelter, dated January 29th, 1830, Goethe wrote:

The world – and I may include myself – is infinitely indebted to our old Kant for the energetic way in which he ranges art and nature alongside each other in his *Critique of Judgment* and accords to both the right to act from great principles, without purpose . . . Nature and art are too great to envisage purposes. They can do well without [them].

In these words, so it seems to me, we have an entirely new attitude (well, perhaps not entirely new, since glimmers of it have appeared in all great ages) concerning the basic autonomy of art and the arts. For centuries they had been largely the handmaid of religion and politics, or the ornament of courts and the aristocratic boudoir, or celebrations of the deeds of great men in peace and war. It was not generally understood, or allowed, that art lived off its own primal energy and did not depend for its validity on the various creeds or codes of value which it had served so well over the centuries. Later in the nineteenth century, as this liberating process slowly advanced, it gave rise to furious debates in which the artist's right to create independently of morals or utility, and free from any obvious aim of bettering society and human nature, was challenged and often condemned by many people who viewed this as a declaration of irresponsibility and amorality. The artist, as they saw it, was claiming a place apart from and above society in general, and the phrase 'ivory towers' came more and more into currency. Yet in spite of loud jeers from moralists and social reformers, traditionalists and crusading journalists, and the whole massed phalanx of public stupidity, the process could not be stopped once its initial momentum had been generated.

This independence, to a great extent, was the fruit of the Romantic Movement, though it had its roots farther back than that (just as many of the socio-political freedoms we take for granted nowadays had their origin in the French Revolution and, further back, in the *philosophes* who were its prophets). In the first half of our century there was a violent reaction against 'aestheticism' as it had come to be called, but if I have read the score correctly, this reaction in turn has been discredited and we are now slowly turning back to the Romantics and their concept of individual liberty applied to artistic creation. Almost anyone who looks over the many cases in the last sixty years or so in which writers and artists (many of them highly gifted) have thrown their talents into the political arena, must admit it has been a sad business on the whole. Sick and tired of their own individuality – the most precious thing they possessed – they were prepared to sacrifice it on what Salvador de Madariaga has called 'the altar of collectivism'.

In middle and late Victorian England the labours of Ruskin, William Morris and other brave prophets drove a wedge of artistic awareness into the stolid roast-beef-and-broadcloth philistinism of the middle classes in particular (the aristocracy by then had largely forfeited their old position as patrons). For a time England, always a creative country but usually a philistine one, became as culture-conscious as France or Germany. To an extent, however, this aestheticism was always a foreign body and with the jailing of Oscar Wilde for homosexuality, the average philistine felt avenged on the Arty Set and what he saw as its subversive affectations. On the Continent, however, the intelligentsia in almost every country felt itself involved in his downfall and Wilde became a martyr-hero of art in France, Belgium, Austria and various other countries. In the eyes of many people today, his wit and frivolity and the fact that he was a successful writer of comedies still over-shadow or even veil the fact that Wilde was an exceptionally clear, even innovative thinker on aesthetic questions. For instance, in the dialogue between two young men entitled *The Critic as Artist*, Gilbert says to his friend Ernest:

> Aesthetics are higher than ethics. They belong to a more spiritual sphere. To discern the beauty of a thing is the finest point to which we can arrive ... Aesthetics, in fact, are to ethics in the sphere of conscious civilisation what, in the sphere of the external world, sexual is to natural selection. Ethics, like selection, make existence possible. Aesthetics, like sexual selection, make life lovely and wonderful, fill it with new forms, and give it progress, and variety and change.

Elsewhere in his writings, Wilde remarks that he is sick and tired of people telling him that beauty is superficial; in his opinion, it is far less so than the morality preached and practised by millions. True beauty, in fact, is lasting whereas most moral systems decay inevitably by the nature of things and the advance, or at least the change, of human thought and behaviour. In historical retrospect, this 'religion of beauty' is one of the most remarkable productions or developments of the whole nineteenth century. Amongst other things, it produced a new type of solitary, dedicated artist and writer willing to work all his (or her, as in the case of the poet Emily Dickinson) life in obscurity and public neglect, or even poverty, purely for the sake of fulfilling his own vision. Such a phenomenon had scarcely existed before in Europe, and to the eighteenth century, which was preoccupied above all with man as a social being, it would have seemed ridiculous or incomprehensible, like the preaching of some isolated religious crank, hermit or mystic.

As this book makes clear, it is largely to the ancient Greeks that we owe the birth of aesthetic thinking. The Romans, while certainly not philistines, were less sensitive to beauty in the higher or ideal sense and more inclined towards political and social areas of thinking, where their practical genius could fulfil itself. (They had, in any case, little flair for the plastic arts apart from architecture, and relied mainly on Greek importations or copies.) In the Middle Ages, religion did not rule out considerable awareness of the beauties of nature and of art. In more recent centuries, it is interesting to watch how national character asserts itself – the Germans tend to theorise too much and the English too little, the French are more critical and analytical, the Italians in general are philosophically humanist and less fond of abstractions than Northern Europeans. No doubt these are generali-sations, but at least it will be admitted that just as all the great European nations have their own artistic traditions, they also have their own traditions of thought. Almost all of these, however, are ultimately growths or offshoots of the great Graeco-Roman tree. It was the Greeks – or at least their artists and philosophers – who first made European man intellectually aware of Beauty. They lit a lamp which cannot be put out, in spite of persecutions and heresy-hunting over centuries and, in our own time, the fearful lunacies of mass political ideology and the destructive powers of modern technology when used by the wrong hands.

1 Introduction and Definitions

Art is man's nature.
(Edmund Burke)

Introduction

Imagine a world without any animate life, apart from human beings: no birds or fish, no mammals, no insects, no bees above the ground nor worms burrowing beneath it. This strange and silent world would soon become even more silent, for the human race would in a short time come to a whimpering end in the midst of a universal desert.

What about a world without art? Here we would have a different kind of desert, one without music, literature, cinema, theatre, painting, sculpture or architecture. Everything even remotely artistic in character would disappear, anything whose ingenuity and skill might awaken in people the shock of the sensuous. We should never more care to rearrange our furniture, nor decorate our dwellings with paint, textiles, paper, plaster or wood. We should never choose our garments to go together, nor have any concern for their cut, colour and shape. None of our possessions would have anything about them of decoration or style. No one would hum, whistle or sing to their children. There would be no storytelling, no drama, no fiction. Language would be an instrument of communication with no character of wit or elegance. There would be no rhythm: no marches, no children dancing, swinging or playing. There would be no pictures of any kind, nor any sort of visual patterns or structures. There would be no games, no rituals, no liturgies, no monuments, no churches to baptise the young nor gravestones to remember the dead.

We can see at once that a species thus denuded of everything artistic in its culture would be, not just the human species deprived of its art, but a species that was no longer human. It would think, behave and imagine in ways entirely alien to our own. A 'human' way of being in the world is inextricably bound up with the work of transforming nature and of introducing into nature both the tools of transformation

and an infinity of new objects and arrangements designed and manufactured for our convenience and delight. Human beings transform
and enrich nature by creating a human culture, and where there is
culture, there also is art and the artistic.

Our physical existence, our spiritual identity, and our history, are
thus inseparable from our artistic activities and achievements. There is
an irrepressible human need to pursue order, to conquer reality
through imagination, to take pleasure in rituals and celebrations, to
enhance our powers of communication and expression, and to seek
out and take delight in beauty. There is an irrepressible desire to transform nature into culture, as if we are unable to accept permanently the
strangeness and the otherness of things. Ideally we both return to
nature and submit to it, and also, at the same time, compel nature to
submit to us. Too often instead we terrorise nature or it terrorises us.
But in the artistic we find something like a perfect balance, a state in
which matter and the imagination combine in the peculiar form of
harmony to which we give the name of beauty.

The ubiquity and necessity of art are well described in the following quotation from Ernst Fischer.

> As a first step we must realize that we are inclined to take an aston-
> ishing phenomenon too much for granted. And it is certainly
> astonishing: countless millions read books, listen to music, watch
> theatre, go to the cinema. Why? To say that they seek distraction,
> relaxation, entertainment, is to beg the question. Why is it distract-
> ing, relaxing, entertaining to sink oneself in someone else's life and
> problems, to identify oneself with a painting or a piece of music or
> with the characters in a novel, play, or film? Why do we respond to
> such 'unreality' as though it were reality intensified? What strange,
> mysterious entertainment is this? And if one answers that we want
> to escape from an unsatisfactory existence into a richer one, into
> experience without risk, then the next question arises: why is our
> existence not enough? Why this desire to fulfil our unfulfilled lives
> through other figures, other forms, to gaze from the darkness of an
> auditorium at a lighted stage where something that is only play can
> so utterly absorb us? (Fischer 1963, pp. 7–8)

Fischer's answer to this cluster of questions is worth quoting also:
'Evidently man wants to be more than just himself. He wants to be a
whole man' (p. 8).

Before concluding this introductory section, let us return to our
thought experiment, but this time invert it. We will suppose that a
party of aliens lands upon an earth whose human population has been

eliminated, but whose property and artefacts are completely intact. As they wander through the empty cities, libraries, museums and factories, they will encounter everywhere the traces and messages of human work, creativity, inventiveness and genius. Before long they will come to know the departed human race almost as well as if they had met them in the flesh: how they looked and dressed and lived, their ways of thinking, loving, feeling, imagining, acting and making. The works of art in particular – literature, drama, music, pictures – would draw the aliens into the very heart of humankind. There they would discover, not just what people knew, looked like and acted, but also what it felt like to be human. Through art and artefacts we fully enter and fully understand the human world. 'In works of art', Hegel said, 'the nations have deposited their richest inner intuitions and ideas' (Hegel [1842](1975) I, p. 7).

Definitions: Aesthetics, Poetics, Criticism

The word 'aesthetics' comes from the Greek word *aísthesis*, which means 'sense perception'. It was used first as a philosophical term by Alexander Baumgarten. Baumgarten took the view that, just as there is a systematic study of intellectual processes called 'Logic', so also there should be a systematic study of sense perception, which he proposed to call 'Aesthetics'. However, when he came to write this study – which he did in a two-volume work entitled *Aesthetica* (1750 and 1758) – he devoted most of his attention to the perception of art and beauty. The reason for this was that he considered the perception of beauty to be the most highly developed form of sense perception, in which the true nature of sense knowledge could be discerned most clearly.

The proposal to create a new branch of philosophy devoted exclusively to sense perception never caught on, but the use of the word 'aesthetics' to refer to the philosophy of art and beauty soon became common practice. Baumgarten's instinct in this matter was well-founded, for aesthetics deals first and foremost with material objects. All works of art are material. Most beautiful objects are material. It may well be the case that there are forms of intellectual and moral beauty as well, but the paradigm cases of beauty are material, and the paradigm forms of aesthetic experience are essentially and profoundly sensuous.

The other part of Baumgarten's instinct is just as important. He regarded aesthetic experience as sensuous *knowledge*. It is not purely and exclusively a state or condition of the senses, but a way in which, through our senses, we come to know the world more fully. Failing to see the beauty of something means failing to know it completely, no matter how well we may know it in other respects. A person blind to aesthetic qualities is a person whose cognitive abilities are defective. This is especially evident in art, more even than in natural beauty, for art explicitly seeks a balance and fusion of sense and intellect. Aesthetic experience, perhaps more than any other human experience, requires the participation of the whole person, body and mind alike.

The appearance of the *word* 'aesthetics' did not mean the birth of aesthetics as a discipline. Reflection on art and beauty has existed since the very beginnings of European philosophy, and even earlier in Greek poetry. Systematic reflection on these matters started with Plato and Aristotle, and it is they who laid the foundations of this branch of philosophy, and who still shape and influence aesthetics as we have it today. Plato returned to aesthetic problems again and again: in his *Ion*, *Phaedrus*, *Hippias Major*, *Symposium*, *Laws* and, most memorably, in two lengthy sections of the *Republic*. Aristotle dealt with various problems in aesthetics in his *Poetics* and, to a lesser extent, in his *Rhetoric*.

The word 'poetics' is therefore much more ancient than the word 'aesthetics'. It was used by Aristotle to refer to the study of all the arts that represent people in action, arts such as literature, drama, dance and music. The surviving part of the *Poetics* deals mostly with drama, and Aristotle's method of explanation was to examine the nuts and bolts of drama – its various parts with their various species and functions, and how they all fit together into a coherent whole. 'Poetics' has therefore come to mean a systematic study of the techniques and processes involved in the construction of works of art, particularly the techniques and processes of a particular artist or a particular movement or period. Some examples of a poetics are Polyclitus' *Canon*, Dante's *Il convivio* and Leonardo's *Trattato della pittura*.

Aesthetics, then, deals with art and beauty in general. Poetics deals with the processes involved in the production of works of art. Individual works of art and artistic movements are dealt with by criticism. Criticism involves two kinds of activity, description and evaluation, each of which is at the service of the other. The critic describes in order to get the reader to notice features of a work of art, and to respond to them in a certain way, and consequently discern the value that the critic believes the work to possess. The critic evaluates in order to justify his decision to describe certain features of a work of art and to ignore others. Ultimately art criticism aims to produce a community, or communities, of shared aesthetic experiences and judgements.

Aesthetics, poetics and criticism are different in their objects and in their methods. None the less, they all pertain to the same realm of human experience, and can easily merge with one another in varying degrees. In all of the great treatises on art of the ancient world – Aristotle's *Poetics*, Horace's *Ars poetica*, Longinus' *On the Sublime*, Demetrius' *On Style* – aesthetics, poetics and criticism flow easily together in the same discourse. Moreover, aesthetics itself has over the centuries assumed protean shapes and forms. Medieval aesthetics was interested primarily, in some cases exclusively, in beauty, whereas Renaissance aesthetics was far more interested in art, so that Renaissance aesthetics and poetics are hard to disentangle. Philosophers such as Francis Hutcheson and Edmund Burke wrote a great deal about beauty, and very little about art, whereas for Benedetto Croce aesthetics was the 'science of art' (Croce 1902, p. 14), and furthermore, coextensive with philosophy as a whole. In the twentieth century aesthetics is nearly always practised as a philosophy of art. Even discussions of aesthetic properties and predicates, and the relatively few discussions of beauty, almost always turn to art for illustration and support.

Definitions: Art and Beauty

The close association, some would say the essential connection, between art and beauty, is deeply rooted in the etymology of the Latin and Greek words whose meaning they render into English. The ancient Greeks used two words for art: *téchne* and *poíesis*. Aristotle adapted *poíesis* to refer to certain kinds of representational arts, but in general usage it, and *téchne*, both signified the production of material objects. They could also refer to the craft or skill required for any kind of material production. Finally, they could signify the knowledge and inventiveness required to make effective use of the craft and skill. (Interestingly, the German *Kunst*, from the verb *können*, has something of a similar etymological flavour and conceptual range). The English word 'art' comes from Latin *ars*, which was employed in senses identical with those of *téchne* and *poíesis*. In addition, *ars* originated from the Greek root *ártios*, an adjective meaning complete, perfect or fitting. This brings it close to the Greek *kalón*, which, in addition to meaning 'beautiful', also connotes excellence or perfection. *Pulchrum*, the Latin for 'beautiful', has a similar range of meanings to *kalón*.

We can thus observe that the Greek and Latin languages reflected in their etymology what Greek and Latin aesthetics were doing on the level of theory: that is, discussing art and beauty in tandem with one another. Art and beauty may be logically and conceptually different, but it is a constant of European aesthetics that artworks are usually taken to be the most paradigmatic and striking instances of the beautiful.

The concept of beauty underwent a significant change in the eighteenth century. Previously it had been taken to refer to a quality or attribute that we discover in things, and that is present in them irrespective of whether it is discovered or not. But in the eighteenth century a number of philosophers claimed that beauty was not a quality in objects but only an Idea in the mind. Francis Hutcheson, for example, said that the Idea of beauty ('Idea' at that time simply meant any mental content) was produced in us by a certain condition in things which he called 'uniformity amidst variety' (Hutcheson 1753, I, § 2). But my awareness of uniformity amidst variety, though it *causes* the Idea of beauty to come into my mind, is quite *different* from the presence in my mind of that Idea. Uniformity amidst variety is ontologically objective, and is discovered in things; whereas the experience of beauty is subjective, so that there would be no beauty (according to Hutcheson) if there were no minds.

From that time onwards, the concept of beauty has been a contested one. For many philosophers outside the field of aesthetics, and for many people without any philosophical training, beauty is subjective. It is 'in the eye of the beholder'. However, if we look at philosophers who have seriously examined the concept of beauty, a clear majority have come to take the view that beauty is ontologically objective. Certainly, subjectivists rarely do more than make the claim that beauty is subjective. They rarely produce arguments, and when they do the arguments are unsatisfactory. It is this that has persuaded a number of contemporary philosophers, perhaps against the spirit of the age, that beauty is a real quality in things. Beauty, however, is a value, and the ontology of values is a notoriously crabbed and difficult area of debate.

As we are going to present and discuss philosophies of art and beauty, it is now time to outline some kind of preliminary conception of what art is, to begin. What is it then? Or, to put it differently, what shall we take as a preliminary definition of art? One answer to this question is that there is no answer, that art cannot be defined. This is a view often held by philosophers of an empiricist temper, and it is supported by two observations which are strongly empiricist in character. One is that works of art are so immensely various – paintings and sculptures, poems and novels, songs and dances, operas and orchestral works, cathedrals and warehouses – that it seems quite impossible that there could be a set of essential properties that they all share. The second observation is that works of art are constantly changing with the passage of time. New kinds of painting, new kinds of music, make their appearance, and subvert all previous conceptions of painting and music. New art forms, such as photography and cinema, are invented, and so all previous conceptions of art have to be discarded. Artists are constantly rebelling against the assumptions and practices of their predecessors, so that just when we think we know what art is we find that some unforeseen artistic novelty comes along and pulls the rug from under us.

In short, it is alleged either (1) that the objects that we call works of art are so various that they do not constitute a single class; or (2) that new artworks and new kinds of art keep appearing, so that the class of artworks is never complete. The first of these amounts to nominalism: that is, the only thing that works of art have in common is the name 'works of art'. The second amounts to the claim that the concept of art is an open concept: that is, it never stays still long enough to be pinned down in a definition.

It should be added that this scepticism about the possibility of definition is found also in the case of individual art forms. It seems difficult to define music if John Cage can compose a work consisting of four minutes and thirty-three seconds of silence; or to define visual art if a pile of bricks is a work of art. As for literature, Terry Eagleton is happy to inform us that it cannot be defined because 'there is no "essence" of literature whatsoever' (Eagleton 1996, p. 8).

This pessimism about definition has been rejected by what has come to be called the institutional theory of art. This is the theory that all works of art have two essential properties in common. One is that they are artefacts. The other is that the status of art has been conferred upon them by an artworld. The 'artworld' is the collection of people who are involved with the type of art in question. For instance, the literary artworld consists of writers and readers, booksellers, publishers' readers, editors and marketing managers, newspaper and radio reviewers, academics and students, agents and translators. There is another, and different, artworld for each of the other kinds of art. If the artworld decides that something is a work of art, then it is a work of art. Otherwise it is not.

The best-known version of this theory is George Dickie's (Dickie 1969; see Davies 1991 and Yanal 1994). Dickie has difficulty in solving some of the problems that the theory generates. For instance, he has to say that people can declare themselves to be members of an artworld, and that even one person can legitimately think of himself as an artworld representative. Dickie also recognises that the definition is circular, but defends the circularity by claiming that at least the definition is informative. He is also extremely vague on whether, when an artworld decides that something is a work of art, it has reasons for doing so or just does it on a whim.

It is fair to say that Dickie's version of the institutional theory has brought down upon his head, if not execrations, at least a good deal of criticism. This is in part because he has not properly tackled, or solved, the many problems that the theory generates. T. J. Diffey developed, independently of Dickie, another version of the institutional theory, which is much more sophisticated and less extreme (Diffey 1969). Diffey, however, is something of a reformed sinner. For, ten years later, he turned again to the problem of the definition of art in another article, and trenchantly disposed of the institutional theory in about half a page (Diffey 1979). His main criticisms are based on the claim that things are works of art independently of human decisions and human behaviour towards them. A thing is a work of art whether we like it or not. Richard Wollheim also points out that an artworld must confer the status of art on a thing either for a reason or without a reason. If there is a reason, then it is that reason, not the artworld's decision, that makes it a work of art. If there is no reason, then the concept of art is emptied of content and the activities of artworlds are arbitrary and meaningless (Wollheim 1980).

The anti-definitionists fare no better. If it were true that works of art had nothing essential in common with one another, then the word 'art' would simply have no meaning. It would, to put it more technically, have reference but no sense. We shall try to show that this is not the case. Also, if we were to refrain from defining art just because a new work of art might undermine our definition the next day, we should be excessively fastidious. Scientists do not refrain from defining particles and forces just because new discoveries might undermine them. In fact, scientists are rather pleased when this happens and feel that it is a sign of intellectual creativity and vigour.

As well as this, there is something in these empiricist approaches to definition which is quite at odds with the role of definitions in theoretical disciplines. Empiricism seems to aspire to a sort of ideal condition in which we examine huge numbers of works of art, take copious notes on what they are like, and then, by careful and systematic induction, discover what is common to them all. As Erich Kahler has pointed out, definitions do not come at the end of years of laborious study (Kahler 1959). Rather, definitions come on the first page. Definitions merely establish, in a provisional manner, what it is that one is proposing to talk about – art, in this case, but not elephants, unicorns or supersonic aircraft. They do not sum up a process of discovery, but start us along the road of discovery. A definition does not *solve* the problem of what art is; it *sets forth* that problem (Davies 1991).

What is Art?

At the beginning of this chapter we spoke of the way in which art is disseminated throughout the entire spectrum of human activities. We arrange our furniture in a room, or redesign our kitchens, not just for convenience, but also to make them look attractive. We choose curtains, tablecloths, china or silverware in such a way that they match one another, and match what we already own. We even arrange our flying ducks upon the wall so that they are displayed to the best advantage. We choose a tie to go with a jacket, with the same care that a composer might exercise in choosing which instruments to go together. The tie and jacket 'look right' just as the musical chord 'sounds right'. Our entire lives, even the poorest lives, are shot through with aesthetic judgements, even if we have never heard of the word 'aesthetic'. Every object, every action, every habit, every ritual, not to mention the great edifices of science and scholarship, that emerge in the course of human history and culture, have aspects of structure and content that are shaped and manipulated in ways that are characteristically artistic.

The ubiquity of the artistic in human culture is recognised in the odd notion of 'minor arts'. We take it for granted that there are indisputable kinds of art such as paintings and sculptures, music, dance, drama, literature. But we also have the uncomfortable awareness that these do not exhaust the realm of art, and so we have invented the category of 'minor' arts such as pottery, glassmaking, weaving, bookbinding, furniture, plasterwork, carpets, posters, packaging, interior design, industrial design. It is easy to see that this list can go on indefinitely - that the realm of the artistic is, in fact, as extensive as the realm of culture as a whole.

It can also be seen that the line dividing 'minor arts' from 'fine art' (a term that we will use for want of a better) is not an easy one to draw. And this brings us back to the problem of definition again. Can we in fact draw that line? Can we delimit and define art in such a way that works of fine art are clearly distinct from the great mass of artefacts which happen to have artistic aspects and properties simply because they are products of human cultures?

We will start on this task in the following way. We begin by claiming that every work of art is an artefact. The word 'artefact' itself requires explanation and debate, of course, but we will assume that everyone has a preliminary idea of what artefactuality connotes. Next, we distinguish between two kinds of artefact, the primarily useful and the primarily aesthetic. We will argue that primarily aesthetic artefacts are works of art, although, as we shall see, they are not the only works of art.

Most of the artefacts that we encounter in life have a strongly util-itarian character: pots and pans, axeheads and flint blades, fishing-rods and fishtanks, roads and gates, houses and churches, bicycles and aeroplanes, and so on endlessly. The predominant motive underlying the universal and obsessive human instinct for making things is the desire to produce objects that are useful and convenient for the conduct of life. Furthermore, the underlying intentionality of useful artefacts is available and evident to observation. We 'see' the function of a hammer or a knife; we 'hear' the function of a doorbell or an alarm clock. Artefacts wear their functions on their sleeves. They are not mysterious. They have a sort of single-minded clarity. We may be occasionally, and momentarily, baffled. We may happen to be on a tour of a Great House and ask what some peculiar implement in the kitchen 'is for'. We know that it is a tool, that it was designed for a function. When we are told that it is a Victorian apple-parer we then see at once how it works, and realise yet again how function determines structure, design, material and size.

Primarily aesthetic artefacts are made for a different reason. When something has a function it points beyond itself, so to speak: the hammer to the nail, the breadknife to the bread, the cup to the coffee, the aeroplane to the journey. Having a function means being related to something else. Primarily aesthetic objects, in contrast, do not have to be related to anything else. They are self-contained and, as it were, self-fulfilling. The intentionality that we observe in them is that they are designed to be experienced rather than used. They are visual objects designed to be looked at, or aural objects designed to be listened to, not for some ulterior purpose, but for their own sake.

Normally, the primary intentionality of objects is easy to discern. I might, for instance, enter a room in a villa in Pompeii. I observe the door, the window, the walls and ceiling. On one wall there is a mosaic, a hunting scene. I have no difficulty in seeing the functional character of the door and window, nor in seeing the aesthetic character of the mosaic. The intentionality in both cases is clear and unambiguous. The mosaic is meant to be looked at, and the door is meant to be used. The conceptual difference between a work of art and a useful artefact is here borne out by the evidence of the senses.

Sometimes, however, the distinction between the primarily useful and the primarily aesthetic is not at all clear. This is the case with a good deal of architecture, but it is to be found also in all of the other art forms. There are huge numbers of religious paintings and sculp-tures which were, and are, designed to educate the faithful, and to induce a state of reflection and reverence. Religious music has the same kind of utilitarian role. Some music is intended to be played on special occasions such as weddings and funerals, and there is music to be danced to. Dance itself has many functions, from courtship to socialising to maintaining a cultural identity to ending a drought. Photography and cinema are the most successful instruments of education and propaganda ever devised. Literature has a great variety of functions: satirical, educational, political, pornographic, philosophical and, in almost every case, the desire to entertain or amuse. Virgil wrote his *Aeneid* to glorify Rome, and Milton wrote *Paradise Lost* to justify the ways of God to men.

There are large numbers of artefacts, then, which are unquestionably works of art, but in which, at the same time, the aesthetic and the useful seem to be inextricably intertwined. It seems impossible to claim that they are primarily aesthetic artefacts. Primarily aesthetic artefacts are certainly works of art, but the concept of the primarily aesthetic is not sufficient, by itself, to define art.

For this reason, we propose to define art in the following way: a work of art is an artefact whose aesthetic properties are essential properties. Thus the dividing line between works of art and other artefacts is the dividing line between essential and accidental properties. For instance, a motor car does not have to look attractive in order to be an efficient motor car (though, of course, attractiveness may help to sell it). Its attractiveness is therefore accidental rather than essential. A piece of dance music, however, must sound attractive, for if it does not people will not want to dance to it nor will the dance-band want to play it. Its utilitarian function is bound up with its attractiveness, which is therefore essential rather than accidental. When defined in this way 'works of art' becomes the name of a category that can include primarily useful as well as primarily aesthetic artefacts, as well as artefacts in which the useful and the aesthetic are inextricably bound together.

This is not the end of the matter, because it is not always easy to determine which of an artefact's properties are accidental and which essential. Let us suppose that I visit the Worcester Museum of Art in Massachusetts. I see an ornate Romanesque doorway, transported from the South of France to the New World. I cannot walk through it because the opening is blocked up. That is, it is no longer a door, even though its function as a door is visible to my eyes. Above my head I also see an intricately painted, fifteenth-century wooden ceiling, taken from the house of an Italian merchant. It is a ceiling, yet it is no longer a ceiling, for it provides no shelter and supports no floor above. It is now just a work of art. And yet it is not essential that a ceiling be beautiful, nor essential that a doorway be ornate.

What is it that has happened here? Oddly enough we are taken back to the institutional theory of art, for there is a little seed of truth in the institutional theory after all. What has happened is that an object has been lifted out of its intended context, and put into another, a museum of art. This does not, as Dickie believed, 'confer the status of art' upon it, for whatever it has of artistic genius and aesthetic value was already there. Rather, its relocation in the museum compels us to focus primarily on its aesthetic properties, and to consider its utilitarian function as secondary. That is, the aesthetic properties *of the object as I now experience it* are essential properties. It is now essentially a work of art, even though it does not cease to be also a doorway or a ceiling, though it is now a doorway or a ceiling accidentally.

This decontextualisation and recontextualisation of artefacts is very common, and, in fact, is one of the most important functions of museums. Altarpieces, chalices, crucifixes, doorways and ceilings, items of furniture, musical instruments, silver and glassware, jewellery and garments: we note their aesthetic properties in everyday life, in their proper and intended context, but when removed to museums their aesthetic properties are transformed. They *become* essential, just because the objects are removed to a place where they are no longer usable. A property may be essential because it was the artificer's intention that it should be so. But it can also be essential because the context compels us to regard it as essential. The museum curator, by depriving objects of their function, can transform them into objects that we are compelled, willy nilly, to regard as artworks. He does not change the objects, but he changes the way in which they are experienced.

Our definition – a work of art is an artefact whose aesthetic properties are essential properties – has thus already raised the problem of essentiality, for 'essence' is a notion that raises profound difficulties. We have adopted the view that aesthetic properties are ontologically objective: that is, they are discovered in things, not projected into them by the perceiving mind. But the essentiality, or otherwise, of aesthetic properties arises in the context of human experience. Sometimes the essentiality is an objective feature of the artefact. In these cases it would be simply wrong if we refused to treat the relevant properties as essential. It would be wrong, for instance, to consider a Rembrandt painting as an object whose aesthetic properties were accidental to its true nature. In other cases the essentiality of the aesthetic properties is contrived by human ingenuity: the artefact 'becomes' a work of art by being placed in a different environment from the one intended by its maker. When this happens, the essentiality is epistemically, but not ontologically, objective. However, whatever is ontologically objective is also, necessarily, epistemically objective. We conclude that aesthetic properties are essential whenever they are perceived as essential (for whatever reason) by the perceiving subject.

We have not actually answered the question, What is art? But we have shown the way to an answer. It is an anthropological rather than a philosophical question. We shall say only that art refers to everything in human culture that possesses or produces aesthetic properties.

Conclusion: The Value of Art

There is one important additional point. A work of art may be an artefact whose aesthetic properties are essential properties, but it does not follow that the work of art is any good. There is an evaluative, as well as a descriptive, sense of the word 'art', and an object may satisfy the latter but fail to satisfy the former. I can include a work by William McGonagall in an anthology entitled *The World's Greatest Poems*, but no amount of concentrating on its aesthetic properties will persuade me of its literary value, whatever its other merits may be. A museum curator can pay a large sum of money for something, exhibit it with the utmost publicity and panache, and even charge extra for getting in to see it, but none of this guarantees that it is worth looking at. All human artefacts have at least some minimal degree of the artistic about them, but in many cases it remains minimal, no matter how we may try to ennoble them by planting them in an art-saturated environment. A sow's ear can never have the aesthetic value of a silk purse.

If the question, What is art? is understood in this evaluative sense, we enter an entirely different realm of enquiry. In fact the question changes its character. It now becomes, What is the value of art? or possibly, What is art *for*? We will not attempt to answer this general question, though it will reappear later, in different guises, when we start to look at the individual arts. Here we will say only that works of art can articulate insights into our deepest human interests: our understanding of ourselves and our purposes, the world and our place within it, nature, history and truth. This is what many works of the past, and of the present, have succeeded in doing. We see no reason why we should demand, from artists and works of art, less than this.

2 From Altamira to Athens: The Ancient World

There is no excellent beauty that hath not some strangeness in
the proportion.
(Francis Bacon)

Introduction

The forms of human consciousness – that is, the external and internal forms assumed by our beliefs and values, our desires and sensibilities, our experiences and modes of behaviour – vary widely through time and across different cultures. The artistic consciousness, rooted as it is in the deepest recesses of the personality, is particularly malleable and protean.

In this and the following three chapters, we explore the development and character of different forms of artistic consciousness as we encounter them in different periods in the history of European culture. We distinguish four major periods: (1) from the Palaeolithic beginnings to classical Greece; (2) the Christian, Byzantine and medieval epoch; (3) the Renaissance and the modern era; (4) the contemporary period.

This fourfold division is adopted partly as a methodological convenience, and is to some extent artificial. It is not, however, totally arbitrary and unjustified, since it corresponds to major shifts in philosophical world-views or paradigms, and reflects major differences in artistic styles and aesthetic sensibilities in successive periods of our history. It is not purely chronological, for it is a distinction also among various forms of aesthetic and artistic consciousness. Furthermore, the divisions must not be taken as water-tight: the story of art is a fluid and plastic continuum of phenomena that often repeat themselves or overlap as one period melts into another, and some features of artistic and aesthetic consciousness can appear or reappear in epochs quite distant and dissimilar from each other. One example of this is a similarity between the Renaissance practice of imitating the art and the canons of classical antiquity, the avant-garde recourse to primitive art in the early decades of this century, and the current programme of postmodernism to revisit and retrieve the past. These are all cases which challenge the historical and cultural divisions that we are adopting here, and highlight instead the strategies of what has come to be called 'intertextuality' in art.

But we will leave intertextuality to one side for the moment, and stay with our fourfold division of historical, cultural and artistic epochs. Each epoch exhibits unifying traits and common characteristics which rest upon underlying philosophical presuppositions. These epochal identities have been referred to by Hegel and other Romantics as 'the spirit of a people' (*Volksgeist*). In a similar spirit, though in a different sense, Jung speaks of a 'collective unconscious'. Each culture and epoch determines, yet is also expressed by, particular forms of artistic and aesthetic consciousness. How, then, can we describe their character and distinctiveness most effectively?

No one would deny the existence of significant differences among successive historical stages *within* cultures, traditions and civilisations. Most societies change with the passage of time – change, for instance, in their manner of dressing, cooking, and building cities, how they manage their work and their economy, how they arrange their social interactions, how they organise their legal systems, how their language develops and mutates, how they worship, how they understand the world and how they express themselves in their artistic endeavours. If changes, mutations and differentiations can be observed *within* the history of the same people, they become much more apparent when we compare the developments of different cultures and traditions. If we consider how the Western world has radically changed since its beginnings in Mesopotamia, Egypt and Greece, up to our own century; or if we consider the whole history of mankind, beginning with the Palaeolithic age or even earlier, we are struck by the remarkable transformations undergone by the human species. At different times and in different places, we have lived in radically different manners and expressed ourselves in radically different ways.

How can we explain and describe these mutations? In what fundamental respect, for instance, do we differ from ancient Athenians or from Renaissance citizens? What distinguishes our ways of thinking, believing and acting, from those of medieval people? How do we differ from the inhabitants of ancient Egypt? Our belief is that all human cultures or civilisations are grounded in certain fundamental presuppositions, certain principles and prejudices that are implicitly or unconsciously adopted by all the members of the particular cultural community under consideration. These presuppositions operate as a guiding principle in all the significant manifestations and expressions of each culture, and are the ultimate determinants of its essential character.

In the next four sub-sections, then, we attempt to identify and define our four spiritual and cultural epochs: classical antiquity (the Greek world, in particular); the Middle Ages; the Renaissance and the modern era; and, finally, our own contemporary culture.

World-views, or Forms of Epochal Consciousness

The Greek World

We know the Greek world very well. Despite massive losses over the centuries, we still possess a substantial body of its literary, scientific and philosophical works, and know a great deal about its religious conceptions, its political and economic structures, social behaviour and organisation, legal systems and works of art. All of this enables us to discern in it a significant degree of unity and homogeneity, resting upon one fundamental idea and a cluster of related principles. That idea is the Greek conception of *being* or *substance*, and the correlative conception of the universe as a closed and finite *cosmos*. The idea of *being/substance* implies that everything is a stable presence in the world, both in itself and as something present for consciousness, and that it manifests itself to us fully and without deception. Everything is transparently self-manifest; it is, as it were, always ready and waiting to be known and understood through and through. This, for the Greeks, was the explanatory principle, ground and essence of all reality. Each thing, and the totality of things, is stable and permanent, structured according to its own internally coherent laws, and intelligible, irrespective of human or divine participation or intervention.

The correlative conception of the universe as *cosmos* points to the same cultural and philosophical presupposition. The word 'cosmos' means 'order', and also 'good order' and 'ornament'. For the Greeks, therefore, the universe comprised all things in an organised, harmonious, intelligible and well-structured whole. Also each part of the universe – all geological, chemical and astronomical phenomena, all plants, animals, humans, gods – reproduce within themselves, in different manners and degrees, the order and structure and intelligibility of being. Even the gods, and the human mind, are subservient to being and posterior to it.

This cluster of presuppositions remained in force through the classical age, though it underwent progressive changes, and, eventually, dissolution.

Christianity and the Middle Ages

With the advent of Christianity, and thereafter up to the culmination of the Middle Ages in the fourteenth century, a new era came into being and a new fundamental presupposition came to be universally adopted, to occupy the central position previously held by the idea of being. This was the idea of *God* as infinite, all-knowing and all-powerful, and the correlative idea of *God's creation*. The very existence and structure of reality were seen to rest upon these two ideas, which were taken as fundamental and never subjected to question or to doubt. The universe was felt to be ultimately dependent on God's intelligent act of creation, and the human world was understood to be informed by the laws of divine order and subject to God's will. Furthermore, human mind and human agency participated in God's attributes.

If classical Greek culture can be called being-centred or *ontocentric*, the medieval epoch was unmistakably *theocentric*. In the Middle Ages, man and the universe and everything in the world was conceived of as a symbol, token and witness of God.

Humanism: The Renaissance and Modern Subjectivity

With the waning of the Middle Ages, a new principle and a new presupposition began to take shape. A revaluation and rebirth of classical ideals led to a reconsideration of human agency in the universe. The central theme unifying all the cultural manifestations of this epoch was that of the *dignity and nobility of mankind*. In this brave new world the human mind and human subjectivity took over, as a universal presupposition, the place previously held by being and by God. The Renaissance thus initiated a new era, one leading directly to our own times, marked by accelerating scientific and technological achievements. Gutenberg's invention of the printing press, transoceanic navigation, Copernicus's, Galileo's and Newton's revolutionary scientific theories, the Protestant Reformation, Descartes's philosophy grounded on subjective certainty, Vico's insights into the historical nature of human experience: these produced a radical reformulation of our understanding of the world. In the modern epoch, the principle of objective reality as stable presence, which had characterised the Greek and classical epoch, was replaced by the principle of spirit or mind. In a parallel manner, the disposition of faith and belief was supplanted by the demands of reason, and the principle of divine authority was replaced by the principle of rational human certainty. If the Greek and classical epoch was primarily and fundamentally *ontocentric*, and if the Middle Ages were deeply *theocentric*, the modern era is unmistakably *anthropocentric*. The human mind and the human agent are now the last court of appeal in matters of truth and falsity, knowledge and action, religious belief and moral values.

The supremacy and centrality of human thought and human subjectivity explain and ground the modern world, in all its manifestations. However, towards the end of the last century and the beginning of our century, a new sensibility began to take shape.

The Twentieth Century and Postmodernism

Even as early as the mid-nineteenth century, man's optimistic reliance on reason and scientific knowledge began to be called in question. The Promethean ideals, claims and aspirations of a supposedly enlightened humanity were subjected to close scrutiny and criticism, and finally rejected by philosophers such as Marx, Schopenhauer, Nietzsche and Kierkegaard. Optimistic notes would continue to sound, but mainly in the halls of science and technology, since these disciplines continued to some extent to develop and change in isolation from the intellectual crises exploding around them.

New theories of the human mind and of the physical universe began to take shape at the turn of the century. In particular, Freud's analysis of the unconscious and Einstein's relativity theory were profoundly to alter our conceptions of reality, both physical and psychical. Nowadays we are inclined to envisage the universe as open-ended and in continuous expansion, ruled by laws of possibility and probability, not necessarily teleological, with elements of chaos as well as structure and order. In an analogous manner we conceive the human agent and the human mind, no longer as a monolithic, unified, autonomous and purely rational entity, but rather as a meeting-point and a sedimentation of social forces, mediated through language, and marked by absence, incompleteness, obscure drives and desires. The self, celebrated by Descartes as the source of rational certainty, is now often thought of as a cultural and linguistic construct, disinherited of internal verification and abandoned to the flux of various and overlapping narratives or discourses.

In the beginning was stable presence for the classical era, God for the Middle Ages, man and reason for the modern epoch. According to postmodernism, in the beginning was chaos, difference, lack and absence.

The epochal distinctions briefly indicated here are to be taken only as approximate guidelines to help us map the territory of art and aesthetics in the Western tradition. But as we know, the map is not the territory, only a useful device to guide us through the complex landscape of the unknown. In what follows, we will examine the conceptions of art and beauty manifested in the artistic practices and the philosophical reflections characteristic of the four epochs that we have now identified.

From Caves to the Parthenon

The Prehistory

Art in a very broad sense refers to the experience and process of making artefacts, and in this sense it is co-extensive with and as old as humanity itself. The sciences of anthropology and archaeology, in fact, infer the emergence of a specifically human intelligence from the presence of tools and artefacts. The first true human being is *homo faber*. The production of tools, however, seems to have gone hand in hand with the production of decorative features. Pottery was thrown in multifarious shapes and adorned with colours and decorative visual patterns; clothes were made in a variety of textures and materials; flints and clubs, spears and boats, the staff of the chief or the sorcerer were carved in elaborate ways. Jewellery and other ornaments, hair arrangements and facial cosmetics were soon to appear, with ritual celebrations, musical instruments and dancing. Finally, with the palaeolithic age – between twenty and forty thousand years BC – there arrived what has rightly been called the golden age of prehistory. In this age we encounter, among other artefacts that are not primarily functional, the almond-shaped carvings of figurines with accentuated physical female attributes, often referred to as primitive Venuses, and the wall paintings in more than 120 caves located primarily in France, across the Pyrenees and in northern Spain. In the words of a renowned anthropologist:

> Religion and art appear in the archaeological record with the appearance of Homo sapiens, religion with Neanderthal man and art with Cro-Magnon or modern-type man. The oldest known paintings have been found in association with occupation layers deposited more than 30,000 years ago, at least 40,000 years after the earliest known burial ceremonies. It seems that some forty millennia of evolution were required before descendants of the first 'philosophers', the first men to think about death and an after-life, found reason to portray things that were important to them. (Pfeiffer 1972, p. 220)

Various interpretations have been given of these ancient artefacts, but all agree on two main points: that the works in question exhibit remarkable formal properties which indicate an advanced stage of intellectual and manual ability; and that they signify the makers' desire to articulate symbolically their mythical, social, propitiatory and celebratory narratives. The palaeolithic Venuses, for instance, are unanimously agreed to be symbols of fertility. More complex, because more structured, is the cluster of meanings attributed to the cave paintings. These animal paintings display an astonishing skill, elegance and compositional structure. They employ formal principles of repetition and difference which, combined with their symbolic content and signification, have led interpreters to read in them the story of struggle and reconciliation between clans or between the sexes. Most are paintings of horses and bisons. The bones of animals found in the vicinity of the caves are not usually those of the painted animals, and from this it has been deduced that the paintings have a primarily symbolic or magical role.

Leaving aside the question of the precise meaning of these prehistoric works, we must note the insights they give us into the minds of their makers. In particular, they show: (1) technical skills in transforming natural material into signifying symbols; (2) intellectual and observational insight, and an ability to handle the formal or structural aspects of visual composition; (3) the makers' attempts to make sense of reality by means of the creative imagination.

What is noticeable also is the total absence, from the cave paintings, of representations of the human figure. This might suggest either an identification of the human agent with the animal figures, or else an inability or unwillingness to portray the human body. Curiously, in one of the caves we find the imprinted depiction of a human hand, perhaps a signature of the anonymous and faceless maker and a symbol of human creativity and presence in art. The cave of Altamira, in particular, has aptly been called the Sistine Chapel of our prehistory. It is a magic chapel, however, inhabited by horses, bison and aurochs, but where the human agent, not represented, is to be found partly by his absence, and partly in the presence, structure and meaning of his works.

Before Plato

The artistic and aesthetic consciousness of our prehistoric ancestors is cryptically encoded in their works. We can only guess at the meaning of the astonishing visual messages that we encounter in palaeolithic caves. But if we leap forward in time, from Altamira to the dawn of classical antiquity, we encounter, in Greek pre-Socratic literature and philosophy, the first explicit attempts to articulate and explain the meaning of art. References to art and craft are to be found in the epic poetry of Homer and Hesiod. In particular, the pseudo-Homeric *Hymn to Hermes* provides a developed and sophisticated conception of art and craft as a creative transformation of nature into culture: a metamorphic process that symbolises the universal laws of death, ritual sacrifice and regeneration. It is a conception of art that implies also an understanding of the linguistic constitution of experience, since it focuses primarily on poetry, which must have been regarded as the paradigm of the artistic (see Santoro-Brienza 1993, chapters 1–3).

'Poetry' in this tradition meant mythological narratives that articulate and universalise the memory of past origins and prophetically anticipate the order of things to come. To borrow the later Latin historian Sallust, poetry, for the Greeks, tells us 'things that never happened, but always are'. The poet embodies the voice of the gods. Inspired by the Muses, daughters of Memory, the poet conveys to fellow humans the meaning of their origin and of their tradition, just as the gods reveal and understand it. The poet is thus conceived as kin to the prophet and seer. He transcends the present in order to reveal what is hidden in the past and the future. For this reason poets, like seers, are portrayed as blind (the name *Homer* – from *hómeros* – means 'blind'), so that their inner vision cannot be distracted by the physical vision of the present and the actual. As prophet and seer, as mouthpiece of the gods and as interpreter of the past, the poet is inspired by the Muses to become a teacher of truth and wisdom. Even Aristotle echoes this archaic conception of poetry and mythology as purveyors of knowledge. 'Mythology', as he put it, 'is also a kind of philosophy' (*Metaphysics* 1005b1).

These early comments on poetry emphasised also the sensuous pleasure that it provokes, and an awareness that poetry could sometimes be a source of falsification and misrepresentation. We can therefore synthesise the views of the earliest Greeks as follows. Poetry is sacred, since it is inspired by the task of interpreting and celebrating the memory of origins and of the past. It is also a repository of collective wisdom and, hence, an instrument of knowledge. It pleases with its delightful sounds. It can also mislead us because it enchants us or distracts us by its purely sensual properties. In this summary synthesis, we can identify two coexisting conceptions of poetry and of art in general: (1) an understanding of poetry and art as autonomously aesthetic, that is, as independently pleasing because of their sensuous properties and sensuous beauty; and (2) more significantly, an understanding of art and poetry as heteronomous, that is, as explicable in terms of knowledge, instruction, moral and social education. These two conceptions of art are not easily reconcilable, and the disparity between them came to haunt the aesthetic theories of Plato.

Pythagoreans

According to Pythagoras and his followers, the entire universe is ruled by and structured by mathematical laws. In the words of Aristotle:

The Pythagoreans, as they are called, devoted themselves to mathematics; they were the first to advance this study, and having been brought up in it they thought its principles were the principles of all things ... Since, then, all other things seemed in their whole nature to be modelled after numbers, and numbers seemed to be the first things in the whole of nature, they supposed the elements of numbers to be the elements of all things, and the whole heaven to be a musical scale [i.e. harmony] and a number. (Aristotle, *Metaphysics* 985b–986a)

However, Pythagorean studies of mathematics, geometry and cosmology were pursued less for their own sake than as a method of sustaining a life devoted to spiritual and ethical ideals. In their constant search for numerical arrangements in the universe, and in their fundamental conviction that numbers are the principles and causes of all things, they happened upon the mathematical laws of music. In the words of Tatarkiewicz:

They established a mathematical order in acoustics because they observed that strings sound harmoniously or otherwise, according to their length. They sound harmoniously if their lengths reflect direct numerical relations. In the relation 1:2 they produce an octave, in 2:3 a fifth, and, when their lengths are in the proportion of 1:2/3:1/2, this produces the chord C-G-c which they call the 'harmonious' chord. Thus they explained the puzzling phenomenon of harmony in terms of proportion, measure and number, and considered that harmony depended on a mathematical relation of parts. This was an important discovery. Thanks to it music became an art: an art in the Greek meaning of the word. (Tatarkiewicz 1970, I, p. 80)

The harmony and order of musical sounds were, for the Pythagoreans, an expression of the universal order of reality itself. They believed that the universe as a whole was constituted and structured in a manner that was exactly reproduced in the canons of musical harmony. This was an unwitting echo of the biblical claim that 'God created everything according to balance and measure' (*Wisdom*, 11:21), and a manifestation of a universal human desire to seek and produce order in things. It is arguable that all artistic and aesthetic experience is the product of a fundamental need to contain and control the disruptive powers of nature and the contradictions in reality. 'Harmony', said Heraclitus, 'consists of opposing tension, like that of the bow and the lyre' (Fragment 51). And this was echoed by Theon of Smyrna when he wrote,

The Pythagoreans, whom Plato follows in many respects, call music the harmonization of opposites, the unification of disparate things and the conciliation of warring elements. For they claim that not only rhythms and melody but in fact the whole system [of the world] depends on music, whose object is unity and harmony. God harmonizes warring elements and this in fact is his greatest aim in music and the art of medicine, namely that he reconciles things which are hostile. (*Mathematica* I, quoted in Tatarkiewicz 1970, I, pp. 87–8)

This passage demonstrates why art in classical antiquity – music for the Pythagoreans and for Plato, tragedy for Aristotle – was thought to have an ethical, educative and cathartic function. The ancient concept of beauty always contained within it the notion of usefulness as well. The Greeks were not inclined, or even equipped, to think of art as fully autonomous.

The Pythagoreans were not primarily and explicitly concerned with aesthetic properties or with art, but we owe to them the axiom that physical beauty consists in order, measure, proportion, harmony. These attributes were destined to survive as essential features in the philosophy of beauty throughout the Western tradition, though often subjected to revisions, reformulations, and even on occasions partial rejection. The connection that the Pythagoreans established between the cosmic order, number and musical harmony, together with the theory that beauty consists in order, measure, proportion and harmony, laid the foundations of European aesthetics. Sextus Empiricus summed up the Pythagorean philosophy of art as follows:

There is no art or craft that has been built up without proportion, and proportion is based on number; so that every art is built up by means of number... There exists in sculpture, and likewise in painting, a certain proportion whereby unvarying resemblance is preserved. And, to speak generally, every art is a system composed of perceptions, and system is a number. Hence it is a sound saying that 'all things are like unto number' – that is, like unto the reason that judges and is akin to the numbers which compose all things. Such is the doctrine of the Pythagoreans. (*Against the Logicians*: I [*Adversus Mathematicos*: VII], 106–10)

The Sophists

For the Pythagoreans beauty was a real property possessed by the universe as a whole as well as by its parts. It might seem to follow that there was no difference between the beauty of art and beauty in general. The Sophists, however, though they agreed that beauty was ontologically real, claimed that works of art also had properties that were specifically artistic. The Sophists were important contributors to the development of aesthetics, although they are sometimes over-looked. Perhaps it is worth recalling that most of the Sophists were contemporaries, not precedessors, of Socrates and Plato, both of whom owed to them much of their own philosophy.

The Sophists were not a movement or school of philosophy. They varied too widely in their interests and outlook. Thus we cannot discover or define something as coherent as a 'Sophist aesthetics'. None the less, we can isolate four theses which were to prove of lasting significance in the history of aesthetics, and whose origin we can attribute to one or other of the Sophists.

The first of these is that the subjective experience of pleasure must be taken into account in any explanation, and perhaps in the defini-tion, of beauty. This, at any rate, is an opinion ascribed by Plato to an imaginary or prototypical Sophist in his *Hippias Major* (289a). It was an opinion that Socrates proceeded to demolish; but the close association of beauty with pleasure never wholly sank out of sight thereafter.

Secondly, more than one of the Sophists distinguished between arts which are useful or instructive and arts whose only purpose it is to give pleasure. Isocrates, for instance referred to arts, 'both those which are useful in producing the necessities of life and those which have been devised to give us pleasure' (*Panegyricus*, 40). And Alcidamas said about statues that they 'are imitations of real bodies; they give joy to the beholder, but they serve no useful purpose' (*Oratio de sophistis* 10, quoted in Tatarkiewicz 1970, I, p. 104).

Thirdly, some of the Sophists remarked upon the illusions generated by representational works of art. Their opinions varied from a sort of grudging admiration to outright suspicion. Thus, in the *Dialexeis* we find, 'For whoever, in tragedy and painting, causes the greatest deception by creating the most realistic work – this man is considered to be the best at his craft' (*Dialexeis* 3.10). But Heraclitus complained that, 'The actor's art deceives those who know. They say one thing and think another; they come on and go off, the same persons yet not the same' (quoted in Tatarkiewicz 1970, I, p. 107).

Finally, it was a Sophist who first expounded a relativist conception of beauty. All relativism in philosophy had its origin in Protagoras' saying that man is the measure of all things, and this is the spirit that we find in another quotation from the *Dialexeis*: 'I think that, if someone ordered every man to throw on a pile whatever each of them considered to be ugly, and then to retrieve from the pile whatever each of them thought was beautiful, then nothing would be left, because everything would have been divided up amongst themselves. For each man has a different opinion' (*Dialexeis* 2.18).

It was against this kind of relativism that Socrates, and more particularly Plato, took a stand.

Socrates

Most of what we know about Socrates we owe to Xenophon and Plato. In Plato's dialogues, however, it is quite impossible to distinguish Socrates' thinking from his own. Xenophon has left us a more detached account of Socrates – although, some would say, his Socrates is a duller person than Plato's Socrates. In Xenophon, at any rate, we find a Socrates who espouses two main propositions about beauty: that the beauty of a thing cannot be separated from its function; and that works of art attempt to represent the ideal rather than the actual. It is very likely that this strong connection between beauty and function expresses an extreme polemical stance against the Sophists' relativism that we have just mentioned. The intended use of a thing is a property that is objectively observable and verifiable, so if use and beauty are then bound tightly together they may come to be regarded as equally objective. However, in this attempt to salvage the objective meaning and value of beauty, Socrates was compelled to ignore the specificity of art, to merge the artistic with the artefactual. In one passage, Socrates replies to the questions of Aristippus in the following fashion.

> 'Is a dung basket beautiful then?'
> 'Of course, and a golden shield is ugly, if the one is well made for its special work and the other badly.'
> 'Do you mean that the same things are both beautiful and ugly?'
> 'Of course – and both good and bad ... What is beautiful for running is often ugly for wrestling, and what is beautiful for wrestling is ugly for running. For all things are good and beautiful in relation to those purposes for which they are well adapted, bad and ugly in relation to those for which they are ill adapted.'
> (*Memorabilia* III.8.6–7)

The same view is expressed on many other occasions, in many other texts, of which we quote one more, from Xenophon's *Banquet* [*Convivium*], (*Memorabilia* V.4): '[Things are beautiful] if they are well made for the respective functions for which we obtain them, or if they are naturally well constituted to serve our needs.'

Socrates' functionalist conception of the beautiful (and the good also) should be read, we have suggested, as a polemical attempt to overcome the risks of Sophistic relativism. Plato's master was too concerned with the universal to allow room for relativism and subjective opinion. But it also reflects the strongly ethical character of Socrates' outlook, which encouraged him to interpret beauty in terms of universal human goals, purposes and aspirations. This element in Socrates was to be explicitly and extensively elaborated by Plato. In both, the idea of moral beauty arises because of their conviction that there is a spiritual as well as a physical beauty: a beauty of mind and character, of laws and societies.

Finally, Socrates suggested that art aims to produce an idealisation of the real, by way of an elevation of the physical to the spiritual, of the temporal to the eternal, of the particular to the universal. In a dialogue with the artist Parrhasius, Socrates is reputed to have said: 'When you copy types of beauty, it is so difficult to find a perfect model that you combine the most beautiful details of several, and thus contrive to make the whole figure appear beautiful' (*Memorabilia* III.10.2). The belief that works of art involve a metamorphosis of reality and experience into an ideal and imaginary form is still as significant today as it was for Socrates, even though contemporary art often rejects the classical conceptions of beauty, and refuses to celebrate order, harmony and the ideal.

Plato's Theory of Forms

Plato achieved a synthesis of all the intuitive and incipient ideas about art and beauty that his predecessors had held in a fragmented and unsystematic manner. For the first time in the classical world, he formulated a mature and complete aesthetic theory, or at any rate a complete philosophical articulation of the aesthetic sensibility of the Greeks.

'If there is anything worth living for', Plato wrote, 'it is to contemplate beauty' (*Symposium*, 211d). This remark is a witness to his passionate interest in the nature of beauty, and, in general, to the importance of beauty and art in classical Greek culture. Plato's account of art and beauty was rooted in his theory of forms. He argued that reality, in its supreme and perfect state, is to be identified with a supratemporal world of ideas. These ideas or forms – which are non-material, eternal, unchanging and intelligible substances – are the supreme archetypes and prototypes, the ontologic and epistemic models, of everything that exists. Even the human mind presupposes and depends upon this objective order of ideas. The material objects that we encounter in the empirical world are mere copies, imperfect reproductions, of the ideas. Physical objects are many and limited, changing and unstable, particular and imperfect, precisely because they are subject to their material constitution. They cannot, on their own, explain and justify their existence or their intelligibility. They exist and are explicable only with reference to the universal substances or archetypes.

Plato's entire metaphysical theory can be seen as a continuous reformulation and modulation of one central theme: *mimesis*. Things in the everyday material world are copies of the eternal ideas. Works of art are also copies. Indeed, they are said by Plato to be copies of copies, imitations of imitations, twice removed from their ideal prototypes and hence twice removed from truth and intelligibility. *Mimesis* became the central principle of Plato's aesthetics, and it was to remain the central principle of all subsequent philosophical reflections on art and beauty throughout the Middle Ages and up to the Renaissance.

Beauty

Plato returned to the question of beauty very frequently. This was partly because the Greek word for beauty, *tó kalón*, could be taken to signify every kind of excellence, not just aesthetic excellence. It was also due to the fact that Plato, like many of his predecessors, believed that beauty, goodness and truth were coextensional terms: that is, while the three values were not identical, each was ontologically dependent on the others and the presence of each necessitated the co-presence of the others. Thus, whenever Plato discussed truth or goodness or any kind of excellence or virtue, he almost invariably discussed beauty as well.

Here, however, we will focus upon beauty as an aesthetic quality in the modern sense, and primarily as a quality in works of art. Plato rejected the functionalist conception of artistic beauty held by Socrates and some of the Sophists. He agreed with the distinction between useful arts and arts intended to give pleasure alone, but he held also that beauty was independent of function, that aptness for a particular function did not in itself constitute the beauty of artefacts (see *Hippias Major* 290d–291c). Furthermore, he rejected the hedonistic conception of beauty held by some Sophists (*Hippias Major* 297e–303e). He recognised that art gives pleasure – indeed, he believed that the pleasure evoked by beauty was one of the keenest and highest pleasures in life. But the pleasure we take in art, though caused by its beauty, does not constitute its beauty. A thing is not good and beautiful because we like it; rather, we like it because it is good and beautiful.

In short, Plato's theory of beauty was objectivist. He adopted the Pythagorean view that beauty consists in order, proportion and harmony, a view particularly evident in the *Timaeus*, where – in 31c – he says that unity in things is brought about by proportion and harmony. Later in the *Timaeus* he also wrote, 'All that is good is beautiful, and what is beautiful is not ill-proportioned' (87c). This conception of beauty was connected with his theory of forms; for he argued that, just as objects are copies or reproductions of the eternal ideas or forms, so the beauty that we find in objects is a copy or reproduction of the eternal idea or form of beauty.

It was in the *Symposium* that Plato expounded his conception of beauty most eloquently and memorably. Here he described, through the words of Diotima – the only female character in Plato's dialogues – how we may progress from the experience and delight of physical beauty to a state in which we contemplate eternal beauty, face to face. In such a state, Diotima is quoted to say, we achieve perfect virtue and a kind of immortality.

> Beginning from obvious beauties he must for the sake of that highest beauty be ever climbing aloft, as on the rungs of a ladder, from one to two, and from two to all beautiful bodies; from personal beauty he proceeds to beautiful observances, from observance to beautiful learning, and from learning at last to that particular study which is concerned with the beautiful itself and that alone; so that in the end he comes to know the very essence of beauty. In that state of life above all others . . . a man finds it truly worth while to live, as he contemplates essential beauty. (*Symposium* 211c–d)

Art, the Arts and Imitation

For Plato, as for Greek and classical culture in general, things were 'real' in so far as their existence was ontologically objective. Subjectivity had no role in defining existence or being, which pre-existed consciousness and was unaffected by experience and knowledge. It followed that the objects produced by human intelligence and skill were not, strictly speaking, 'new' realities, but were rather copies or rearrangements of the ontological order of things. This was Plato's metaphysics of art: whatever was objectively real predetermined the possibilities of art and craft, but remained itself ontologically unaffected by art and craft.

Plato, as we have said, adopted the Sophist distinction between the useful arts and the arts intended just to give us pleasure, but he altered the distinction in one significant respect. The latter category, which had been defined by the Sophists in terms of pleasure alone, was redefined by Plato in terms of imitation. In the *Sophist*, for instance, he writes, 'There are two kinds of art . . . There is agriculture, and the care of living creatures, and the art of making or shaping vessels; and there is the art of imitation' (219a).

Plato is here moving to the view that a certain category of the arts, what we would now call the fine arts, can be defined as imitative or mimetic. However, one must be careful about this point, for Plato used the term 'mimesis' in more than one sense. There is a sense in which *all* arts are mimetic, because they all produce copies, to a greater or lesser degree, of the ideas or forms. A carpenter, for instance, when he manufactures a bed manufactures a material copy of the idea of a bed. In this sense, the products of art and craft are mimetic in exactly the same sense that natural objects are mimetic, since they too are material copies of the ideas. Even here, however, Plato places a different value on nature and art, for he believes that the copies produced by art can never measure up to the copies found in nature:

> The greatest and most beautiful things are the work of nature and of chance, and the lesser things that of art – for art receives from nature the great and primary products as existing, and itself moulds and shapes all the smaller ones, which we commonly call 'artificial'. (*Laws* 889a)

Art, then, is inferior to nature. But Plato makes a further subdivision within the arts themselves, between those which are purely imitative and those which, as he puts it, 'lend their aid to nature'. It is clear that by the former he means the fine arts, and he deals with these at length in his *Republic*. Here we will quote one further passage from the *Laws*, in which this distinction is clearly set forth:

> Art . . . produces playthings which share little in truth . . . such as images in painting and music, and the arts which accompany these. The arts which produce something serious are those that lend their aid to nature – like medicine, agriculture, and gymnastic. (*Laws*, 889d)

Imitation, Appearance and Falsification

All arts and crafts, then, are imitative in some sense, and to some degree, of the ideas. But Plato considers the fine arts – music, painting, poetry, drama – to be primarily and fundamentally mimetic. The useful arts aid and complement the real world. The fine arts exhaust themselves in the exercise of imitation alone. This kind of mimesis, as we saw, is described by Plato as 'a kind of production, but of images, not of real things' (*Sophist* 265b). It is worth noting that the Greek word translated here as 'image' is *eídolon*, literally 'a small idea'. From this same root comes the word 'idol' – a small or false god! This conception of art as imitation, art as the production of 'small ideas' – semblances, copies of copies, toys, falsifications – is presented in highly critical and polemical terms in Books 3 and 10 of the *Republic*. But it is only natural to expect such a negative evaluation of art in a work that maps the structure of a perfect society, a society ruled by ideal moral values and educative goals.

In Book 10 Plato distinguishes three kinds of bedstead. One kind is made by god, namely the eternal and immutable idea of a bedstead. A second kind is manufactured by a carpenter, and is a piece of furniture upon which people can actually sleep. It is a material copy of the idea. Thirdly, a painter makes a representation of a bedstead. Thus the artist's production is far removed from the idea, and has not even got the value of utility. It is not even a very good copy of the carpenter's bed, for the requirements of pictorial perspective mean that the bed is painted from only one particular visual point of view.

It follows, for Plato, that art is deficient in truth and in usefulness, and deficient even as a copy of a copy. This is why it is a mere distraction in an ideal city-state, and is in general a distraction for anyone who genuinely seeks truth and the good.

> Paintings and works of art in general are far removed from reality, and ... the element in our nature which is accessible to art and responds to its advances is equally far from wisdom. The offspring of a connection thus formed on no true or sound basis must be as inferior as the parents ... This will be true not only of visual art, but also of art addressed to the ear, poetry as we call it. (Plato, *Republic* 603b)

Condemnation and Celebration of Art

The passage just quoted introduces yet another element in Plato's discussion of art: namely, that there is a part of the human psyche which is strongly attracted and affected by art, but which, according to Plato, has nothing to do with the pursuit of knowledge and wisdom. This passionate, irrational and intuitive element in human nature can produce powerful and alluring excitements. Art is a distraction from the pursuit of wisdom just because it excites this irrational and affective part of the mind.

It is often suggested, therefore, that Plato wanted to suppress this affective part of the mind, that he advocated a life of reason independent

of the emotions. The truth, however, is more complex and more interesting. Plato *was* censorious and moralistic about art. But in several of
his works he also celebrated its genius and its power. There is in fact
a radical ambiguity in Plato's responses to art, between the philosopher
and moralist on the one hand and the poet and connoisseur on the
other.

His condemnation of art is strong and explicit, and is found mainly
in the *Republic* and the *Laws*. The reasons for his condemnation are
by now clear. In the first place, works of art are copies of copies of the
ideas, so they embody and communicate only pale, fleeting glimpses
of the truth. It is only through reason that we can see the essences of
things in their fullness and purity. In the second place, art is so glori-
ously warm and exciting that it distracts us from the exercise of reason
and makes us wallow instead in art's sensuous and emotional pleasures.
Plato therefore held that art should be severely controlled in an ideally
ordered society, or even excluded altogether if the artists are, so to
speak, too good at their job.

> We have, then, a fair case against the poet and we may set him down
> as the counterpart of the painter, whom he resembles in two ways:
> his creations are poor things by the standard of truth and reality,
> and his appeal is not to the highest part of the soul, but to one
> which is equally inferior. So we shall be justified in not admitting
> him into a well-ordered commonwealth, because he stimulates and
> strengthens an element which threatens to undermine reason.
> (*Republic* 605a–b)

On the whole, however, Plato was inclined not so much to banish
artists completely as to compel them to produce only edifying and
morally improving works:

> In dealing with the poet, the good legislator will persuade him, or
> compel him, with his fine and choice language to portray by his
> rhythms the gestures, and by his harmonies the tunes, of men who
> are temperate, courageous, and good in all respects, and thereby to
> compose poems aright. (*Laws*, 660a)

All of this has drawn down weighty criticisms on Plato's head. But
a number of points are worth noting. In the first place, the controls
that he would place upon art are not as restrictive as they may seem.
Even if they were rigorously implemented, there would still remain a
very significant body of artworks – one that would nowadays include
such works as Milton's *Lycidas*, Aquinas's hymns, Dante's *Commedia*,

numerous poems by Donne, Herbert and Gerard Manley Hopkins, as
well as a multitude of paintings and sculptures from the classical,
medieval and Renaissance periods. Secondly, Plato spends a good part
of Book 3 of the *Republic* explaining that an education in literature
and music is essential in the preparation of young children for the life
of reason. Thirdly, Plato's criticisms of art in the *Republic* occur almost
in the same breath as his insistence that the experience of beauty is
essential in a well-lived life, that it is an essential constituent in the life
of reason, that love of truth and love of beauty feed upon one another,
and that the aim of education is to produce a love of beauty. Plato was
unlike almost any other aesthetician before or since because of this
radical dualism between art and beauty; and whatever we may think
of this dualism, he did succeed in defining the two fundamental categories of aesthetic discourse.

Fourthly, and most importantly, there are some other works in
which Plato praises art, especially poetry, above all other pursuits. In
the *Ion*, the *Symposium* and the *Phaedrus*, artistic creativity is linked
to the idea of divine inspiration or *manía*. This was not meant to be
a denigration of art in favour of reason, but an exposition of art's
specific character and value. Poetry is described in the *Ion* as an activity in which reason plays no part, but this is not because it is inferior
to reason, but because it goes beyond reason.

> A poet is a light and winged and sacred thing, who is unable to
> compose until he has been inspired and put out of his senses, and
> his mind is no longer in him ... God takes away the mind of these
> men and uses them as his ministers, just as he does soothsayers and
> godly seers, in order that we who hear them may know that it is not
> they who utter these words of great price, when they are out of
> their wits, but that it is God himself who speaks and addresses us
> through them ... These beautiful poems are not human or the
> work of men, but divine and the work of gods ... The poets are
> merely the interpreters of gods, according as each is possessed by
> one of the heavenly powers. (*Ion* 534b, e)

The poet's power is a mysterious gift whereby reason and reflection
are taken over by divine enthusiasm and inspiration. Reason surrenders
and withdraws. The inspired artist shares in divine powers and par-
takes in divine wisdom. With this kind of narrative we are far removed
from the conception of art as an inadequate imitation. The principle of
inspiration and divine participation replaces the principle of mimesis.
In the *Symposium* and the *Phaedrus*, art is regarded as a specific kind
of divine mania, closely associated with love. Poetic creation demands

the abandonment of human reason and the adoption of a non-rational, un-dialectical, intuitive disposition. And this is far from being defective or evil. On the contrary, divinely imbued 'madness' or manic enthusiasm is a highly desirable state, for 'the best things come to us through madness, when it is sent as a gift of the gods' (*Phaedrus* 244a).

This theory of a divinely inspired mania, granted as a gift, was the foundation of all subsequent mystical and ecstatic theories of art. It also laid the foundations for subsequent theories of non-intentional and non-conscious elements in the mental processes required for artistic production. Mediated through Neoplatonists such as Plotinus and the Pseudo-Dionysius, it strongly influenced the early Middle Ages – the Victorines for instance – and reappeared in the Renaissance and again in the Romantic period. Its latest manifestation is in the theories of unconscious inspiration or influence espoused by Freud and Jung.

We conclude by summarising four central points in Plato's contribution to the history of aesthetics: (1) his two conceptions of art, one grounded on the principle of mimesis, the other on the principle of inspiration; (2) the radical dependence of art upon pedagogical and moral concerns; (3) the dualistic separation of art and beauty; (4) his central preoccupation with the idea of beauty and his relatively peripheral concern with the problem of art.

Finally, his metaphysics, which was congenial to the spirit of Christian theology, and his aesthetics, mainly concerned with the essence and definition of beauty, came to inform a large part of the Western tradition, and survived the centuries in the form of a variety of metaphysical, transcendental and dualistic conceptions of being and of beauty.

Aristotle: From Aesthetics to Poetics

Diogenes Laertius (V.1.20) tells the story that, when Aristotle was asked why anyone should spend so much time reflecting on the meaning of beauty, he replied, 'This is the question of a blind person'. The anecdote is a witness both to Aristotle's interest in the nature of beauty and also to the highly developed aesthetic consciousness characteristic of Greek culture. Plato had concentrated on the question of *kalokagathía* – a composite term, made up from the Greek words for 'beauty' and 'goodness', which referred to the quality in things which arises from the integration and interdependence of these two values. Plato thus paid more attention to beauty than to art. Aristotle, in contrast, wrote very little about beauty and a great deal about art. Aristotle, we might say, constructed a poetic theory ('poetic' comes from a Greek verb meaning 'to make'), whereas Plato constructed an aesthetic theory ('aesthetic' comes from a Greek word meaning 'to perceive'). Plato and Aristotle together drew up the basic principles and parameters of all subsequent philosophical reflection on art and beauty in the Western tradition. The Platonic and Neoplatonic assumptions that beauty is the pre-eminent artistic value, and that art shares in a metaphysically transcendent beauty, survived strongly up to and during the Renaissance. A secularised version appeared again in Hegel, and some element of Platonism can be found in all philosophies of beauty. Aristotle's poetic approach to art, which was largely ignored through-out the Middle Ages because of the unavailability of texts, re-emerged strongly in the Renaissance, and then again in the nineteenth century. Our own century, too, is Aristotelian in spirit; for, like Aristotle, we are interested primarily in the structures and semiotics of art.

Aristotle's Poetic Approach: The Meaning of Art

In the previous chapter we mentioned two Greek words for art, *téchne* and *poíesis*. Aristotle's definition of *téchne* was as follows.

> All art [*téchne*] is concerned with coming into being, that is, with contriving and considering how something may come into being which is capable of either being or not being, and whose origin is in the maker and not in the thing made; for art is concerned neither with things that are, or come into being, by necessity, nor with things that do so in accordance with nature, since these have their origin in themselves. (*Nicomachean Ethics* 1140a)

This passage distinguishes sharply between art and nature. The distinction was already widespread in Greek thought and was to be found in Plato and the Sophists generally. But Aristotle was the first to exploit its full potential, because he was the first philosopher to give a satisfactory explanation of nature. Plato's metaphysics was dominated by the concept of transcendent and eternal ideas, and this discouraged any systematic reflection on the properties of material things, natural phenomena, and nature in general. Aristotle, in contrast, achieved for the first time a detailed and convincing metaphysics of nature. This was the most radical of the differences between these two great philosophers, the master and his pupil.

Art and Nature

We must therefore consider, first of all, Aristotle's conception of nature. At the beginning of Book 2 of the *Physics* he writes:

> Some things exist by nature, some from other causes. By nature the

animals and their parts exist, and the plants and the simple bodies (earth, fire, air, water) – for we say that these and the like exist by nature. All these things plainly differ from things which are not constituted by nature. For each of them has within itself a principle of motion and of stationariness, in respect of place, or of growth and decrease, or by way of alteration. (*Physics* 192b)

Shortly afterwards he pulls these ideas together into a definition: 'Nature is a principle or cause of being moved and of being at rest ... in virtue of itself and not accidentally' (*Physics* 192b).

Nature, therefore, is the indwelling or immanent principle of organic beings, and so an immanent ontological process of self-unfolding and self-completion. Nature, that is, is its own beginning or principle and its own end or *télos*. Natural organisms have their principle of growth within themselves and aim at reproducing themselves, so achieving the self-preservation of the species. The acorn has within itself the power to develop into an oak tree, and also strives to reproduce itself by means of the mature tree, which produces further acorns.

Natural beings come into being and pass away. But Nature, the universal process, abides in every change and motion and in everything that moves, lives, grows and develops. Interestingly, and perhaps surprisingly, Aristotle often explains what he means by nature and natural beings, by comparing them with artefacts – a bedstead, a garment, a house, a statue. He does this throughout Book 1 of the *Physics*, and frequently elsewhere in his writings. The main purpose of the analogy, perhaps its sole purpose, is to stress that all material entities, whether in nature or in art, have a particular end or *télos*.

Despite this analogy, however, Aristotle persists in distinguishing between natural beings, which have the principle of their coming to be and change within themselves, and artificial products, which have their principle and cause in some external agent. Natural beings come into existence according to necessity, since they are ruled by immanent or internal causes, while artefacts may or may not come into existence, since they are produced by causes external to them. Eggs and acorns have within themselves the power to grow, change and mature into animal and vegetable organisms, but blocks of marble and random collections of words do not have within themselves the power to transform and organise themselves into statues or poems. While *nature* is a form of immanent and intrinsic production, *art* is a form of external and extrinsic production. In this sense, a work of art or craft possesses and manifests a lower degree of ontological perfection. Unlike nature and natural organisms, it is not self-constitutive, it does not immanently abide by itself in autonomy and self-sufficiency, and does not come into existence by its own internal causes. Art does not have the substantial or ontological perfection of nature.

Instead, art involves a kind of confederation between the properties of the materials used by the maker and the plan or *eídos* in the maker's mind. This *eídos*, Aristotle reminds us in the *Nichomachean Ethics*, involves 'a true course of reasoning' (1140a). Art, therefore, implies and requires knowledge – a knowledge of how to organise and transform materials so as to achieve a form and a goal. Aristotle distinguishes five kinds of such productive skills: 'Change of shape, as a statue; addition, as things which grow; taking away, as the Hermes from the stone; putting together, as a house; alteration, as things which change in respect of their matter' (*Physics* 190b).

Despite the complex ontological differences between the products of nature and of art, there is one respect in which they are closely analogous, and this is indicated in the following passage:

> If a house had been a thing made by nature, it would have been made in the same way as it is now by art; and if things made by nature were made not only by nature but also by art, they would come to be in the same way as by nature . . . If, therefore, artificial products are for the sake of an end, so clearly also are natural products. (*Physics* 199a)

The analogy is that they are both teleonomic. That is, art and nature are both driven by a goal-oriented dynamism, a dynamism that is immanent in nature but externally derived in art from the maker's design. It is this analogy that allows Aristotle to draw a well-known comparison, in the *Poetics*, between a tragedy and a natural organism:

> Just . . . as a beautiful whole made up of parts, or a beautiful living creature, must be of some size, but a size to be taken in by the eye, so a story or plot must be of some length, but of a length to be taken in by the memory. (*Poetics* 1451a)

Mimesis

For Plato, *mímesis* signified a passive and subservient copying of something else, whether it be an artefact, a natural phenomenon, or an idea. Aristotle's conception of mimesis is often held to be the same as Plato's. We shall demonstrate, however, that this was not the case, that Aristotle developed a meaning for the term that was a great deal more sophisticated, and which made it the defining characteristic of fine art. It thus enabled him to distinguish sharply between the broader and the narrower senses of art – *téchne* and *poíesis* respectively – and even to conceive of art as an autonomous form of experience and as an independent field of enquiry (see Santoro-Brienza 1993, pp. 38–46).

His distinction between useful crafts and fine arts is stated in the following terms: 'Art [*téchne*] either brings to an end [it realises and fulfils] what nature cannot achieve, or it mimesises nature' (*Physics* 199a). The word 'mimesise' translates the Greek term, and is deliberately used here in order to avoid the prejudicial connotations of the verb 'to imitate'. The central role of mimesis is emphasised in a passage from the *Poetics*: 'Epic and tragic poetry, as well as comedy, dithyramb, and most music for aulos and lyre, are all, taken as a whole, kinds of mimesis' (1447a). Such is the importance of the concept of mimesis that we must now examine its meaning more closely.

Mimesis as Imitation and Reproduction

It cannot be denied that Aristotle sometimes uses the term 'mimesis' to signify, or to signify in part, an act of reproductive copying – for instance in the miming skill of actors. This is explicitly stated when Aristotle is discussing the origin of poetry and art.

> It is clear that the general origin of poetry was due to two causes, each of them part of human nature. Imitation is natural to man from childhood, one of his advantages over the lower animals being this, that he is the most imitative creature in the world, and learns at first by imitation. And it is also natural for all to delight in works of imitation. (*Poetics* 1448b)

This, however, is only the beginning, for Aristotle tells us more than once that mimetic representation is also an instrument for the articulation and communication of knowledge. The following quotation is typical:

> To be engaged in learning something is the greatest of pleasures not only to the philosopher but also to the rest of mankind, however small their capacity for it. The reason for delight in seeing a picture is that one is at the same time learning, gathering the meaning of things. (*Poetics* 1448b)

His concept of mimesis is further elaborated when he claims that mimesis is not simply or exclusively cognitive, but also involves the formal properties of the mimetic object.

If one has not seen the thing before, one's pleasure will not be in the picture as an imitation of it, but will be due to the execution or colouring or some similar cause. (*Poetics* 1448b)

If we take these three quotations together we find that, so far, mimesis involves: (1) copying; (2) the expression and communication of knowledge; and (3) the construction of an object with formal properties that give pleasure.

Mimesis as Production of Verisimilitude

The full character of Aristotelian mimesis, however, is revealed when we turn to consider the objects of mimesis – the objects 'mimesised'. Aristotle mentions two such objects: nature (*physis*) and action (*práxis*). The first of these is mentioned in the *Physics*, in which we find the famous statement *he téchne mimeítai tén physin*. It is usually rendered in English as 'Art imitates nature', but this can be a very misleading translation. It should be noted that Aristotle does not say that art mimesises *natural objects*, but that it mimesises *nature* – that is, nature itself, the universal immanent process of self-unfolding, the internal principle that produces and manifests itself in natural beings. Nature, understood in this way, is not a thing or an object, nor a set of things or objects. It is not an empirically observable object or phenomenon at all, nor any kind of datum or given. And nature in *this* sense cannot be copied or imitated or represented by any kind of concrete image.

What art 'imitates' is, rather, the teleological dynamic of nature. Let us recall again the analogy that Aristotle repeatedly drew between nature and art:

Nature [*physis*] is the end or that for the sake of which. For if a thing undergoes a continuous change toward some end, that last stage is actually that for the sake of which ... The arts, too, make their material (some simply make it, others make it serviceable), and we use everything as if it was there for our sake. For we also are in a sense an end. (*Physics* 194a)

That is, while natural processes have their goal within themselves, artificial processes have mankind as their goal and aim, since they emerge from an *eídos*: a mental picture, plan and model in the artificer's mind. So, however we choose to translate the words of the sentence *he téchne mimeítai tén physin*, its meaning is *Art produces extrinsically as nature unfolds immanently*. Art mimesises nature because it proceeds towards a goal, just as nature does. Nature does it immanently; art does it by a creative human decision.

The second object of artistic mimesis that Aristotle mentions is action or praxis. 'Action' might seem at first sight to be more concrete than 'nature', since it suggests that artists produce copies of people talking, laughing, fighting and so on. However this is not the case, since 'action' here connotes, not individual and concrete human actions, but action in general, action as the human dimension of nature. Action in this sense is part of the human essence and of human identity. That this is what Aristotle means by art mimesising action is shown by the following quotation.

> The unity of a plot does not consist, as some suppose, in its having one man as its subject. An infinity of things befall that one man, some of which it is impossible to reduce to unity; and in like manner there are many actions of one man which cannot be made to form one action ... In writing an *Odyssey*, he [Homer] did not make the poem cover all that ever befell his hero – it befell him, for instance, to get wounded on Parnassus and also to feign madness at the time of the call to arms, but the two incidents had no necessary or probable connection with one another – instead of doing that, he took as the subject of the *Odyssey*, as also of the *Iliad*, an action with a unity of the kind we are describing. (*Poetics* 1451a)

This long passage should resolve the ambiguity, sometimes real, sometimes apparent, in Aristotle's employment of the words 'action' and 'actions' in the singular and the plural form. It is clear that Aristotle is not talking here about individual actions understood as *behaviour*. Instead, he emphasises that *poetry mimesises one single action*: that is, a single spiritual event, a coherent set of existential experiences, a mental project, one single immanent order of events, one *mythos* and one fundamental plot. Action or praxis is the unfolding of the immanent energy and activity of the psyche. Obviously, the internal operations and the immanent energy of the soul cannot be 'copied' or 'imitated' in the sense of duplication in an image.

This interpretation of Aristotle is further confirmed by his comparison of poetry with history.

> The poet's task is to describe, not the thing that has happened, but a kind of thing that might happen, that is, what is possible as being probable or necessary ... One [The historian] describes the thing that has been, and the other [the poet] a kind of thing that might be. Hence poetry is something more philosophical and of graver

import than history, since its statements are of the nature rather of universals, whereas those of history are singulars. (*Poetics* 1451a–b)

Although the word 'mimesis' does not appear in this passage, it helps none the less to explain what mimesis is. History gathers and reconstructs particular events, embedded in particular contexts and linked to particular agents. Poetry, in contrast, gathers and grasps what could happen according to probability, and what must happen according to necessity. In so far as the poet does not deal with given facts and events, with empirical data, his activity of mimesising cannot be understood as the activity of copying or representing. This must be so, because the objects of poetic mimesis – the possible, the probable, the necessary, what could be and what ought to be – *are not empirically observable facts, data and phenomena*. This point is made yet again in another passage of the *Poetics* (1460b8), where Aristotle distinguishes three objects of mimesis:

The poet being a mimetist, like painters and any other artist, must of necessity mimesise one of three objects: things as they were or are, things as they are said or thought to be, or things as they ought to be.

It is obvious that 'things as they are said or thought to be', and 'things as they ought to be' are not the kind of concrete events or objects that can be copied or reproduced.

Aristotle, then, did not hold a representationally realistic conception of art. He did not accept Plato's conception of art as the production of simulacra. Instead, he insisted that artists deal with probability, possibility and inner necessity: in a word, with verisimilitude, that is, with the imaginative, creative, fictional constructions of symbolic and ideal worlds. A probable impossibility, he wrote, is to be preferred to something possible but improbable. 'It may be impossible that there should be men such as Zeuxis painted. "Yes", we say, "but the impossible is the better thing; for the paradigm or ideal type must go beyond [reality]"' (*Poetics* 1461b).

Artistic Verisimilitude and Beauty as Ideal Epiphany

For Aristotle, we conclude, art does not consist in the copying or reproducing of a pre-existing state of affairs, but rather in forming and producing an ideal state of affairs. Through art we encounter metaphors and epiphanies of probable and possible worlds. This is what is meant by art's verisimilitude: that it follows the laws of ideal probability and necessity, and so engenders in us a heightened experience of knowledge and delight. Aristotle, in fact, stresses both aspects of art: both its objective properties and its relation to the human subject. Its objective properties ensure that art is autonomous, that its value depends upon its intrinsic properties rather than upon its utility. 'The products of art', he wrote, 'have their goodness in themselves' (*Nicomachean Ethics* 1105a). Thus he differed decisively from Plato, for whom the edifying and educational role of art was a crucial determinant of its aesthetic value. For Aristotle, utility was accidental rather than essential. Young people may be taught drawing, he said, because it makes them judges of the beauty of the human form, and 'to be always seeking after the useful does not become free and exalted souls' (*Politics* 1338a–b). As for music, it should be studied, 'not for the sake of one, but of many benefits, that is to say, with a view to education, or katharsis . . . Music may also serve for intellectual enjoyment, for relaxation and for recreation after exertion' (*Politics* 1341b).

The relation of art to the human spirit, therefore, was one that subsisted as much within an autonomous realm of the aesthetic as in its pedagogical benefits. Aesthetic delight, coupled with knowledge and intellectual insight, was the aim of art and the effect of beauty. Beauty is, of course, one of the objective properties of art, and was described by Aristotle as 'order, symmetry and definiteness' (*Metaphysics* 1078a). This, as we have seen, was a commonplace of the classical world, and we find it also mentioned in the *Poetics*:

> Beauty is a matter of size and order, and therefore impossible either in a very minute creature, since our perception becomes indistinct as it approaches instantaneity; or in a creature of vast size – one, say, a thousand miles long – as in that case, instead of the object being seen all at once, the unity and wholeness of it is lost to the beholder. Just in the same way, then, as a beautiful whole made up of parts, or a beautiful living creature, must be of some size, but a size to be taken in by the eye, so a story or plot must be of some length, but of a length to be taken in by the memory. (*Poetics* 1450b–1451a)

As we have already noted, Aristotle here uses an analogy with natural organisms to explain the properties and criteria of artistic beauty. He also refers, yet again, to the role of human perception and experience in beauty's definition. The properties of beauty are determined in relation to what is required in order to perceive the properties. Finally, the properties in question are structural as much as individual properties. This last point reappears in a passage from the *Politics* (1284b):

The painter will not allow the figure to have a foot which, however beautiful, is not in proportion, nor will the ship-builder allow the stern or any other part of the vessel to be unduly large, any more than the chorus-master will allow anyone who sings louder or better than all the rest to sing in the choir.

Works of art, therefore, are co-realities or verisimilitudes of reality. They have a structural coherence and unity comparable to that of natural objects. They have a teleological, goal-directed character analogous to the immanent teleology of nature. Art is thus a spiritualised nature, a production of the ideal. So we arrive finally at the theory that works of art, though ontologically inferior to natural beings, succeed by their mimetic power in creating spiritual ideals embodied in physical forms, and are thus in a sense spiritually superior to natural beings. As Aristotle put it, works of art differ from realities, 'because in them the scattered elements are combined, although, if taken separately, the eye of one person or some other feature in another person would be fairer than in the picture' (*Politics* 1291b).

Poetic Strategies and Rhetorical Devices

Aristotle's remarks on literature, drama, tragedy and epic have proved to be the most influential part of his aesthetics. In both the *Poetics* and the *Rhetoric* he examined literature in detail, especially tragedy and epic poetry, as well as the formal strategies that give to verbal texts their aesthetic value and persuasive power. The *Poetics*, in the single extant section that has reached us, deals partly with epic poetry but mostly with tragedy. It is, by now, widely accepted that the work contained also a study of comedy, which has not survived. After some introductory remarks about how to define art, mimesis and poetry, Aristotle gives his famous definition of tragedy:

A tragedy, then, is the mimesis of an action that is serious and also, as having magnitude, complete in itself; in language with pleasurable accessories, each kind brought in separately in the parts of the work; in a dramatic, not in a narrative form; with incidents arousing pity and fear, wherewith to accomplish its katharsis of such emotions. (*Poetics* 1449b)

In this definition we can identify the following elements: (1) tragedy is a form of mimesis; (2) its object and theme is human action, more precisely serious or noble action; (3) it employs ornate, poetic and not prosaic language or diction; (4) it is structured according to a certain order and size; (5) it induces feelings of pity and fear, and a kathartic final resolution. Although Aristotle's conception and definition of tragedy have been widely accepted in the Western literary tradition, they have also given rise to a huge variety of interpretations and voluminous debate. The concept of katharsis in particular has preoccupied a host of commentators and theorists, not least because Aristotle never properly explained what he meant by it.

More important for our purposes, however, is Aristotle's analysis and discussion of diction [*léxis*] (see Santoro-Brienza 1993, pp. 29–37). We quote a central passage in this discussion:

> The excellence of diction is for it to be at once clear and not mean. The clearest is diction made up of ordinary words for things, but it is also mean . . . On the other hand diction becomes distinguished and non-prosaic by the use of unfamiliar terms, that is, strange words, metaphors, lengthened forms, and everything that deviates from the ordinary modes of speech. But a whole statement in such terms will be either a riddle or a barbarism . . . A certain admixture, accordingly, of unfamiliar terms is necessary. These – the strange word, the metaphor, the ornamental equivalent, and so on – will save the language from seeming mean and prosaic, while the ordinary words in it will secure the requisite clearness. (*Poetics* 1458a)

This passage deals with a topic to which Aristotle returned on many occasions and which he treated systematically in his *Rhetoric*. Diction must be clear, familiar, hence readily decodable, on the one hand. However, a diction that had nothing other than these properties would be commonplace and prosaic. On the other hand, diction could be rare, strange and unpredictable. In this case we would have what Aristotle calls barbarism or jargon – a private dialect in danger of collapsing into meaningless noise. If the strangeness were sustained by a relentless use of metaphorical devices, we would have enigmas, riddles and undecodable puzzles. Poetically effective diction cannot be prosaic language, nor can it be a semi-private dialect or jargon. The clarity of ordinary diction, sustained by familiarity of code or convention, can avoid banality and the commonplace, and thus produce poetic utterances and aesthetic effects, only when adequately combined with unfamiliar, unexpected, metaphorical or other figurative elements.

Centuries before structuralism, linguistics and semiotics, Aristotle had already seen that a work of art can produce the shock of epistemic discovery and delight only if it employs a diction that is both surprising and familiar. Effective poetic diction requires a symbiotic interaction of estrangement, violation, and deviation, with the obvious and the conventional (see, in particular, *Rhetoric* 1422a12ff.). As Umberto Eco puts it:

> What happens in the aesthetic message is what happens also in tragic plots, according to the precepts of Aristotelian poetics. The plot must bring about something that surprises us, something that goes beyond our expectations and is therefore paradoxical and contrary to common opinion. But if this event is to be accepted, if we are to identify with it, it must also, however incredible, conform to certain conditions of credibility. It must be endowed with a certain verisimilitude. It is stupefying, incredible, that a son should return home after long years of war, savagely intent on killing his mother, with the help and encouragement of his sister. Confronted with a fact so contrary to any expectation, the spectator grows tense, shocked by the ambiguous informational power of an extraordinary situation. The event must be made credible and probable, lest it be rejected as mere madness. And in fact the son intends to kill his mother, because she had induced her lover to kill her husband. (Eco 1968, p. 63)

3

From Byzantium
to Chartres:
The Middle Ages

All things are artificial, for nature is the art of God.
(Sir Thomas Browne)

Introduction

This chapter deals with the long and varied period of European history that is usually, and misleadingly, known as the 'Middle Ages'. The name is misleading in part because it might suggest that for a thousand years there was little change or development in European thought or behaviour. In fact it was a period marked by frequent and radical changes, and by an inventive genius in technology, agriculture, urbanisation and education, civic structures and financial practices, that laid the foundations of the modern world.

In one respect, however, the Middle Ages did constitute a single epoch. For, as we said in the last chapter, its fundamental world outlook was theocentric. Medieval Europe was scarred by frequent theological controversies, and conflicts between Church and State, but it was profoundly Christian in every aspect of its life and thought – although, it must be remembered, it was a Christianity marked by its intellectual, political and military encounters with the brilliant and expansive civilisation of Islam.

The Middle Ages produced a variety of aesthetic theories, all of them flowing from its theocentric world-view. Beauty was held to be objective, just as in the classical world, but also to be transcendent, since it was an attribute of God, and a sign of the divine origin of the universe. This complex thesis – that earthly beauty is both a sign of divine beauty and also, ultimately, identical with it – is the single most characteristic thesis in medieval aesthetics. It was articulated in a rich variety of philosophical and theological works, some influenced by Plato, and others, after the twelfth century, by Aristotle. We cannot give an exhaustive survey of medieval aesthetics here, so we will not deal with the three most important schools of aesthetics in the monastic tradition: the Cistercians, the Victorines and the School of Chartres.

Nor will we discuss in detail important thinkers such as John Scottus Eriugena, Bonaventure and Duns Scotus. We choose instead four representative figures, and will deal with each in turn. These are Plotinus, the Pseudo-Dionysius, Augustine and Aquinas.

Plotinus: Between Classical Antiquity and the Middle Ages

Most historians emphasise the classical foundations and character of Plotinus' thought, the influence upon him of Aristotle and, to an even greater extent, of Plato. He was one of the last heirs of the classical tradition. But here we want to focus instead upon Plotinus' originality, as the founder of Neoplatonism and the earliest exponent of a new sensibility that was to develop subsequently throughout the Middle Ages. His belief in a transcendent and unitary source of being, with its strongly spiritualistic and mystical overtones, made him congenial to the theocentric medieval vision of the universe. Although Plotinus did not himself embrace Christianity, he strongly influenced and informed the Christian sensibility of the early Middle Ages.

The entire philosophy of Plotinus was inspired and sustained by a search for unity in all things. He observed and analysed the teleological dynamism of human experience, and, at the same time, aimed to devise a metaphysics that could explain and account for apparently conflicting ontological and existential categories, such as unity and diversity, singularity and plurality, totality and particularity, harmony and dissonance, light and darkness, perfection and imperfection, spirit and matter. In order to make sense of all of these, and to provide a metaphysical foundation of being, Plotinus conceived the ultimate origin of things as a self-sufficient and perfect unity or, as he called it, the *One*.

The 'One' is the primordial source of all reality, and also the final goal to which all reality aspires. The manifold plurality of distinct beings emanates from the One. They are produced or generated by its super-abundance, only to return to it again as their source and goal, there to find rest, fulfilment and final verification. Just as the sun cannot but diffuse its rays of light, so the One cannot but diffuse existence. And we humans, as pilgrim rays of the One, cannot find rest in the multiplicity, dispersion and fragmentation that we experience in our everyday lives. We carry within ourselves a deep nostalgia for the infinite and perfect unity that is our ultimate source. Imperfect and limited as we may be, unable to speak of or even to know the One as it is in itself, we have, all the same, an intuitive inner sense of it. The One is unutterable, and is describable only in terms of what it is not;

but it is somehow present to us by way of an intuitive and connatural sympathy.

The One does not abide in a condition of solitude beyond being. Rather, it generates its first opposition, its Other – for, as Plotinus put it, in a remarkable and lapidary sentence, 'If you take away otherness, it will become one and keep silent' (*Enneads* V.1.4). The first Other that emanates from the One is *Intellect* or, in the Greek original, *Nous*. Nous contemplates the One eternally, and in doing so it thinks the totality of all eternal ideas. It is similar to the One in that it beholds in perfect unity the multiplicity of all purely intelligible thought. Nous also acts as an inward, silent poet and craftsman, for it generates in turn the Soul, which is the third actor in this metaphysical drama. The Soul is the intermediary link between intelligible ideas and empirical or sensuous reality. In fertile contemplation of the Intellect, the Soul, with an unconscious and extrovert poetic power, generates the realms of sensory experience. It is eternal, yet it operates in time and history. Eternally contemplating the eternal Intellect that makes her pregnant with perfection and unity, the Soul generates both the cosmic *anima mundi* and the individual souls of individual beings. Though itself one and eternal, like the One and the Intellect, the Soul produces a multiplicity of embodied living souls. From it proceed all visible, tangible, perceptible things, and it holds all things in perennial life, order, harmony and beauty. Everything, immersed in the emanated flux of participated perfection, carries within itself the mark of its unitary origin and a nostalgia to return to perfect one-ness. Everything is organically linked to the total order of being and is, therefore, the sign, symbol and messenger of everything else.

Beyond and below the three unitary hypostases of the ontological order – the One, the Intellect, the Soul – lies the empty, boundless, indeterminate simplicity of matter. This is the realm of human beings, of individual human souls. These souls, Plotinus tells us, are ashamed of being in the body, weakened and isolated by their separation from the All-Soul from which they emanate. Yet persons are protagonists in the Plotinian universe. For, despite their material nature, persons participate also in Soul, Nous and ultimately the One. The human soul attunes itself to truth, goodness and beauty, and so readies itself for contemplation of the supreme One. The path leading to this end is the pathway of art. For beauty is a reflection in the human world of its ultimate source.

Sensory Beauty and Spiritual Beauty

Art and beauty therefore occupied a central position in Plotinus' philosophy, and he devoted two of the fifty-four treatises of the *Enneads* to them (I.6 and V.8). This entire work, it should be added, is one of the most elegant and inspiring works in the philosophical literature of the West. Plotinus echoed Plato in distinguishing between a purely spiritual world and a material and sensory world. But he also believed that the material world possessed a unity and perfection that flowed into it from Intellect and Soul. He placed a high value on sensuous beauty, and considered it to be the most perfect property of this world. Because of its beauty it carries the imprint of the spiritual world and participates in that world. Physical beauty is thus a sign of spiritual beauty and a participation by the physical in the spiritual.

Most of Plotinus' predecessors had accepted the Pythagorean definition of beauty, that it consists in order, measure, proportion and harmony. Plotinus disagreed. He argued that we can predicate these properties only of material objects, but not of simple entities – that is, entities without parts – and not, therefore, of spiritual entities either. It does not make sense to call light or colour symmetrical, nor to call virtue and truth symmetrical. Yet light, colour, virtue and truth can be called beautiful. Beauty must therefore be different from symmetry or any comparable property.

> Nearly everyone says that it is good proportion of the parts to each other and to the whole, with the addition of good colour, which produces visible beauty, and that with the objects of sight and generally with everything else, being beautiful is being well-proportioned and measured. On this theory nothing single and simple but only a composite thing will have any beauty. It will be the whole which is beautiful, and the parts will not have the property of beauty by themselves, but will contribute to the beauty of the whole. But if the whole is beautiful the parts must be beautiful too; a beautiful whole can certainly not be composed of ugly parts; all the parts must have beauty. (*Enneads* I.6.1)

Plotinus concluded, in the light of this argument, that even when physical beauty is accompanied by symmetry, symmetry is not the cause of beauty but only one of its manifestations. Matter symmetrically structured is beautiful, not in itself and not for its symmetry, but only if it possesses spiritual perfections such as unity, truth, reason and form. Plotinus concluded that beauty cannot be understood and defined in terms of structure and relationship. Instead, beauty is a quality. The primordial quality and the fundamental metaphysical attribute of all reality is unity. Beauty also, as a universal characteristic of all reality, consists in unity. Thus, since matter in itself has no metaphysical unity, beauty cannot come from matter, but has its source in the soul: 'Soul makes beautiful the bodies which are spoken of as beautiful; for since it is a divine thing and a kind of part of beauty, it makes everything it grasps and masters beautiful' (*Enneads* I.6.6).

For Plotinus, therefore, beauty is the manifestation in matter of an inner, ideal form or image of perfection. This concept of beauty, as revelation of soul and spirit in matter, has proved to be particularly fortunate, significant and lasting in the history of aesthetics.

Art and the Arts

The originality of Plotinus' aesthetics, especially when compared with Plato, is strongly evident in his conception of art. He divided the arts into two main categories: those that make and employ their own specific tools, and those that exploit the forces and powers of nature. He then distinguished five types of arts and crafts: (1) those that produce physical objects, such as architecture; (2) those that improve nature, such as medicine; (3) those that induce a sense of harmony and rhythm, such as music and dance; (4) those that primarily generate beauty, such as the fine arts, poetry and music; (5) finally, those primarily concerned with knowledge, such as geometry. Two central ideas are particularly relevant here. In the first place, Plotinus rejected the Platonic assumption that fine art is fundamentally mimetic and imitative of pre-existing reality. In the second place, he believed that the defining role of the fine arts is that they produce or manifest beauty in the material world. We shall comment on these two central propositions, and then conclude our presentation of Plotinus' aesthetics by looking at his description of aesthetic experience.

Art, Mimesis and Beauty

We have already remarked upon the complex meanings of *mimesis* in classical antiquity, particularly in the theories of Plato and Aristotle. Plotinus' understanding of this concept was significantly closer to Aristotle's than to Plato's. He rejected the widespread idea that fine arts are simply forms of representation. As well as redeeming the value of physical beauty, Plotinus also stressed the autonomy of art, just as Aristotle had, and considered that the products of art belonged to, because they were generated by, the realm of the artist's soul and intellect. It followed that 'the arts do not simply imitate what they see, but they run back up to the forming principles from which nature derives; then also . . . they do a great deal by themselves, and, since they possess beauty, they make up what is defective in things' (*Enneads* V.8.1).

Art is thus a creative process of imbuing matter with form and spirit. The following passage is particularly worthy of attention, for it sums up the main points in Plotinus' conception of art.

> Let us suppose a couple of great lumps of stone lying side by side, one shapeless and untouched by art, the other which has been already mastered by art and turned into a statue of a god or of a man . . . and if of a man not just of any man but of one whom art has made up out of every sort of human beauty. The stone which has been brought to beauty of form by art will appear beautiful not because it is a stone . . . but as a result of the form which art has put into it. Now the material did not have this form, but it was in the man who had it in his mind even before it came into the stone; but it was in the craftsman, not in so far as he had hands and eyes, but because he had some share of art. So this beauty was in the art. (*Enneads* V.8.1)

In this passage we can see how emphatically Plotinus correlated art with beauty, and also how close his conception of art was to our own conception of fine art. Plotinus understood, better than any previous philosopher of art and beauty, that the primary task of art consists in the creation of beauty by the process of informing and spiritualising matter.

Aesthetic Experience: Empathy, Cognition and Intuition

For Plotinus the source of sensuous beauty is the artist's mind and spirit. It is also the mind and spirit in us that acknowledges and rejoices in the beauty of nature and of art, even though we may also make use of the senses in order to do so. This spiritual ability, however, must undergo a process of refinement in order to be empathically or con-naturally attuned to beauty. Plotinus explained this in metaphorical language.

> One must come to the sight with a seeing power made akin and like to what is seen. No eye ever saw the sun without becoming sun-like, nor can a soul see beauty without becoming beautiful. You must become first all godlike and all beautiful if you intend to see God and beauty. (*Enneads* I.6.9)

This passage perfectly reflects the overall structure and spirit of Plotinus' philosophy, centred as it is upon the concept of effusive participation and therefore of universal sympathy and attunement among all the orders of being. Empathy is, furthermore, a kind of cognition: not scientific, discursive, mediated knowledge grounded on observation and logically structured explanations, but a direct, immediate and intuitive apprehension of reality and truth by means of images. Plotinus understood that art and the contemplation of beauty afford us an intuitive insight into reality and constitute one of the highest forms of human experience.

The Pseudo-Dionysius

Plotinus' ideas exercised a powerful influence on the entire Middle Ages, in part because they were adopted and transmitted by an anonymous Christian writer of the fifth century who was familiar with the writings of the Fathers of the Church, and was mistakenly identified with Dionysius the Areopagite, the first Bishop of Athens. This anonymous author, now known as the Pseudo-Dionysius, left a series of treatises containing important metaphysical and theological reflections on art and, especially, beauty. There emerged from these writings a transcendental conception of beauty – that is, a conception of beauty as an attribute of all being – which was eventually given its final and most complete expression by Thomas Aquinas.

The Pseudo-Dionysius' aesthetic ideas are to be found in his *Ecclesiastical Hierarchy*, the *Celestial Hierarchy*, the *Mystical Theology*, but particularly his *Divine Names*. In all of these works he fused together classical Greek thought, Plotinus' Neoplatonism and Christian ideas. He conceived of beauty as one of the attributes of God – one of the 'divine names' – and devised a transcendental metaphysics that proved to be congenial to the new religious aspirations and experiences of Christian Europe.

Transcendental Beauty

The Pseudo-Dionysius borrowed his metaphysics mainly from Plato and Plotinus, and like many of his contemporaries he tried to formulate a theological conception of beauty which identified it with God, the origin of being. 'Whatever there is, whatever comes to be', he wrote, 'is there and has being on account of the Beautiful and the Good' (*Divine Names* 705D). His reflections on the aesthetic were not based upon the sensory experience of beautiful things, nor were they concerned with the nature of physical beauty. He was interested first and foremost in divine beauty, which he described in a hyperbolic language crowded with superlatives, such as *super-substantial beauty*, *universal beauty* and *super-beauty*. This is a beauty larger than life, a transcendent and abstract beauty, a beauty of the terrible and the sublime.

Beauty... in itself and by itself is the uniquely and the eternally beautiful. It is the superabundant source in itself of the beauty of every beautiful thing... From this beauty comes the existence of everything, each being exhibiting its own way of beauty. For beauty is the cause of harmony, of sympathy, of community. Beauty unites all things and is the source of all things. It is the great creating cause which bestirs the world and holds all things in existence by the longing inside them to have beauty. And there it is ahead of all as Goal, as the Beloved, as the Cause toward which all things move, since it is the longing for beauty which actually beings them into being. (*Divine Names* 704A)

In his descriptions of this transcendent beauty, the Pseudo-Dionysius often employed the metaphor of light. It was a metaphor derived in part from Plotinus, and in part a reflection of the Byzantine sensibility, which was disposed to think of light as a symbol of the heavenly kingdom and of God. That sensibility was perfectly expressed in the golden, glittering brilliance of the icons and mosaics of the time, whose luminosity was intended to symbolise divine or spiritual perfection. Byzantine artists aspired to conceal matter – or, to put it differently, to transform matter into light.

The Pseudo-Dionysius also defined beauty, in a manner inherited from the classical tradition, as consonance, harmony and proportion.

The 'beautiful' which is beyond individual being is called 'beauty' because of that beauty bestowed by it on all things, each in accordance with what it is. It is given this name because it is the cause of the harmony and splendour in everything, because like a light it flashes onto everything the beauty-causing impartations of its own well-spring ray. Beauty 'bids' all things to itself (whence it is called 'beauty') and gathers everything into itself. (*Divine Names* 701C–701D)

Art and Sensuous Beauty as Symbol

The Pseudo-Dionysius followed Plotinus in holding that beauty originates in God, emanates from God, and returns to God. Physical beauty, though imperfect and opaque, carries within itself the imprint of its participation in the spiritual beauty of the divine. Divine beauty, for all its transcendence, resonates throughout the physical world. Forms created by an artist, therefore, 'even those drawn from the lowliest matter, can be used, not unfittingly, with regard to heavenly beings. Matter, after all, owes its subsistence to absolute beauty and

keeps, throughout its earthly ranks, some echo of intelligible beauty'
(*Celestial Hierarchy* 144B).

Visible things, therefore, are images of invisible things. In more general terms, everything is the symbol and sign of something else, and
ultimately of God. Art and physical beauty are one of the means by
which we come to understand and contemplate the divine. Once again,
as in Plato, art and physical beauty are supposed to serve a function
beyond that of inducing an independent and self-sufficient aesthetic
experience.

> Any thinking person realises that the appearances of beauty are
> signs of an invisible loveliness. The beautiful odours which strike
> the senses are representations of a conceptual diffusion. Material
> lights are images of the outpouring of an immaterial gift of light.
> (*Celestial Hierarchy* 121D)

From this it also follows that the primary and essential task of the
artist consists in copying and reproducing the paradigmatic perfections
of absolute beauty.

> The Word of God makes use of poetic imagery... but, as I have
> already said, it does so not for the sake of art, but as a concession
> to the nature of our own mind. It uses scriptural passages in an
> uplifting fashion ... to uplift our mind in a manner suitable to our
> nature. (*Celestial Hierarchy* 137B)

In the Pseudo-Dionysius' reflections, as in all Byzantine aesthetics,
and later throughout the entire Middle Ages, the task of art was to
produce images and symbols of spiritual reality, or of God, so that
people's minds might be edified and elevated from their worldly
concerns to the contemplation of theological and religious truths.

Augustine: The Great Synthesis

Augustine is rightly considered a primary figure in the shaping of
medieval thought. His main intellectual achievement was to synthesise
the pagan Greek, Hellenistic and Roman traditions with the sources
of Christian thought – the Bible, the Fathers of the Church – and also
the Pseudo-Dionysius in so far as he was mediator of the Platonic and
Neoplatonic metaphysics.

Augustine's intellectual journey, from ancient philosophy to
Christian theology, corresponded to his existential journey from
scepticism and paganism to religious conversion. By an interesting

coincidence, even the historical events through which Augustine lived registered a profound transition in the Western world. In his lifetime, he witnessed the final dissolution of the classical world, and the collapse of the waning Roman Empire. His intellectual masterpiece, *The City of God*, is a wonderful meditation on the nature of history, and a reflection on worldly events that were unfolding under his very eyes.

Schooled in the ancient art of rhetoric and hence influenced by ancient wisdom in general, and by Cicero and Horace in particular, Augustine is reputed to have written a work specifically dedicated to the problem of beauty. That work, not preserved in its entirety, carried the title *De pulchro et apto* (On Beauty and Suitability). Two other works, *De ordine* (On Order) and *De musica* (On Music) also devote considerable space to aesthetic issues. Numerous references to art, literature and beauty can be found in all of his writings, especially the *Confessions*, *The City of God*, *De vera religione* (Of True Religion) and his commentaries on the Scriptures. We must particularly note that, after his conversion, and hence after considerable exposure to the Bible and the theological writings of the Fathers of the Church, Augustine became acquainted also with Plotinus, whose discussions of beauty in the *Enneads* strongly influenced his views.

The Objectivity and Transcendence of Beauty
Augustine's explanation of beauty combined and consolidated all of the philosophies that preceded him. It synthesised four main ideas: objectivity, transcendence, harmony and pleasure. The first of these he took for granted, like virtually everyone else in the classical, medieval and Renaissance periods. '[Things] give pleasure', he wrote, 'because they are beautiful' (*De vera religione* xxxii: 59). Neoplatonism then brought with it a reason or ground for the objectivity of beauty. In its Christian version, first in the Pseudo-Dionysius and then more systematically and accessibly in Augustine, the ground of beauty was identified with God. God's perfect beauty was the source of beauty in everything else, and so the beauty of objects was a token or sign of their creator. To love and enjoy material beauty was to be touched and entranced by God himself. 'The eyes delight in beautiful shapes of different sorts and bright and attractive colours', Augustine wrote. But he went on,

> The beauty which flows through men's minds into their skilful hands comes from that Beauty which is above their souls and for which my soul sighs all day and night. And it is from this same supreme Beauty that men who make things of beauty and love it in

its outward forms derive the principle by which they judge it.'
(*Confessions* X.34)

Beauty is perceived by the eyes of the mind rather than the eyes of the
body, and to experience beauty is to encounter something that transcends our own embodied existence.

Augustine was particularly taken by the notion that beauty was a
form of harmony or measure. The word he often used for this quality
was *convenientia*, which means a fitting together of parts. He sometimes referred to it also as *copulatio*, that is, an intimate coalescence into
a unified whole. Thus the concept of unity came to occupy a central
role in his aesthetics. 'Every form of unity', he wrote in one of his
letters, 'is a form of beauty' (Letter 18). And he frequently invoked
the concept of unity whenever he was expounding the nature of
aesthetic harmony:

> In all the arts it is symmetry that gives pleasure, preserving unity
> and making the whole beautiful. Symmetry demands unity and
> equality, the similarity of like parts, or the graded arrangements of
> parts which are dissimilar. (*De vera religione* xxx.55)

The concept of unity, since it meant a unity produced by the coalescence of parts, also generated the concept of order. 'There is no ordered
thing', Augustine wrote, 'that is not beautiful' (*De vera religione*
xii.77).

This group of concepts – harmony, unity, and order – defined the
essential criteria of beauty for Augustine, and they clearly reveal the
lasting influence of Pythagoreanism in the aesthetics of the classical
world to which Augustine still, in part, belonged. For Augustine the
criteria meant that the experience of beauty was not exclusively sensuous, but required an element of intellectual insight. The senses may
apprise us of raw colours, shapes and sounds, but only the intellect
can apprise us of unity and order.

> Reason came to the assistance of the eyes, and, observing the
> heavens and the earth, knew that they gave pleasure because of
> their beauty, and their beauty because of their shapes, their shapes
> because of their dimensions, and their dimensions because of their
> number. (*De ordine* II.15.42)

Aesthetic apprehension is therefore a process that is as much intellectual as sensuous; it involves a level of cognition whose object is available to the intellect alone. To experience beauty is to know something

about the world, not just to luxuriate in sensations. Thus we return again to the transcendence of beauty. For Augustine it was the intellect, the faculty that people share with God, that perceived beauty, the revelation of the divine in the physical world.

Beauty and Aesthetic Experience

Augustine possessed one of the great intellects of European history, but he was also a passionate and emotional man. He was well aware, and knew from his own experience, of the physical effects of beauty upon people. He did not, therefore, neglect or disregard the role of the senses in aesthetic experience. But sensuous delight, for Augustine, was not aesthetic in itself. He distinguished between the beautiful (*pulchrum*) and the pleasant (*suave*). The latter was a purely sensuous affair, whereas beauty was sensuous and intellectual at one and the same time. He also distinguished the beautiful from the useful (*aptum*). The usefulness of an object was judged by the intellect alone, and did not require any involvement with sensuous pleasure. Aesthetic experience for Augustine was something that demanded the presence of the whole person, body and spirit. After all, its object was the presence of the divine in the universe. Interestingly, Augustine was one of the few philosophers who have considered the notion of ugliness. He thought of ugliness, rather as he thought of evil, as a sort of ontological deficiency: it existed whenever the properties required for the fullness of being – properties such as harmony, unity and order – were absent or defective. Nothing could be completely ugly, however, because if a thing existed at all it retained some degree of harmony and order, and so some residual trace of beauty.

Art and the Arts

Augustine, like Plato, feared and distrusted the 'illusions' of art – or, rather, some of the effects that these illusions could have upon us. On the other hand, he was disposed like Plotinus to associate the artistic with the beautiful. The reason for this was that he thought of God as the supreme artist, and of the whole cosmos as a work of art. Thus, instead of art imitating nature, nature was itself a creation of art. The human arts were in some way similar to divine art, in that their primary function was to create traces, tokens and symbols of the beauty which was a mark of God's nature and presence.

As for the illusions produced by art, these were inevitable in an activity involving artifice and imaginative invention. There was a kind of falsehood in art. However, this falsehood was a condition of there being any art in the first place: a painted object, after all, is definable in part by the fact that it is not a real object. One of the most remarkable passages about art in all of Augustine's writings occurs in his *Soliloquia*.

> The picture of a man, though it tries to be like him, cannot be a true man any more than a character in the books of the comedians. These things are false, not from any will or desire of their own, but from the necessity of following the will of their authors. On the stage, Roscius wants to be a false Hecuba, but by nature he is a true man. By so wanting, he is also a true tragedian, so far as he fulfils the part. But he would be a false Priam if he gave himself out as Priam and was not ... In all such matters truth and falsehood are inevitably intertwined; indeed, if there is to be truth in one respect there must be falsehood in another. How could Roscius be truly a tragic actor if he refused to be a false Hector, Andromache, Hercules or the like? How could a picture of a horse be truly a picture if the horse were not false? (*Soliloquia* II.10.18)

In this passage, Augustine secured for his successors an idea that came to occupy a central role in aesthetics and poetics: that there is a kind of truth specific to art, a fictional and invented truth, a truth created by the human mind and hand.

The High Middle Ages: The Thomistic Synthesis

The various aesthetic theories that emerged or survived in the Middle Ages found their most complete formulation and synthesis in Thomas Aquinas. Aquinas was strongly influenced in his thinking by Platonism and Neoplatonism. But he was also influenced, and just as strongly, by Aristotle. He had been introduced to Aristotle by his teacher, Albert the Great (Albertus Magnus), and then himself became the most important figure in the Aristotelian Revival of the late twelfth and thirteenth centuries. So far as aesthetics is concerned, his Platonism is evident in his conception of beauty, and his Aristotelianism can be seen in his analysis of aesthetic perception and experience. It is a matter of regret, all the same, that Aquinas did not know of Aristotle's *Poetics*.

We will begin by looking at two important themes in Aquinas's philosophy: the principle or concept of analogy, and the problem of the transcendental properties of being.

Metaphysical Presuppositions: Analogy and Transcendentals

In the medieval Christian world, God was not just the maker, but the existential source, of everything that there is. Everything participated, in varying degrees, in the divine perfection of being. For this reason, the multiplicity of different entities in the universe were understood to share their being with one another, regardless of their concrete diversity. This is what the principle of analogy signifies: a participation in a common pool of existence, a universal mutuality that coexists with universal difference. All things in the universe differ from one another, are distinct from one another, and are identical only with themselves, and yet at the same time they mutually refer and point to one another across the vast universe of being.

In so far as being is present in varying degrees in different things, analogy implies a hierarchical structure of the universe: a kind of ladder ascending from inorganic matter, through organic matter, plants, living animals, humans, angelical substances and finally God. It is in the light of the principle of analogy that we must understand the medieval preoccupation with symbolism in general, and the conviction that everything is fundamentally linked to everything else. The principle of analogy produced the metaphysical lyricism of a well-known poem by Alan of Lille (Alanus de Insulis):

> Omnis mundi creatura
> quasi liber et scriptura
> nobis est in speculum;
> nostrae vitae, nostrae mortis
> nostri status, nostrae sortis
> fidele signaculum.
> Nostrum statum pingit rosa,
> nostri status decens glosa,
> nostrae vitae lectio;
> quae dum primo mane floret,
> defloratus flos effloret
> vespertino senio.
>   (Quoted in De Bruyne 1946, II, p. 338)

> [Every creature of this earth
> is like a picture or a book;
> it is a mirror of ourselves.
> It is a faithful sign
> of our life and of our death,
> of our condition and our fate.
> The rose is a picture,
> a fitting image of our state,
> a lesson on our life;

for it flowers in early morning,
and the fading flower blooms
in the evening of age.]
(trans. H. Bredin)

This poem could serve as a manifesto of the medieval sensibility, articulating as it does an analogical order of reality, and thus the possibility of a universal symbolism.

The principle of the analogical structure of all reality points in turn to the other fundamental medieval assumption, encoded in the notion of the transcendental properties of being. This theory, Aristotelian in its provenance, was given its definitive form by Aquinas. The theory held that being in general – and hence each individual being or thing – is one, true and good. Being and unity, just like being and truth, and being and goodness, *convertuntur*: that is, they are interchangeable and co-extensive. Unity connotes a thing's identity with itself and distinctness from everything else. Truth means an absence of contradiction, and thus an intelligibility or knowability and openness to the enquiring mind. Goodness means appetibility, desirability and therefore the capacity to serve as a goal for the will. Being is unified within itself and distinct from what is not; it is free from contradiction, and therefore an object of intellection; it is a positive value and the object of will and desire. Everything that is, precisely in so far as it participates in the activity of being, by the same token participates – analogically – in the transcendental properties of being: it is one, true and intelligible, good and appetible. It has also been convincingly argued that Aquinas considered beauty to be yet another transcendental property of being (Kovach 1963). From this it would follow that, as Aquinas put it, 'There is nothing that does not participate in beauty' (*Comm. Div. Nom.* IV.5).

Beauty: Vision and Delight

Aquinas's reflections on beauty and art were never set forth systematically or thematically, but are dispersed through his works in a fragmentary and occasional fashion and in a variety of different contexts. Many are to be found in his commentaries on Aristotle. Others occur in his commentary on the Pseudo-Dionysius' *Divine Names*. Pre-eminently they appear in his *Summa Theologiae*, a mature work in which we find Aquinas's most developed and definitive views on aesthetics, poetics, beauty and the meaning of art.

Aquinas has two complex definitions of beauty, both of which require further analysis. The first is as follows.

Goodness has to do with appetite/desire [*appetitus*] ... Beauty, on the other hand, has to do with the cognitive powers, for we ascribe beauty to things which give us pleasure when they are seen. Thus beauty consists in due proportion, because the senses take delight in things duly proportioned as being similar to themselves – for the senses, and every cognitive power, are a kind of reason. Cognition takes place through assimilation, and assimilation pertains to order, so beauty properly belongs to the realm of formal causes. (*Summa Theologiae* I.5.4ad1)

This is a passage of some density, but we can extract from it the core of a definition: *those things are called beautiful which, when seen, grant us pleasure*. It should be noted that this is an objectivist definition of beauty, since the logical subject of the sentence is 'things which give pleasure when seen'.

The second definition, in contrast, has a subjectivist character, since it focuses upon the experiential side of the equation. When extrapolated from its context, it is as follows: *let that be called beauty, the very apprehension of which pleases*. Here, *apprehension* is the subject of the sentence and is clearly indicated as the cause of delight. Let us now quote the text more fully:

It is part of the nature of beauty that, in seeing or knowing it, the will and desire [*appetitus*] come to rest. The senses involved in the experience of beauty – sight and hearing – are those particularly involved in cognition. Thus we speak of beautiful sights and beautiful sounds. In the case of the other senses we don't speak of beauty; we don't call tastes and smells beautiful. What the notion of beauty adds to the notion of good is an involvement with the cognitive powers. We call something good when it satisfies the will and desire [appetitus]; but we call it beautiful when the simple apprehension of it gives us pleasure. (*Summa Theologiae* I–II.27.1ad2)

The central elements in these two definitions are: sight or vision [*visio*], and pleasure or delight [*complacentia*], in the first definition; and apprehension or sense-perception [*apprehensio*] and again pleasure or delight [*complacentia*], in the second definition. A detailed analysis of these elements, together with some reference to Aquinas's conception of the human faculties, will bring to light the richness and complexity of the definitions. To begin with, *visio* in the first definition is refined in the second into the notion of *apprehensio*: sight [*visio*] stands for perception in general, but particularly for the senses of sight and hearing, and not for taste, touch and smell, not if the object of perception is the beautiful. *Visio* also refers to intellectual apprehension, which is a form of cognition. Modern linguistic practice also warrants the metaphorical use of the word 'seeing' to signify intellectual grasp and understanding. Thus we talk of 'seeing' the point that Aquinas is making. It is a usage that is entirely consistent with Aristotle's observations and with Western tradition, according to which knowledge is a kind of sight, an 'insight' as we say. For Aquinas, moreover, the analogy between sight, sense-perception and intellectual insight does not rest solely on a metaphorical transposition and displacement. For Aquinas understood that sense-experience cannot be separated from cognition, but rather is related to and structured by intellectual experience. The senses, as he put it, are a kind of reason. He also wrote:

> The word seeing or vision indicates [*patet in nomine visionis*] that it refers in the first instance to the activity of the sense of sight. But because of the dignity and certainty of this sense the name is extended, in accordance with linguistic usage, to all cognition by the other senses ... and ultimately even to intellectual knowledge. (*Summa Theologiae* I.67.1c)

Let us now turn our attention to the second vital element in the definition of beauty: pleasure and delight [*complacentia* or *delectatio*]. As we saw a moment ago, Aquinas holds that in seeing or knowing beauty 'the will and desire [*appetitus*] come to rest'.

Pleasure and delight refer to: (1) the gratification of the senses when confronted by objects that have certain properties, and that we call beautiful; and (2) the mental satisfaction we experience when we have adequately grasped the form or internal structure of a physical object presented to the senses. More importantly, however, pleasure is produced by (3) the satisfaction of 'appetite'. This term, a translation of the Latin *appetitus*, means both 'desire' and 'will' taken together. It is the movement of the will to possess what one desires because one judges it to be good. More succinctly, Aquinas says in one place that pleasure comes from the possession of what we love: 'The cause of pleasure is love. For everyone takes delight in whatever he possesses and loves' (*Comm. Nic. Eth.* III.19.6).

We can therefore conclude that, for Aquinas, beautiful things are objects of love and desire. They are not only sensuously perceptible and knowable, but also lovable and good. For, as he frequently remarked, goodness has to do with *appetitus*, with desire and will. There is goodness in beauty, and so the experience of beauty involves our desires and our will as well as our cognitive faculties. Aquinas, following Aristotle, is quite clear about the conceptual distinction between goodness and beauty: goodness is the proper object of the will, while beauty is primarily the proper object of sensation and cognition. But at the same time, he identified in the beautiful object the presence of goodness, without which we could not feel the sense of emotional delight, pleasure and well-being that aesthetic experience brings. As he put it:

> Beauty and goodness are the same thing in an object, for both clarity and consonance are contained within the concept of goodness. But they differ conceptually [*ratione*], because beauty adds on to goodness a reference to the knowledge that something is the way it is. (*Comm. Div. Nom.* IV.5)

The Harmonious Synthesis of Beauty

We are now in a position to reconstruct Aquinas's conception of aesthetic experience. In the presence of beauty, whether natural or artistic, we perceive sensible properties that stimulate and gratify our senses. Sensory experience leads to an intellectual insight into the structure, order and form of the object, so that the intellect is stimulated and gratified in its turn by its intuitive grasp of the form. Anything that is perceived, and whose form is intuitively known, is experienced as desirable, and, as a result, stimulates our emotions also. The harmonious correspondence between the object and our faculties brings it about that our senses, our intellect, and our will are satisfied, and this generates a sense of pleasure and delight.

It is an experience in which all of our faculties are active and perfectly harmonised among themselves, just as they are perfectly attuned to the object of contemplation. We experience an intuitive, gratifying unity of all our faculties with all the aspects of an object which exhibits truth, in so far as it is intelligible and open to the intellect, and exhibits goodness, in so far as it is desired by our will and grants delight. The aesthetic experience is a harmonious and unifying experience in which subject and object cannot be separated and distinguished. (As Yeats put it, *How can we know the dancer from the dance?*) That experience of fusion is kin and analogous to the experience of love, both physical and spiritual, and to the experience of deep reflection, prayer and anticipated beatific vision.

We can now appreciate the claim that Aquinas regarded Beauty as a fourth transcendental property of being – and even more spectacularly, that Beauty is the synthesis of the other three transcendentals (Unity, Truth and Goodness). If we were to accept this claim, we would be compelled to hold that everything is beautiful in its own way. This, however, would turn the specifically aesthetic meaning of beauty into a metaphysically transcendent category applicable to everything that is. Aquinas seems at times to be quite close to this position, which was congenial to the medieval conception of the universe as a beautiful masterpiece issuing from the hands of God, the supreme artist.

Objective Properties: Integrity, Proportion, Clarity

Aquinas believed that objects had to possess certain properties in order to be beautiful. Two of these, proportion and clarity, he took directly from the Pseudo-Dionysius:

> From what Dionysius has written we can gather that the notion of beauty involves both clarity and proportion – for he says that God is called beautiful because He is the cause of consonance and clarity in the universe. (*Summa Theologiae* II–II.145.2c)

And elsewhere he wrote:

> We call a man beautiful because of his correct proportions in size and shape, and because he has a bright and glowing colour. So it should be accepted in other cases that a thing is called beautiful when it possesses the clarity of its kind, whether spiritual or corporeal, and is constructed in the correct proportions. (*Comm. Div. Nom.* IV.5)

Two things are worth mentioning in these passages. First, the properties of clarity and proportion are not just material properties, but can be properties of material and non-material entities alike. Aquinas was keenly interested in the nature of material beauty, to a much greater extent than most of his medieval predecessors; but he did not think for a moment that beauty was merely physical. Secondly, both of these passages – just like the two definitions of beauty in the section 'Beauty: Vision and Delight' – emphasise the semantic function of the word 'beauty'. Aquinas, that is, seems to be concerned with the meaning of the term, the reasons why we *call* something beautiful. In contemporary philosophy, the distinction between the semantic and the ontological is thought to be significant. For Aquinas, however, the semantic presupposes and is grounded in the ontological. We should not be misled by his manner of writing into thinking that Aquinas was a closet sceptic about the objectivity of beauty.

To the concepts of clarity and proportion, taken from the Pseudo-Dionysius, Aquinas added a third property, integrity. All three properties are defined in a frequently quoted passage from the *Summa Theologiae*:

> Three things are necessary for beauty. The first is integrity or perfection; for whatever is defective is therefore ugly. The second is due proportion or consonance. The third is clarity, so that whatever has a bright and clear colour is called beautiful. (*Summa Theologiae* I.39.8c)

We will now briefly consider each of these properties.

1. *Integrity or perfection* signifies the completeness of something. It signifies that an object can be called beautiful provided that it exhibits all the structural and organic elements that its specific nature or essence requires. It cannot be beautiful if it lacks any of its ontologically necessary attributes and elements. A human body is disfigured by the absence or privation of a limb or organ, and is thus imperfect and ugly. Beauty is grounded in ontological completeness and perfection. Obviously, this criterion is particularly and primarily applicable to natural organisms and phenomena, rather than to works of art.

2. *Proportion or harmony* had already been identified as an aesthetic property by the Pythagoreans. The Pythagoreans, however, understood proportion primarily in quantitative and mathematical terms. In Aquinas we find rather a qualitative conception of proportion, which had been adumbrated by Augustine before him. This he called *convenientia*, which means an intrinsic attunement and correspondence, whether in the physical or the spiritual world, a correspondence between inner and outer reality, appearance and essence, matter and form.

3. *Clarity*, finally, was explained in the first instance in terms of bright colours – scarcely surprising in view of medieval visual taste, some trace of which can still be witnessed, with spectacular effect, in the vibrant flags, scarves and costumes at Siena's *palio*. Aquinas also spoke of the clarity and beauty of virtue and, more radically, stated that 'the clarity of a glorified body derives from the clarity of the soul' (*Summa Theologiae* III.45.2ad1). In this sense, clarity signifies the shining forth of form or essence in material and physical appearances. Augustine had defined beauty as 'the splendour of order' and Albert the Great had defined it as 'the splendour of form'. Aquinas was aware of these predecessors and, hence, could understand clarity as the splendour of an intelligible form shining through material

appearances. Clarity is the self-revelation and the self-transparency of inner truth, in its material embodiment. The splendour of physical and bodily appearances is due to the clarity of the spiritual principle – soul and essence – which manifests itself in every material body or structured artefact. Beauty is the splendour of unity, truth and goodness.

Art and the Arts

Aquinas's conception of art and the arts was profoundly influenced by Aristotle, and most of his numerous references to art are to be found in his Commentaries on Aristotelian texts, especially the *Physics* and the *Nicomachean Ethics*. There is no evidence that he knew, or knew of, Aristotle's *Poetics*, even though partial translations and paraphrases of that work were available during his lifetime. His definition of art, as *recta ratio factibilium* (the rational knowledge of how to make things) was, however, entirely conventional in medieval times. It was Aquinas's understanding of the definition, not the definition itself, that had an Aristotelian flavour.

The phrase *recta ratio factibilium* refers to art in the broad sense of all arts and crafts, all manufacturing and purposeful manipulation of the physical world. It emphasises the role of knowledge and intellect in these processes. The structure of artifacts, he wrote in one place, 'derives from the ideas of their makers, and consists of composition, order and shape' (*Summa Theologiae* II–II.96.2ad2). But he also followed Aristotle in connecting art with nature. It was just because art was a rational process that it fitted in with the intelligible order of the created world. Aquinas therefore explained Aristotle's claim that art imitates nature in the following way:

> Art imitates nature. The reason is that the principle of artistic activities is knowledge . . . Natural things can be imitated by art, because, by a certain intellectual principle, all nature is directed to an end, and a work of nature has the character of a work of intelligence: it moves to its certain goal by determinate methods. Thus, art imitates nature in its activity. (*Comm. Phys.* II.4.6)

Art imitates nature, that is to say, by deploying the same rational purposefulness that we can observe at work in the natural world. One significant modification that Aquinas made to this theory is in the phrase 'by virtue of a certain intellectual principle'. The intellectual principle is God. For Aristotle the teleological character of nature is just the way nature happens to be, whereas for Aquinas it signifies the creative intellect of the divine creator. For Aquinas, therefore, when art imitates the intelligent order of nature it is exercising an intelligent creativity that bears the mark of its source in the divine.

Aquinas did not have a clear concept of what we now call fine art. He did reflect from time to time upon representational art, for instance when he wrote, 'An image is called beautiful if it represents its object, even an ugly object, perfectly' (*Summa Theologiae* I.39.8c). But it should be remembered that, whenever Aquinas wrote that art aims to produce arrangement, order and shape, this also meant that art aims to produce something beautiful. All works of art were, like nature itself, signs of the divine. The human artist resembled the divine artist. Every creature of the world, as Alan of Lille put it, was a book and a script. The medievals knew that the art of their time was the Bible of the poor.

4 From the Renaissance to Idealism: The Modern Era

The artist determines beauty, but does not take it over.
(Goethe)

Introduction

The Renaissance gave birth to a new kind of philosophical consciousness, grounded upon the centrality of the human subject. This new focus on the subject, accompanied by a continuing belief in a transcendent God, was to find its prophet in Descartes and its ultimate incarnation in Hegel's Idealism. Not surprisingly, the Renaissance has been called the age of Humanism. The name 'Renaissance' – which means 'rebirth' – reminds us that the new age was regarded as a renovation and rebirth of humanity, and its elevation to a higher level of consciousness. It was also believed to be a rebirth of earlier values and ideals, since it claimed to have rediscovered the Greek and Roman roots of Western culture and therefore also of Western art. The word 'Humanism' points to its overriding interest in the powers, beauty and nobility of human beings. The human agent came to be understood as a microcosm or miniature synthesis of all the perfections of the cosmos. In the Renaissance we encounter the most luminous era of artistic achievement in the Western world. We also encounter a mature aesthetic and poetic consciousness, in the light of which art came to be regarded as autonomous – that is, as an independent human activity – and beauty was thought of as a specific characteristic and product of artistic endeavours, whose aim it was to celebrate the order of the cosmos in general as well as the nobility of mankind.

Dante Alighieri: Crown of the Middle Ages and Forerunner of the Renaissance

Deeply rooted in the medieval tradition, well schooled in Scholastic philosophy and theology, an encyclopaedic genius of his age, Dante has given us the poetic *Summa* of the Middle Ages in his sublime

67

Divina Commedia. This monumental epic poem, one of the greatest masterpieces of literature, articulates and synthesises the entirety of medieval culture and history, and is the most perfect expression of its spiritual, religious and aesthetic sensibility. Particularly indebted to Aquinas – and, through him, to Aristotle, the Pseudo-Dionysius, St Bernard, Richard of St Victor, Augustine, Albert the Great and others – Dante defined beauty, in traditional Scholastic terms, as order, consonance and clarity. He conceived of art in Aristotelian terms, as analogous to nature and natural processes, as daughter of nature and therefore, in Dante's striking image, 'grandchild of God', that is, second in descent from God (*Inferno* XI.105). Art comes after nature, and nature is the work of God. In this statement we encounter again the medieval conception of God as supreme artist. In a famous passage in the *Divine Comedy*, Dante writes:

> E se tu ben la tua Fisica note,
> Tu troverai non dopo molte carte
> Che l'arte vostra quella, quanto puote,
> Segue, come il maestro fa il discente,
> Sì che vostr'arte a Dio quasi è nepote.

> [If you read your *Physics* carefully
> you will find, within a few pages,
> that art follows [nature], as the disciple
> follows a master;
> so that art is like a grandchild of God.]
> (*Inferno* XI.101–5)

Dante also investigated the problem of the interpretation of literature. Ever since Philo of Alexandria, it had been customary to find in the Scriptures a complex structure of layered meaning, four levels in all. Dante seems to have been the first to apply this hermeneutical principle to all writing – not just to biblical texts, but also in the decoding of any literary document and, by extension, to any work of art or human message. The key passage goes as follows.

> Texts can be understood and should be explicated primarily on four levels. The first of these is called the literal level, the level which does not extend beyond the letter . . . The second is called allegorical, and is hidden under the cloak of these fables, a truth disguised under a beautiful lie . . . The third sense is called moral, and it is this one which teachers should seek out with most diligence when going through texts, because of its usefulness to them and to their

pupils ... The fourth sense is called the anagogical, or the 'sense beyond'. This occurs when a spiritual interpretation is to be given a text which, even though it is true on the literal level, represents the supreme things belonging to eternal glory by means of the things it represents. (*Convivio* II.1)

This fourfold distinction is a remote ancestor of the view that poetry and art are allegorical – or, to put it differently, metaphorical – discourse, and therefore that they articulate their own kind of truth and reality. Art and poetry, that is, are *that which we invent*. In this way Dante signalled the emergence of a new aesthetic sensibility, one that came close to affirming the autonomy of art.

Art and Love, Art and Beauty

Although he was steeped in medieval culture and thought, Dante enlarged the medieval conception of art and beauty in two ways. First, he connected the idea of love, both human and divine, with the production and expression of beauty. (It is worth noting that *amor* is one of the most frequently used words in Dante.) In the *Divina Commedia* there are constant references to divine love, which is conceived of both as God's creative love and as the Neoplatonists' universal power or cosmic force that leads us to God. But Dante also introduced the conception of love as a human passion, echoing in this his contemporaries the troubadours, and like them writing in what was called the *dolce stil novo* (sweet new style). Dante's poems in *La Vita Nuova*, which celebrate the beauty of Beatrice as *donna angelicata* (angel-like woman), portray with profound psychological insight the vicissitudes of human love as a source of beauty and as an inspiration of artistic beauty. This psychological, secular and human conception of love allowed Dante to formulate the novel idea that poetry, and art in general, are products and expressions of feeling. Poetry expresses in words what love and the heart dictate. This was the beginnings of an expression theory of art, and makes of Dante an ancestor both of Renaissance and of modern art theory.

The second original element in Dante was the close relationship that he established between art and beauty. In fact he was far less interested in natural beauty than in the beauty of art. In the *Convivio*, where we find Dante's mature poetic theory, he abandons pedagogical, theological and moral considerations, and interprets poetry purely in the light of its formal and aesthetic properties. Poetry, he writes, is valuable for its beauty, and is written in order to be pleasing in form. Poems can be beautiful even if their deepest meanings remain obscure. They please us – and so are 'understood' – simply because of their formal beauty. This belief was to become central both in Renaissance and modern aesthetics, and is clearly an early formulation of the principle of the autonomy of art. After Dante his two successors, Petrarch and Boccaccio, developed these ideas more explicitly, especially with reference to poetry, and ushered in the new era of Humanism and the new aesthetic consciousness that marked the birth of modern aesthetics and poetics.

Renaissance: The New Sensibility

The Renaissance was an era marked by the retrieval of classical Greek and Roman traditions, in the arts as much as in philosophy. It began in Italy, and its highest achievements were Italian. Coincidentally, perhaps, Italy's social structures emerged in relatively small republics or city-states, not unlike the Greek *polis* of classical antiquity at its peak. In these socially coherent small communities the arts thrived, sponsored by affluent communes, citizens and patrons. The wealth of artistic achievement, and the importance given to art and artists, was so great in Italy that, when visiting Bologna in 1495, Albrecht Dürer wrote, 'Here I am a lord, and at home I am a parasite'.

The rediscovery of classical roots led also to a preoccupation with human values and human agency. Renaissance sensibility tended towards the naturalistic and the secular, and thus to a strong sense of self-assured individualism. This outlook produced an aspiration to elegance and perfection, and an all-pervasive sense of *joie de vivre*. Its religion was not one of mortification or asceticism. It rejoiced in the beauty, nobility and dignity of mankind. Its spirit is perfectly expressed by Miranda's cry in *The Tempest*:

> How many goodly creatures are there here!
> How beauteous mankind is! O brave new world,
> That hath such people in it!
>
> (V.1.183–5)

It is therefore not surprising that the primary subject for visual art in the Renaissance was the human body set within nature. The Renaissance gave birth to the thematic study and representation of the nude, explorations into the human passions, and, in general, the celebration of human beauty. Leon Battista Alberti expressed well this widespread feeling of celebration, when he suggested that, although the body will decay to dust, to despise it while it breathes is to despise life itself. On the contrary, he argued, to love our bodies and keep them in health is sure wisdom.

Underpinning this secular interest in humanity and the human was the concept of man as microcosm, found in philosophers such as Marsilio Ficino, Giordano Bruno, Tommaso Campanella and Giovanni Pico della Mirandola. The human soul, poised as it is between time and eternity, was regarded as a microcosm – a miniature version and synthesis of the whole universe. It was believed to imitate God because of its unity; to imitate the angels with its intellect; to imitate itself thanks to its reason; to imitate the animal kingdom because of sensation, and plant-life because of its power of nutrition. Finally, the soul imitated inorganic matter by simple existence. Expressions of this kind of thinking abounded in Shakespeare as well as in many other Renaissance poets and dramatists. As André Malraux remarked, there appeared in Renaissance art, for the first time in the history of visual art, the human smile.

The New Aesthetics and Poetics: Petrarch and Boccaccio

The year 1400 is generally and conveniently regarded as the end of the Middle Ages and the beginning of the Renaissance. It is an artificial boundary, since the fourteenth century, marked as it was by catastrophes such as the Black Death, poverty and war, saw both the overwhelming achievements of Gothic art, and also the appearance of Petrarch and Boccaccio, two writers and poets who were crucial to the development of the Renaissance sensibility. In both of them we find ideas that are no longer medieval. Some of these ideas had already been formulated by Dante, but others were new. We will present their thinking here in summary form.

One of their most important innovations arose from a determined attempt to distinguish between fine art and art in the broad sense of arts and crafts. Medieval thinkers had distinguished between the liberal arts and the mechanical arts – roughly, between rational and autonomous arts such as music or astronomy, and useful or manual arts such as carpentry or agriculture. Painting, sculpture and architecture were held to be mechanical arts. In the Renaissance, however, they came to be considered as liberal arts, and so to possess an autonomous status and value. The artist, as a result, acquired a new, socially independent status. In classical antiquity, and particularly in the Middle Ages, painters, sculptors and architects were often anonymous. In the Renaissance they became celebrated figures. Vasari's *Lives of the Artists* epitomised the spirit of the times.

If art was autonomous, it followed that it was not always a means to an end, but corresponded to a spontaneous human need, one involving distinctive modes of feeling and experience. It followed also that art could articulate and communicate its own kinds of truth, which sometimes differed from scientific or philosophic truth. It followed, finally, that art was not wholly a matter of following rules, but required the exercise of talent, imagination and skill.

From these beginnings, a new set of aesthetic and poetic theories evolved to articulate and explain the new aesthetic and artistic sensibility.

Birth and Rebirth: Platonism and Aristotelianism

Dante, Petrarch and Boccaccio were late medieval figures who laid the foundations for Renaissance aesthetics and theory of art. All three of them were interested primarily in literature, although what they said about literature could be extended in principle to the other arts. In the case of architecture, an enormous influence was exercised by Vitruvius, and the theory of painting was powerfully influenced by Cennino Cennini. We will look at these two in a moment. First of all, something must be said about Platonism and Aristotelianism in the Renaissance.

Plato and Neoplatonism had been the dominant influences on medieval philosophy and theology, up to and including the twelfth century, although they were known for the most part in Latin translations, and strongly coloured by Augustine's interpretations of Plato and Plotinus. The Aristotelian revival in the late twelfth and thirteenth century generated an enormous amount of commentary and debate, not least by Thomas Aquinas, and radically changed the direction of medieval thought. The Renaissance was to produce further changes of direction. The full corpus of extant works by both Plato and Aristotle was recovered, largely due to the efforts of medieval scholars. Knowledge of the Greek language became more widespread, and translations became more accurate. After two centuries of Aristotelianism, from the thirteenth to the fifteenth, there was then a return to Platonism, although Aristotelianism survived and coexisted with it. Thus, Platonism and Aristotelianism became the two most powerful philosophical influences upon Renaissance thought. The outstanding Platonists were Nicholas of Cusa, Marsilio Ficino and the members of the *Accademia* in Florence. The Aristotelians included philosophers such as Giordano Bruno and Tommaso Campanella and, in the arts, Leonardo da Vinci.

So far as the arts were concerned, Platonism suggested the theory of a manic and erotic inspiration. According to this view, the inspiration of love produces a *fantasia* and *fervour* in the artist which inform his representations with an eternal, ideal and ultimately divine beauty. An Aristotelian like Leonardo, however, understood things quite differently. Aristotelianism maintained that art has to start from experience of the sensible world, and from a scientific understanding based upon observation of empirical data. As a consequence of this, art imitates nature and learns from nature by decoding its internal processes. Art, however, also reproduces and perfects nature. In fact, it is more truthful and more permanent than nature itself. As Leonardo put it, 'In nature beauty perishes, not in art.' 'How many paintings have preserved the image of divine beauty of which time or sudden death have destroyed Nature's original; so that the work of the painter has survived in nobler form than that of Nature, his mistress' (Leonardo da Vinci 1952, pp. 197–8).

Vitruvius

Vitruvius' *De Architectura* (first century AD), which synthesised the major aesthetic and technical theories of architecture in classical antiquity, has had an enormous influence on the theory and practice of architecture over the centuries. During the Renaissance it influenced aesthetic theory as well. It had been influential during the Carolingian Renaissance, and a great many early medieval manuscripts of the work have survived. But it was largely forgotten in the later Middle Ages until it was rediscovered in 1414, in the library of the Abbey at Monte Cassino. All the great architects of the Renaissance – Alberti, Brunelleschi, Bramante, Peruzzi, Palladio and Vignola, to mention only the most prominent – adopted the techniques, models and measurements outlined in Vitruvius. His influence on the theory of art was also considerable. It was evident initially in Alberti's treatise on architecture, *De re aedificatoria* (1452), and from him it spread to others. Plato and Aristotle gave a general theoretical foundation to aesthetics and poetics in the Renaissance, but Vitruvius provided the specific and detailed precepts that gave life and meaning to the philosophical ideas.

Vitruvius restored to architecture its rightful place among the fine arts, by insisting that good architecture was beautiful architecture. Utility alone was not enough. But almost in the same breath he transformed the concept of beauty from a transcendental property of being into something of human dimension. Beauty for Vitruvius signified a congruence with human lives, human needs and human occupations. Art and nature, particularly human nature, went hand in hand. The human body, for instance, could be a model for a fine building: in architecture, he wrote, 'symmetry and good proportions should be solidly based on the proportions of a well-built man' (*De Architectura* III.1). Beauty was not something that objects merely shared in, or that emanated from on high. It was instead part of the essential nature of everything that plays a role in the drama of human history.

The human dimension of beauty was so important for Vitruvius that it could interfere with and amend the laws of symmetry. Beauty certainly meant symmetry, but it was also a property that necessarily evoked an inner state of pleasure, a state that Vitruvius called *eurythmia*. Eurythmia, he believed, justified deviations from a strict adherence to a mechanical or mathematically correct symmetry. Beauty could not be fully captured in a set of impersonal laws, but must be determined in part by its relations with people and with society.

A New Aesthetic Consciousness: Cennini

Cennino Cennini's treatise on painting, *Il libro dell'arte*, appeared at the end of the fourteenth century. At first sight it seems to be just another medieval manual on painting, full of practical advice, recipes and tricks of the trade. But it was much more than that, and turned out to be as innovative in the theory of visual art as Petrarch and Boccaccio were for literature. For a start, Cennini invoked the canonical rules of antiquity, particularly regarding the mathematical relations among the parts of the human body. Secondly, he engaged in theoretical comparisons among different forms of art. This was not a new preoccupation. Petrarch had already debated the relative merits of science, poetry and painting, and had placed poetry above both of the others. Cennini, however, argued that painting is superior to both poetry and science. This was in part an interpretation of the ancient dictum *ut pictura poesis*, meaning that poetry should aspire to imitate the character and effects of pictures. More significantly, though, Cennini argued that painting requires and exhibits more scientific knowledge than poetry does, that it is the equal of science in manifesting the order of things, and superior to science in its production of beautiful objects. The painter is a scientific expert who is also a creator.

> There is an art called painting, which calls for imagination, and skill of hand, in order to discover things not seen, hiding themselves under the shadow of natural objects, and to fix them with the hand, presenting to plain sight what does not actually exist. And it justly deserves to be enthroned next to science, and to be crowned with poetry. The justice lies in this: though the poet has but one science, it makes him free and worthy to compose and bind together as he pleases, according to his inclination. In the same way, the painter has the freedom to compose a figure, standing or seated, half a man or half horse as he pleases, according to his imagination. (*Il libro dell'arte*.I.1)

Cennini also introduced a new term into art theory, *disegno*. This word had, in Cennini's usage, a complexity of meaning which to some extent it still has, even in English: compare 'book design', 'industrial design', 'he had designs upon her'. It connoted both a shape or pattern and also a project or intention. It was a powerful concept, easily applicable to a wide range of arts. Music is a case in point. Music in Renaissance times manifested the same mixture of scientific laws with creative inspiration that were to be found in architecture and the visual arts. The invention and development of polyphony and counterpoint, which mark the origins of modern Western music, combined a rigorous and scientific arrangement of sounds with the human elements of expressiveness and feeling. The English word 'design' nowadays refers primarily to the visual features of artefacts, but it still retains the twin connotations of scientific order and artistic inventiveness, and thus betrays its Renaissance ancestry.

Cennini's seminal ideas developed to their maturity in the sixteenth century. The Platonists, such as Marsilio Ficino, were interested primarily in the nature of beauty, but the Aristotelians concentrated on knowledge and technique in the arts. They also discussed and refined the concept of mimesis, both the mimesis of nature and mimesis of the great artworks of the past. Platonism and Aristotelianism were to some extent rivals, and to some extent complementary to one another. In the end, however, and certainly by the sixteenth century, Aristotelianism was the more influential. This was due to the widespread dissemination of Aristotle's *Poetics* and *Rhetoric*, works which inspired a large number of commentaries, and whose ideas were particularly evident in literary theory. Needless to say, of all the themes contained in the *Poetics*, mimesis was the one most debated and puzzled over. But despite this, Renaissance theorists never forgot that art is also a human invention which expresses human emotions and feelings. They understood, in their various ways, that art is a kind of autonomous creation, and that 'imitation of nature' implied an understanding of the internal order of natural processes and a harmonious re-creation of that internal intelligibility. What the artists imitated was the dynamic order of nature, rather than the objects of which nature is superficially composed. Art does not *copy* nature and reality, but rather produces *veri-similitudes* of the world, that are themselves 'worlds' in their own autonomy.

The Seventeenth Century: The Subject in Art

The Renaissance world-view involved both a shift from a transcendent God to earthbound humanity, and also a shift from objective nature to subjective action, knowledge, experience and feelings. This led in turn to a new conception of art centered on invention and expression rather than on imitation. The human agent himself came to be regarded as the creator of his own destiny, so that in a sense the totality of human life was a work of art – and not just in artistic or cultural pursuits, but also in ethics and philosophy, science and politics. Machiavelli's portrait of the Prince, and Castiglione's celebration of the aristocratic courts where art and beauty flourished, perfectly illustrate this point. The move to subjectivity was more evident still in the seventeenth century, and was eventually to achieve its most mature and complete systematisation in Hegel.

The seventeenth century was, in many respects, an extraordinary era. The transoceanic journeys of discovery, the large-scale development of printing, the Galilean revolution, the Protestant Reformation, the development of mathematics and the pursuit of empirical observation in the physical and natural sciences are some of the remarkable occurrences that both strengthened and expressed a new consciousness grounded upon the primacy and centrality of the human subject. That new consciousness found its seminal formulation in Descartes's conception of the thinking subject which from doubt derives certainty, and which therefore claims to be the last court of appeal in matters of truth and falsehood, good and evil, right and wrong. And along with Descartes's rationalism, the seventeenth century saw also the emergence and development of modern empiricism.

So far as aesthetics was concerned, the seventeenth century began to take a turn towards the human subject. It produced and explored subjectivist terms and ideas such as taste, ingenuity, wit, conceit, phantasy, imagination, sensibility, feeling, emotion. At the same time, both then and in the century following, a great deal of effort was devoted to the concept of beauty, usually by way of distinguishing it from derivative, but not identical, concepts such as nice, pleasant, graceful, elegant, attractive, sublime. Even these terminological distinctions – at times subtle and perceptive and at other times precious and boring – point to the pervasive interest in subjectivity. The classical and Renaissance concept of verisimilitude came to signify the result of unbridled imagination, and hence the wonderful, the magical, the surprising, the theatrical, the fantastic. These were, after all, the centuries of Mannerism, Baroque art and Rococo ornamentation, the age of theatre, wigs and social display. This era of extreme subjectivism and its extravagant imaginative expression was, on the other hand, also the age of reason and observation, of rationalism and empiricism. The seventeenth and eighteenth centuries were, in the end, too deficient in overall cohesion to produce fully elaborated theories either in philosophy or in aesthetics and poetics. We shall therefore summarise the aesthetics of rationalism and empiricism in only the most general way.

The Aesthetics of Rationalism

The philosophy of subjectivity found its earliest and most explicit expression in Descartes's *je pense donc je suis*, better known as the sentence *cogito ergo sum*: I think, therefore I am. Here, subjectivity is identified with thought and reason, at the expense of other kinds of human or subjective experience and activity. In this perspective, there is little room for feeling, emotion, sense perception, imagination or art. At best, these kinds of experiences were seen in the light of, and as dependent upon, the primarily rational structure of the thinking subject which, Descartes claimed, entertains only clear and distinct ideas. The most representative expression of Cartesian rationalism in aesthetics and poetics is to be found in Nicolas Boileau's *L'Art poétique* (1674). Boileau subjected the creative inventiveness and the imaginative freedom of artistic experience to the rigours of intellectual and mathematical classicism. Of course, Descartes was not insensitive to the power of imagination. He was, however, compelled – by the intentions and goals of his general philosophical assumptions – to the view that the imagination belongs to the realm of dreams. In a letter to his friend Balzac, written in 1630, Descartes describes the value and significance of artistic imagination as similar to that of dreams, which 'lead the spirit into woods, gardens, enchanted palaces, where we experience all the pleasures that are imagined in fairytales' (Descartes [1631] 1969, I).

Beauty was another matter. Here, Descartes was a relativist (see Descartes [1630] (1970)). In fact he can be regarded, along with Montaigne, as one of the originators of aesthetic relativism in modern times. In his *Compendium musicae* (1618) he argued that there are different conceptions of the beautiful in different epochs, countries and cultures. His illustrations of this are interesting: he notes that in some non-European cultures large lips, a large and flattened nose, large ears or painted teeth are considered to be beautiful. It is not surprising, then, that Descartes also emphasised the notion of taste.

Leibniz, although a rationalist also, was concerned to avoid its most extreme consequences, and in particular to preserve the value and autonomy of sense perception, affective experience, imagination and artistic inventiveness. He followed Descartes in likening imagination to the world of dreams, which he contrasted with the world of conscious reason. However, he ascribed great importance to these 'small perceptions' as he called them – that is, the unclear and indistinct ideas and sensations involved in feelings, tastes, emotions and sensory experience (*Monadology* 20–3). He described them as direct, intuitive, and immediate, unlike the experience of reason. Beauty he regarded as a form of harmony, defined as the immanent presence of logic in the sensible world. It is a striking definition, which foreshadows Kant's efforts to reconcile the reason with the sensibility.

Baumgarten also belonged to the rationalist tradition. He is generally held to have coined the term 'aesthetics', but, ironically, he also assigned an inferior role to art and to aesthetic experience in general. He defined aesthetics as *scientia cognitionis sensitivae*, the study of cognition acquired through the senses. However, he considered that the realm of sense experience, and the knowledge acquired in the course of sense experience, were inferior to rational knowledge. Art and beauty were in the end subordinate to the rational. Their autonomy, as well as their value, was thus undermined.

The Empiricists and Vico

The seeds of modern empiricism – which must be viewed as an offspring of Aristotelianism – are to be found in the philosophy of Tommaso Campanella. They were later reformulated by Francis Bacon and, after him, by Hobbes, Locke, Berkeley and Hume. Echoing Campanella, Bacon held that our knowledge of particulars rests upon sense experience, and that sensory impressions are the raw material of reason and imagination alike. He believed in the superiority of reason over imagination, and also thought of these two faculties as forces that produced two different epochs in the history of mankind. There was, according to him, an initial age ruled by the power of phantasy and imagination, an age of poetic invention and mythical narratives. This was followed by a later epoch of thought, reflection and scientific endeavour. The age of poetry engaged in the free expression of the imagination, by producing subjective and mythical inventions. The age of philosophy came to understand the objective reality of nature and, by discovering its internal laws, learned how to control and master it. It was not an altogether happy division, either of history or of the mind. On the one hand, Bacon valued art as the realm of imaginative expression in a sensuous medium, while on the other hand he held that only through science and the new 'universal knowledge' [*mathesis universalis*] could mankind free itself from the 'idols' or false representations of religion, rhetoric, ideology, myths, imaginative intuitions and poetic narratives.

Bacon's insights were to be developed further by his successors. Hume, in particular, stressed the importance of sensory experience, and argued even for the superiority of sense experience over intellectual and abstract discourse. He went so far as to state that all abstract ideas are feeble, obscure and undefined, while all impressions and sensations, whether internal or external, are sharp, strong and lively. Of course, we need abstract ideas in order to engage in philosophical and scientific reflection, but these will eventually fail us. In the end, our life unfolds and is situated in the realm of immediate experience. In this realm, beauty, taste, imagination and sensibility find their proper dwelling. Another theory of Hume's, which was developed at some length by Francis Hutcheson, was that there is in human experience a distinctively aesthetic feeling or sentiment. This is very close to the concept of aesthetic taste, and it signifies that we are able to make the judgement of beauty because we are endowed with a specific faculty for doing so. This belief was later developed by Hogarth, Hume and Burke, who influenced, in turn, Immanuel Kant.

The empiricists, for all the fertility of their ideas, have never succeeded in formulating a completely systematic aesthetics. It was Giambattista Vico who provided the first complete systematisation of aesthetic and poetic reflection in the modern period. Vico distinguished between two kinds of truth; or rather, two ways in which we can entertain a knowledge of the truth. One is the method of abstraction, through which we come to understand the truth about the world as it already exists. The other is the method of praxis, through which we create and shape the world, and, by so doing, come to know it. In the latter case, truth coincides with what we create: as he puts it, *verum ipsum factum* (Vico 1982, p. 51). Human creativity is most perfectly exercised, Vico believed, in 'poetic' discourse, by which he meant artistic expression in general. 'Art', he wrote, 'is entirely a product of the imagination, be it the art of the painter of non-pictorial ideas or of the painter of representations. This resemblance to God the creator explains why poets, like painters, are called "divine"' (Vico 1982, p. 142).

Art, therefore, is the activity through which we participate in the process of creating history and creating the world. The artist uses intuition rather than abstraction, and through intuition achieves a knowledge of truth that is felt or imagined rather than abstracted or reasoned. Vico in this way established, for the first time in modern aesthetics, the view that art is a kind of knowledge, or a means for the acquisition of knowledge. It is a view that we encounter again and again in the modern period, and especially in Hegel. The artist, with his ability to articulate a creative and factive truth, becomes the true protagonist of human history and also the true philosopher, the maker and custodian of an active wisdom articulated in metaphors, myths, images and art. The early ages of mankind were poetic cultures, guided by intuition and creative or poetic genius. Only in the later stages of history, at twilight, do we find the emergence of scientific and philosophical reflection. This, however, has dispensed with creative genius by pursuing *verum* at the expenses of *factum*.

For Vico, artistic experience is an essential ingredient in the constitution of human nature and of human history. After Vico, the concept
of art as creation became central in modern aesthetics. As Croce put
it:

> The real revolutionary who by putting aside the concept of
> probability and conceiving imagination in a novel manner actually
> discovered the true nature of poetry and art and, so to speak,
> invented the science of Aesthetic, was the Italian Giambattista
> Vico. (Croce 1902, p. 220)

Kant and Idealism

Kant's aesthetic theory was a synthesis and a development of ideas
formulated earlier by the philosophers of the seventeenth and eighteenth centuries. Leibniz in particular had said that beauty consists in
a harmony between the rational and the sensible. Hutcheson had
separated beauty from the realm of passion and desire. Burke had distinguished between beauty and perfection. Various other predecessors
of Kant – Sulzer, Winckelmann, Mendelssohn, Dubos, Tetens and
Baumgarten – produced in piecemeal fashion a heterogeneous collection of claims about art and the aesthetic: that art is not teleological;
that artistic form is of central importance; that appearance (*Erscheinung*)
is of central importance; that aesthetic taste pertains to feeling rather
than intellect; that the experience of beauty is essentially subjective.
All of these propositions, although they were articulated by various
thinkers in an unsystematic and fragmentary manner, collectively
suggested a subjectivist and psychologistic conception of art and
beauty. One problem, however, remained unsolved, a problem which
had to do with the subjectivist notion of aesthetic taste. Taste meant,
on the one hand, an individual and subjective faculty which produced
affective or emotive experiences – hence something contingent, par-
ticularised and arbitrary. On the other hand, it was felt that aesthetic
taste should sustain some degree of universality, even necessity.
Otherwise aesthetic judgements would be private and relativistic.
Beauty would be entirely in the eye of the beholder. Kant set out to
resolve this impasse, to resolve the antinomy between, on the one
hand, the individual and contingent, and on the other hand the universal and necessary, functions of aesthetic taste. He believed firmly
that, although the experience of beauty is inevitably *my* subjective
experience, unique to myself, I also expect and even demand that
others should agree with my aesthetic judgements.

In solving this problem, Kant succeeded also in synthesising the aesthetic ideas of his immediate predecessors. Thus, even more than Vico, Kant's *Critique of Judgement* was a sort of new beginning for aesthetics. With Kant also there began the truly grandiose stage of Western philosophy, roughly identifiable with Idealism. Hegel, the last of the great German Idealists, was to construct for the first time (and, some would say, for the last time) a fully comprehensive and systematic philosophy.

Taste, Feeling, Beauty and the Third Critique

In the *Critique of Pure Reason* Kant had investigated the nature and structure of knowledge, and in the *Critique of Practical Reason* he had studied the faculty of will and desire. In 1787 he became acquainted with Moses Mendelssohn's writings on psychology, in which Mendelssohn presented a threefold conception of the soul or mind. He argued that between knowledge and the will there is a third faculty, namely the faculty of feeling, which gave to us the ability to experience pleasure and delight. In Kant's third critique, the *Critique of Judgement*, he explored the nature and structure of this third faculty, the faculty of affectivity, an autonomous and quite specific faculty which he defined as 'the feeling of pleasure or displeasure' (Kant [1790] (1952), p. 38).

In order to appreciate fully the significance of Kant's aesthetics, we must first of all note that the fundamental and all-pervasive idea in the third *Critique* is that of teleology. Teleology is a universal principle governing all that there is, and is the guarantor of an ultimate harmony in all things. In Kant's aesthetic theory, this principle is the ground and justification of aesthetic experience, which achieves a harmony between nature and mind, imagination and understanding, affectivity and the will, universality and particularity, subjectivity and objectivity.

The *Critique of Judgement* is a monumental, highly original and extremely complex work. Because of its rigorous, at times obscure argumentation, and its elaborate scholastic structure, it demands close and extensive scrutiny. We can only indicate, in this panoramic overview of aesthetic ideas, the main conclusions reached by Kant after detailed and laborious arguments articulated particularly in the first part of the work, entitled 'The Critique of Aesthetic Judgement'. The following are the central tenets of this section.

The aesthetic judgement has the form 'This is beautiful'. This is a judgement of taste. That is, it is an articulation of a feeling of pleasure in the object about which the judgement is made. However, it is a peculiarity of this kind of judgement that it prescinds from any use or value, or even the existence, of the aesthetic object. It is a 'disinterested' pleasure that gives rise to the judgement, a pleasure detached from any kind of utilitarian or moral significance that the object may have.

Since the judgement is based upon, and expresses, a feeling of disinterested pleasure, it is also a subjective judgement. That is, it is not open to verification in the way that an objective judgement such as 'This is made of wood' would be. Yet despite this resistance to verification, the aesthetic judgement is a universal one. For, since all human minds are alike, they can all agree on which objects are beautiful and which are not. If 'This is beautiful' is true for one person, it must be true for all persons (although some may be blind to the object's beauty for reasons of personal history).

Because of its subjectivity, the aesthetic judgement is not a cognitive one. Cognitive judgements about things are judgements that certain concepts are true of them – for instance, that the concept *wood* is true of a wooden object. This is not the case with the aesthetic judgement, since 'beauty' is not the name of a concept, but an expression of a feeling of disinterested pleasure. None the less, when I say 'This is beautiful' about a beautiful object I am saying something true about the object, albeit a truth expressed without the use of a concept. The aesthetic judgement, that is, expresses a genuine understanding of its object. On the other hand, the object has become an object of consciousness in the first place through the activity of my imagination. It follows that aesthetic experience is an experience of the harmony that exists between my imagination and my understanding. Thus the ancient, Pythagorean conception of harmony finds in Kant a new form and a new articulation.

So far as art is concerned, Kant considered artistic aesthetic objects to be, like natural aesthetic objects, detached from utilitarian and moral considerations, to be objects of a free and joyous play of the mind. To a large extent, therefore, we ignore the content of works of art – since content might generate utilitarian or moral judgements – and take pleasure instead in their formal properties. The art object becomes an aesthetic object in virtue of these formal properties alone.

To sum up: Kant's monumental aesthetic theory rests upon the central idea of a subjective harmony. The aesthetic sentiment or feeling of pleasure depends upon and derives from the free, non-conceptual and harmonious interplay of the imagination and the understanding. The spiritual power that creates artistic ideas and masterpieces consists in the perfect harmonisation of imagination and understanding. In so far as this harmony is beyond the boundaries of subjective individuality, the feeling of pleasure elicited by beauty is an *a priori* faculty that grounds the universal and necessary validity of aesthetic

judgements. Finally, in the light of the idea of teleology, Kant understood art to be the conscious creation of objects that engender, in those
who contemplate them, the impression that they have been created
without intention, freely, as if they resembled natural processes.

Idealistic Developments: Schiller and Schelling

In the fertile artistic and intellectual climate of German Romanticism,
Kant's third *Critique* attracted considerable attention and became
enormously influential. So far as aesthetics was concerned, his most
significant successors were Schiller, Schelling and Hegel. We conclude
this chapter by looking at Schiller and Schelling and postpone our
study of Hegel until the next chapter.

Hegel paid tribute to Schiller's contributions to the philosophy of
art and beauty in the following words:

> It is Schiller who must be given great credit for breaking through
> the Kantian subjectivity and abstraction of thinking and for ven-
> turing on an attempt to get beyond this by intellectually grasping
> the unity and reconciliation as the truth and by actualizing them in
> artistic production. (Hegel [1842] (1975), I, p. 61)

Schiller agreed with Kant that aesthetic experience, whether of artistic
or natural beauty, had as its goal and its achievement a harmonious
reconciliation of the human faculties with one another. This was best
achieved, he argued, by freeing ourselves from any practical or intellectual judgements about the value or function of the aesthetic object.
It should be experienced as if it were autonomous and self-produced,
freed from its web of connections with other things. Such a state of
mind is like a supreme form of play, in which we enjoy a mental freedom and harmony and an independence from our practical selves.

He pursued the implications of his aesthetic theory in two great
works. In one of these, *Letters on the Aesthetic Education of Man*
(1793-4), he argued that art and beauty should lie at the heart of the
education and development of mankind. The perfecting of human
nature requires that we find a way of harmonising our reason with our
sensibility, and this is just what aesthetic education can bring about.
We have two basic impulses: a physical instinct for self-preservation
and material success, and a formal instinct for inner stability and
moral freedom. Schiller said that a third, aesthetic impulse is required,
to effect a synthesis of the other two. This impulse to aesthetic play
enables the human spirit to enjoy a harmony of reason and sense,
freedom and law. The education of this impulse, aesthetic education,

is therefore the means through which mankind reaches its highest perfection.

In *Naive and Sentimental Poetry* (1795) Schiller set forth many of the most central themes of Romantic and Idealist aesthetics, and also exploited his own ideas on aesthetics in a theory of cultural history. He began with the assumption, common at the time, that the most perfect manifestation of mankind's aesthetic impulse was to be found in Greek art. Human history, therefore, began with a state in which people had achieved, at least in their art, a perfect unity and harmony of the spirit. After that there was a regression, a separation and division of soul and world, the ideal and the real. Art is the means by which the original harmony embodied in classical Greece can be recovered.

In the light of this, Schiller distinguished between two kinds of art and poetry. Greek poetry was *naive*, since it was unaware of conflicts and division. Romantic poetry, on the contrary, was *sentimental*, since it was generated by division. Greek poetry *is* nature, Romantic poetry *seeks* nature. Greek art *is* unity, Romantic art *seeks* unity. Greek art is a representation of nature and of a finite world-order, while Romantic art is an expression of the infinite. Naive, natural and objective art was complete and self-contained, while sentimental and subjective art attempts to represent the absolute as a distant and transcendent ideal, and is therefore open to new varieties and reformulations. Schiller understood clearly that classical art was grounded upon ontological and closed world-orders, while modern art rests upon a subject-centred and open-ended conception of the human world.

Fichte and Schelling

Fichte was, along with Schelling and Hegel, one of the three great Idealist philosophers who succeeded Kant, but he paid relatively little attention to the problems of art and beauty. He did, however, stress the importance of feeling, intuition and imagination in the life of the mind, and regarded them as complementary to speculative thinking and necessary for the apprehension of truth. In perfect correspondence with the prevailing Romantic sensibility, and in agreement with Kant's project, Fichte suggested that the ideas of science must be produced in each individual that wants to pursue it, by means of creative imagination. This is unavoidable in a science that aims to return to the first and final principles of human knowledge.

Schelling, unlike his predecessor, devoted a great deal of attention to aesthetic theory, and he expanded in particular Fichte's suggestion that the artistic and the intellectual are complementary and interactive. He argued that philosophy is dependent upon art, since art is able to

satisfy fully our aspirations to the infinite, and to unify the oppositions within ourselves and between ourselves and the world. The subjective internal world and the objective external world are produced by
one and the same activity of the spirit, though it is an activity that
operates both consciously and unconsciously. Knowledge is conscious,
intuition and feeling are unconsious, but together they constitute a
single movement of the spirit, which is nothing other than artistic
creation. For Schelling, art is the foundation of consciousness, and
therefore also of the world. Objective and external reality is an incipient and primitive artistic production, as yet unconscious, of the
spirit. As for human culture, philosophy is born from poetry and
aspires to return to poetry – that world of spontaneous creation and
final reconciliation of inner and outer reality, subject and object,
feeling and form, truth and sensibility, thought and emotion. In art
reality is fully manifested, for the artist, more than the philosopher,
achieves the supreme synthesis of all differences and oppositions. Of
course, it is the philosopher who scientifically and consciously articulates that supreme synthesis. But the artist is not and does not need
to be a philosopher, because true genius is his alone.

5

From Hegel to Semiotics: Art and Crisis

In art we are dealing with an unfolding of truth.
(Hegel)

Introduction

Idealism, especially in Hegel's systematic presentation, marked the final affirmation, in philosophy, of reason and of subjectivity, and their final expression in a comprehensive explanatory system. It was the end of an intellectual journey that had begun in the Renaissance, took a decisive turn with Descartes, and assumed a canonical form in Kant. Post-Kantian Idealism often considered art, along with religion and philosophy, to be one of the supreme expressions of the human subject. For Hegel in particular, art was a manifestation of the Absolute – a term which he used to denote a consciousness freed of all limiting conditions or necessities, and to mean the totality of reality. It is sometimes said, in anglophone discussions of aesthetics, that modern aesthetics began with Kant. But Hegel has been far more influential than Kant, and Hegel still remains the starting-point for all subsequent reflections upon art.

Hegel's Aesthetics: Art, Religion and Philosophy

The cultural movement known as Romanticism, and the philosophical movement known as Idealism, were always tempted to abolish the traditional boundaries inscribed within the human spirit, as well as the boundaries between the human spirit and nature. They liked to think that intellect and imagination were ultimately absorbed into and superseded by intuition, whose role it was to reveal to us, in a direct unmediated fashion, our unity with nature and God. The truth lay within, and the truth was that we are at one with all things.

Hegel, although he was permeated with the spirit of the time, did not accept that this all-encompassing unity described how things actually are in everyday life, or even in the life of the mind. For Hegel, everything that exists certainly constitutes a single totality, but it does not manifest itself to us in an undifferentiated manner. Art, religion and philosophy are all ways in which the intelligibility of things is grasped by the human spirit. But in art truth is manifested in the element of sensibility; in religion truth is revealed in the element of myth and images; while in philosophy truth is given to us in its most adequate element, rational thought. Art is thus in some measure inferior to religion and philosophy, since its material and sensuous nature is less connatural with and less adequate to the nature of the Absolute.

Art, Beauty and Truth

Hegel's conception of beauty both preserved and enlarged the traditional conception. He thought of beauty as symmetry and order, but also as a revelation of the spiritual in the material, as a synthesis of matter and spirit. For Hegel, and perhaps for philosophers throughout the ages, one of philosophy's central problems is that of explaining and reconciling the divisions and oppositions within the world, particularly the divisions between persons and nature, between mind and matter, and between the particular and the general. He believed that art was one way of overcoming these divisions, since art achieves a synthesis of spiritual content and material form. Art spiritualises the physical and makes the spiritual tangible. The human imagination produces sensible images, and these are filled with the deepest truths that are comprehended by the spirit. 'In works of art', he wrote, 'the nations have deposited their richest inner intuitions and ideas, and art is often the key, and in many nations the sole key, to understanding their philosophy and religion' (Hegel [1842] (1975), I, p. 7).

History of Art, History of Truth

Hegel's monumental *Aesthetics* is divided into three parts. The first, called 'The Idea of Artistic Beauty or the Ideal', deals with theoretical and definitional problems. The second, 'Development of the Ideal into the Particular Forms of Art', deals with the history of art as it is related to the philosophical development of human thought. The third, 'The System of the Individual Arts', considers the particular forms of art. Here we shall briefly summarise the second part.

The spiritual contents of art are what Hegel describes as 'moments' in which the mind reveals itself and becomes conscious of itself. They are the deepest, most fundamental conceptions of the real, which define different epochs and different cultures, the varying models and forms through which reality reaches the light of human consciousness and assumes the distinctive character that it has for its time and place. These conceptions, which predispose us to adopt a particular way of addressing reality, are the determinants of what Hegel calls *Volksgeist* – literally, 'the spirit of a people'. Hegel is thus led to distinguish three artistic epochs in the history of mankind: the symbolic, the classical and the romantic. This should not be understood as a rigid separation of successive historical periods. Rather, it identifies three different ways of making art, three modes of artistic sensibility and expression. The basis of the distinction rests upon the relation between the ideal content of works of art, and their physical form.

All forms of art, Hegel claimed, seek a perfect balance and attunement between idea and form. In some cases, however, the ideas remains too abstract, too formless, to find their perfect physical expression. The physical comes to dominate, while the idea remains shadowy and inchoate. Art of this kind – Hegel calls it symbolic art – has a tendency to physical monumentality and formal stylisation, a certain rigidity and geometrical simplicity. It is characteristic of pre-Greek and non-Greek cultures of the ancient world, such as Egypt, Mesopotamia, the Cyclades.

Classical art – the art of Greece, Rome and the Renaissance – is an art in which the idea and the physical form are in perfect attunement with one another. It is an art that characteristically uses the human body, which is presented as a perfect physical expression of thought, virtue and all the varied movements and aspirations of the spirit. The physical work of art and the meaning that it expresses and communicates to us are completely at one.

Finally, Christian or Romantic art is an art in which the idea of reality is highly developed and sophisticated, and fails by a kind of excess to find a perfect expression in physical form. It bursts through the bounds of the physical, as it were, and overwhelms matter by its splendour. One might think here of Byzantine art, which transforms matter into light, or of Gothic cathedrals in which the weight of the physical seems to be transcended by its spiritual meaning, of Romantic literature with its explorations of every detail and recess of the human mind. With this kind of art, the artistic harmony of the classical world is disrupted, and even the institution of art itself begins to come under strain and to crumble. The perfect articulation of the spirit in art gives way to other forms of expression, notably science and philosophy. As Hegel wrote:

> There is a deeper comprehension of truth which is no longer so akin and friendly to sense as to be capable of appropriate adoption and expression in this medium. The Christian view of truth is of this kind and, above all, the spirit of our world today or, more particularly, of our religion and the development of our reason, appears

as beyond the stage at which art is the supreme mode of our knowledge of the Absolute. (Hegel [1842] (1975) I, pp. 9–10)

A dramatic ambiguity thus emerges in Hegel's aesthetics. Hegel
formulated a comprehensive and systematic justification of art as an
expression of the Absolute, and yet at the same time, as a result of this
very justification, he concluded that art was being absorbed into philosophy. The very fact that art is the most characteristic and perfect
expression of a historical epoch inevitably leads, in the fullness of
time, to its demise.

> In the case of the Greeks, art was the highest form in which the
> people represented the Gods to themselves and gave themselves
> some awareness of truth . . . In general it was early in history that
> thought passed judgement against art as a mode of illustrating the
> idea of the Divine . . . indeed even with the Greeks, for Plato
> opposed the Gods of Homer and Hesiod starkly enough. With the
> advance of civilization a time generally comes in the case of every
> people when art points beyond itself . . . When the urge for know-
> ledge and research, and the need for inner spirituality, instigated the
> Reformation, religious ideas were drawn away from their wrapping
> in the element of sense and brought back to the inwardness of
> heart and thinking. Thus the 'after' of art consists in the fact that
> there dwells in the spirit the need to satisfy itself solely in its own
> inner self as the true form for truth to take. (Hegel [1842] (1975) I,
> pp. 102–3)

For Hegel, the modern world is a world in which art is no longer
capable of expressing fully our understanding of ourselves or of reality.
'Art', wrote Hegel, 'is something of the past.'

Art is Dead

Hegel's announcement of the so-called 'end of art' is closely related to
the highly critical attitude that he adopted towards what he saw as a
new artistic sensibility, already present at the end of the eighteenth
century and more strongly affirmed during the first decades of the
nineteenth. Hegel identified features of the art and literature of his
contemporaries which, he argued, undermined and contradicted the
formal harmony and the universality of meaning implied in the ideal
of beauty. He criticised in particular the lack of cohesion and the
fragmentary character of contemporary artworks: their prosaic, mun-
dane, inessential and 'particular' themes, their excessive irony, their

derisory use of realism in caricature, their capricious, superficial and ineffectual self-indulgence, their technical virtuosity and refinement, as if art were an amusing and decorative game without serious content. He spoke of

> the vanity of everything factual, moral, and of intrinsic worth, the nullity of everything objective and absolutely valid. If the ego remains at this standpoint, everything appears to it as null and vain, except its own subjectivity which therefore becomes empty and hollow and itself mere vanity. (Hegel [1842] (1975) II, p. 66)

At times his criticism could be venomous. As Romanticism waned, he wrote, 'fools, louts, all sorts of everyday vulgarities, taverns, carters, chamber-pots and fleas' made their appearance on the stage of art. And as a result,

> the latest poetry has screwed itself up to endless fantasticalness and mendacity which is supposed to make an effect by its bizarre character, but it meets with no response in any sound heart, because in such refinements or reflection on what is true in human life, every genuine content is evaporated. (Hegel [1842] (1975) II, p. 233)

Hegel, in short, was convinced that much of the art of his own time had entered a stage of serious crisis. He believed that this had occurred in part because of the social and political convulsions of the time. Like Schiller, he understood that art is deeply rooted in its own time and place – that works of art are, in Umberto Eco's brilliant formulation, 'epistemic metaphors' of the culture from which they emerge, and which they express figuratively. He was dismayed by the developments in art and literature that he could see around him, and his criticisms of them anticipated the reactions that many people later had to the avant-garde in the twentieth century.

Hegel was not in fact the first to voice alarm about the way that art was going. Friedrich Schlegel, in his short treatise *On the Study of Greek Poetry* (1795–6) had already castigated the state of aesthetic culture, which, he said, was marked by a sense of derisory and solipsistic irony, and, at its worst, by a descent into anarchy:

> When we consider with equal attention the uselessness and the lack of rules – the anarchy – of the totality of modern poetry and, on the other hand, the perfection and refinement of its individual parts, its mass appears like an ocean of contrasting forces in which float and interact, in a turbid mixture, the particles of decomposed

beauty, the fragments of shattered art. We could call it a chaos of all
sublime, beautiful and charming things . . . (in Minor 1882, I, p. 112)

Schlegel believed that there was a movement in art towards fragmentation, associated with an ironic and solipsistic attitude adopted by the
artists of his time. He wrote of 'the aesthetic culture of modernism'
which, he said, tended towards the category of the 'interesting'. But
it is always possible, he added, 'to find something even more interesting . . . Our taste, accustomed to old stimuli, will seek new, more
violent and sharper stimuli. Soon it will pursue the piquant and the
surprising. Piquant is that which spasmodically excites a sensation
that has become dull; the surprising, in like manner, stimulates the
imagination' (Minor 1882, I, pp. 110–11).

The concepts of the interesting and the piquant were not the only
contribution made by Schlegel to the vocabulary of criticism. He also
used terms such as boring, shocking, adventurous, disgusting and
horrid. It is chastening to discover that the critical categories often
used in descriptions of late twentieth-century art were devised some
two hundred years ago.

Then, as now, the use of this vocabulary was connected to a dissolution of the ideal of beauty – a dissolution, it must be said, that is
even today far from complete – and the appearance of aesthetic theories which laid stress upon other features of art. After Hegel, the
concept of beauty did not go away, but it started to fall out of favour.
Late nineteenth- and twentieth-century theories are closer to poetics
than aesthetics. That is, they focus upon the processes of artistic
production, the sociohistorical properties and functions of art, and
the formal and structural features of artistic artefacts. They write of
aesthetic experience, not of beauty, and interpret that experience
subjectively rather than objectively. Beauty, of course, has not vanished from the vocabulary of criticism, but its role and significance
have altered.

Another aesthetic category that emerged in post-Hegelian times
was that of the ugly. Traditionally, ugliness was considered simply to
be an absence of beauty, and this was Hegel's view as well. But Hegel's
biographer, Karl Rosenkranz, thought otherwise, and wrote a treatise
about ugliness, *Aesthetik des Hässlichen* (1853), in which he argued
that it had a positive character, a presence, which made it aesthetically
interesting in its own right. He argued that:

Ugliness is not a simple absence of beauty, but its positive negation.
What does not fall under the category of beauty cannot be comprised under the category of ugliness either . . . For instance, a

mathematical point is not beautiful, but it is not ugly either. (Rosenkranz 1853, Introduction)

Ugliness, he went on to say, has an existential reality just like disease, selfishness, injustice or cruelty. Aesthetic theory had therefore to take account of it. His own analysis of the ugly is at time laborious, but also enlightening. Ugliness, he concluded, has three main properties. First, it means *Formlosigkeit*: lack of form and symmetry. Secondly, *Inkorrektheit*: a mismatch between an idea and its physical expression; thus, in art, an internal dissonance or imbalance or incoherence. Thirdly, *Verbildung* or *Defiguration*: a qualitative property which included the vulgar, the disgusting, the boring, lifelessness and bad taste. Rosenkranz, finally, thought that ugliness was an essential property of caricature, and this led him to a consideration of the comical and thus also of parody and satire.

The Foundations of Formalism: Herbart and Hanslick

With Hegel, aesthetics came to assume its proper and permanent place within philosophy. It also achieved what was in a sense its highest point. It never subsequently found an exponent who could confer upon it the kind of systematic coherence that it had in Hegel. Hegel discerned a crisis in the art of his time, and after Hegel there was a sort of crisis, certainly a fragmentation, in aesthetics also. In Hegel, everything had been unified. After him, some thinkers focused on the ideological contents, others on the formal properties, of art. Some spoke of art for art's sake, or of art as play, while others were concerned with the techniques of art, thus turning aesthetics into poetics. Some understood art as a means of discovering values, others explored the psychological mechanisms involved in the making and in the consumption of aesthetic objects. Some insisted on the autonomy of art, others demanded that art should deal with social reality. Some saw aesthetic experience as a step towards mystical liberation, others concentrated on empirical observation and description. Aesthetics became enormously complex and various after Hegel, and correspondingly harder to survey or summarise. Hence we shall look at only a few of the most influential and significant developments. We shall start with Formalism.

Johann Friedrich Herbart, a contemporary of Hegel and successor to Kant in the chair of philosophy at Königsberg, is rightly regarded as the founding father of aesthetic formalism. Herbart believed that philosophy's concern is not with particular or specific objects of investigation, but with every possible object. It encompasses the totality of the real and the totality of all possible concepts. In practice, however, he took this to mean that philosophy consists in the clarification and elaboration of concepts. Some concepts require clarification and differentiation, while others demand transformation and interpretation. Logic is concerned with the first kind of concept, while metaphysics deals with the second. There are, however, other concepts that require neither logical clarification and classification, nor metaphysical transformation. These are concepts which produce judgements of approval or disapproval. They are the objects studied in aesthetics, for Herbart understood aesthetics to be a science of values and of value-judgements, and so inclusive of ethical reflection and evaluation. Concepts that produce in us a sentiment of approval are applicable to beautiful objects. Beauty is a structure of formal relations which are capable of stimulating a positive aesthetic evaluation and a pleasurable appreciation of the object. Aesthetic formal relations can be either coexistent and simultaneous or linked in a sequential chain. The first kind gives rise to simultaneous or static beauty, while the second generates successive or dynamic beauty. Static beauty is to be found in nature and in the figurative arts, while dynamic beauty is encountered in music, poetry, literature. We should note that this distinction echoes one already made in Lessing's *Laocoön* (1766), according to which the arts can be classified as either spatial or temporal. This distinction was to be adopted in many subsequent attempts at constructing a system of the arts.

Herbart's aim was to provide an objective science of what pleases and what displeases. As a psychological science, aesthetics investigates events in order to discover the elements of beauty and their condition of possibility. He paid close attention to music, an art which had not been adequately considered by his predecessors, especially Kant and Hegel. (Hegel was a contemporary of Beethoven, and was even born in the same year, 1770, yet he never once mentioned the name of this musical genius.) Unlike Hegel, Herbart recognised and appreciated the value of Beethoven's revolutionary music. Herbart's aesthetics of music functioned as a matrix and general methodology for the understanding of other forms of art, for he believed that music was a system of measurable relations that can be objectively identified in their formal organisation and development.

For Herbart, then, the proper object of aesthetics is the study of those relational structures or forms in things which are responsible for inducing a sense of approval and delight or of disapproval and displeasure. These structures or forms must be sought among various material elements, such as sounds, colours, volumes or words. But relational form is not independent of the material elements in which it is found, and it therefore follows that the arts have a degree of independence from one another, and must be investigated individually and separately.

> There is not just one form of universal relations independent from the matter of each art. Against the abstract generalisations of idealistic aesthetics, against the Romantic fusion of the arts, and against the use of emotive language . . . Herbart retrieved the specificity of beauty in the single arts and the specificity of the pertinent judgement on each art. The heterogeneity of the arts is quite total: the poet and the musician 'pursue beauty in completely different manners', and 'we cannot give only one answer, for all cases, to the question of what beauty is'. (Dufrenne and Formaggio 1981, I, pp. 245–6)

Herbart opposed, not just Idealism in general, but Idealist concepts such as expressiveness, inspiration, feeling, phantasy, imagination, creative genius. He stressed instead the importance of technique, skill, poetic rules and practices. In the case of music, an art which he looked upon with special favour because of its clearly defined formal structures, he argued that the essence of this art does not consist in the emotive and affective responses that it triggers in us, as the Romantics thought. Rather, the essence of music is a purely formal essence, consisting of relational structures such as those found in counterpoint. Herbart argued that the aesthetic judgement has nothing to do with feelings, just as beauty has nothing to do with the emotionally moving. Finally, Herbart's formalism led him to believe firmly in the autonomy of the arts. He repeatedly stressed his conviction that the work of art triggers in us a judgement of approval, on its own formal merit, without signifying – and without reference to – anything else outside of itself. This statement perfectly captures the very essence of formalism in aesthetics, and its transformation into poetics. This process of gradual metamorphosis can be further observed in most of his successors, and must be considered as one of the most significant developments in nineteenth-century debates on art and beauty.

Another influential formalist in aesthetics, Eduard Hanslick, also considered that each of the arts had its own specific kind of beauty, with its own distinctive formal structure and poetics, and he devoted his *On the Musically Beautiful* (*Vom Musikalisch-Schönen*) (1854) to the study of form and beauty in music. Hanslick was extremely hostile to the view that it was the aim of music to arouse feeling and emotion, to provide musical 'descriptions' of nature, to complement and illustrate myths or stories, or to aspire in any way to ideological or programmatic content. He opposed these views, not merely as propositions in the theory of music, but also as practical goals for composers or musicians. Thus, he was a vigorous supporter of Brahms and a virulent critic of Liszt, Schumann and Wagner. He believed that the essence of music lay in its formal properties and structure alone. We shall not present and discuss Hanslick's formalism at this point, but will deal with his aesthetics and poetics of music in Chapter 9.

Schopenhauer and Nietzsche

One of the most fundamental propositions in Kantian metaphysics, certainly one of the most influential, was his distinction between things as they are in themselves, which he called *noumena*, and the appearances that things have in our experiences of them, which he called *phenomena*. Kant further argued that the noumena are unknowable, since we cannot stand outside of our own experiences in order to observe them. By definition, all that can ever be present to consciousness are the phenomena.

Arthur Schopenhauer partly accepted, and partly amended, this distinction. He amended it because of his reflections upon the way in which we know ourselves. In my experience of myself I can observe myself externally – that is, as a material body subject to the laws of physics. But I can also observe myself from within – that is, as a subject rather than an object. But to know myself as a subject is to know my very essence, and thus to know myself as noumenon rather than phenomenon. Furthermore, my essential self, everyone's essential self, the self as such, is Will – a will to live, a will to exist. The external body and its behaviour is simply the phenomenal appearance of my will. Schopenhauer concluded that the entire phenomenal world is an objectification of Will, that its essence, its true character, is Will. The world is Will. All our other mental faculties, such as intellect, emotion and imagination, are subservient to and at the service of Will.

However, the intellect can sometimes free itself from subservience to the Will. This occurs whenever it adopts a 'contemplative' mode in which it puts to one side everything pertaining to Will: desires, goals and purposes, hope and dread. In this state of mind, the quality of knowledge itself is altered, for we become aware of the permanent essences that underlie the phenomenal particulars of everyday life. These essences or 'Ideas' are aesthetic objects, and this state of Will-free contemplation of essences is an aesthetic state. Aesthetic experience thus enables us to achieve a form of knowledge far superior to that of the natural sciences, which are confined to the phenomenal world. It follows that art brings about a revelation of the real world freed from the veil of the phenomenal, and freed thus from causal determination, time and suffering. Artistic and aesthetic experience, moreover, is accessible to everyone.

On the basis of this theory of the aesthetic, Schopenhauer devised a system of the arts. The system depends on the view that the Ideas objectify Will in different degrees. Architecture, for instance, enables us to contemplate the laws of space and matter. Tragedy enables us to contemplate the terror of life. Music is superior to all the other arts, since it expresses and enables us to contemplate, not just Ideas, but the Will itself; it is the image and revelation of the Will itself. Music expresses in a language immediately intelligible, though not translatable into the language of reason, the deepest and most intimate essence of life. Music embodies Will, or, as Schopenhauer puts it, 'The world is embodied music' (Schopenhauer [1818] (1886), I, § 52).

It is not surprising that Schopenhauer's aesthetics influenced Nietzsche and Wagner, Thomas Mann and the Symbolists, and the aesthetic psychologists of the nineteenth century. The metaphysical and mystical overtones of Schopenhauer's aesthetics reflected, and also helped to bring forth, a new sensibility which subsequently acquired the name 'aestheticism'. From the point of view of aestheticism, art and aesthetic contemplation are existential and lived experiences. The separation between life and art is blurred. Life must aspire to the condition of art and, particularly, of music. Aestheticism also gave rise to the idea of 'art for art's sake', and the further idea that life imitates art. Finally, to Schopenhauer's influence we must ascribe the subsequent aestheticist ideals of transfiguration of life into form, and the transformation of ethics into aesthetics.

The anti-Idealist and anti-Rationalist character of Schopenhauer's philosophy became more overt in Friedrich Nietzsche, who is rightly considered to be the forerunner or even the initiator of Existentialism, and the father of Nihilism. In his deliberately fragmentary and aphoristic writings, Nietzsche often reflected on the nature of art and beauty. He was as much a literary as a philosophical writer, and his works are replete with classical references and overtones. *Thus Spoke Zarathustra* (published in stages between 1883 and 1891) is still read as much for its poetic vision and style as for its intellectual content. To some extent he married the poetic with the philosophical, and overcame the traditional opposition between concept and image, idea and intuition.

His reflections on art and beauty, scattered though they are throughout his voluminous writings, are also like a thread that runs through and unifies his intellectual journey. He considered that science, philosophy, religion and morality are lies and forms of ideological repression. Truth itself, on the other hand – the truth of a nihilistic world devoid of absolute values – is too frightening. Hence 'we possess art lest we perish of the truth' (Nietzsche [1901] (1967), p. 822). Unlike abstract knowledge and unlike philosophy, which are caught in the prison of language, art goes beyond the boundaries of discursive knowledge and unfolds as immediate intuition, unmediated expression. It embodies the primordial energies of the 'will to power'. All previous absolutes are obsolete, and the supreme value is art alone: 'the great means of making life possible, the great seduction to life, the great stimulant of life' (Nietszche [1901] (1967), p. 853).

We shall limit ourselves to a brief examination of one of Nietzsche's works, namely *The Birth of Tragedy* (1872), partly because of its seminal importance for the understanding of Nietzsche's whole philosophy, but mainly because it contains something like a coherent aesthetic theory. The central theme of the book is the origin of tragedy, but Nietzsche expands his analysis far beyond this topic alone. He has much to say about Greek tragedy, of course, so that even as a study of this literary genre alone the book is innovative and informative. But his study of Greek tragedy allows him also to pursue a series of other considerations: on mythology, on Greek art, on German culture, on philosophy, on civilisation, on Schopenhauer's nihilism, on Wagner's music, on the relation between tragedy and music, finally on art in general. A recurrent idea is that art is the most powerful way to justify existence: that it is the aesthetic that best makes sense of the world.

Nietzsche said that Greek culture, and in fact the whole of Western culture, is ruled by two fundamental impulses which he identified, metaphorically, with two gods: Dionysos and Apollo. The Dionysiac impulse produces images and actions in which we abandon ourselves to a sense of universal oneness, and absorption in the totality of all things. The Apollonian impulse produces images and actions which assert our individuality, our separateness from the rest of nature. The Dionysiac urge may find primitive expression in orgy, frenzy and trance, or a more cultivated expression in music. The Apollonian urge seeks expression in order and form: epic and sculpture are Apollonian arts.

Tragedy combines the two. It is an art form in which Dionysiac man discharges his energy in Apollonian images. It is an Apollonian embodiment of Dionysiac insights and powers. In tragedy, the hero expresses his Dionysiac side by seeking to overwhelm nature, to impose his will upon it (hybris). He seeks unity with it by making it subject to him. Thus his actions are against nature – 'unnatural' acts, or what is conventionally called 'sin' or 'crime'. But it is a delusion to attribute an ethical content to tragedy. It is beyond good and evil. Its message is: Whatever exists is both just and unjust, and equally justified in both' (Nietzsche [1872] (1956), p. 65).

In tragedy, therefore, it is disclosed that man's highest good must be bought with crime and paid for by suffering. Its content is ugliness and disharmony. It has no moral effect upon us. It does, however, give us delight, but a purely aesthetic delight. It is the delight we take in a sublime spectacle, in the energy and power of existence, in 'an aesthetic game which the will, in its utter exuberance, plays with itself' (Nietzsche [1872] (1956), p. 143). Tragedy for Nietzsche is a sort of paradigm of human artistic culture, and therefore of human culture in general. He conceives of human history as a struggle and a periodic reconciliation between the Dionysiac and the Apollonian impulses. If either impulse overwhelms the other, there is a period of maladjustment and imbalance. Nietzsche believed that the Apollonian impulse was in the ascendant and had increasingly prevailed, since the days of Socrates. He argued that reason had supplanted intuition, while science and morality had weakened creativity. What others regarded as a triumph of Enlightenment values, Nietzsche regarded as a state of decadence.

The Birth of Tragedy deals with all the themes in Nietzsche's account of art and beauty. Here we encounter the idea of the Dionysiac as the primordial artistic power of ecstasis and of sexuality, the autonomy of art from morality and its superiority over science and knowledge, art as an affirmation of life, the critique of contemporary culture as decadent, reflections on music and mythology, the relation between art and cultural identity. Here we also encounter his conception of art as a supreme and mysterious play enacting the harmony of man and world. In later writings, Nietzsche focused on the crisis of art in his own time, and went so far as to prophesy the death of art. He wrote: 'Just as in old age we remember our youth and celebrate festivals of memory, so in a short time mankind will stand towards art: its relation will be that of a *touching memory* of the joys of youth. Never, perhaps, in former ages was art dealt with so seriously and thoughtfully as now when it appears to be surrounded by the magic influence of death' (Nietzsche [1876–8] (1910), Vol. 6. part 1, § 223, pp. 205–6).

Kierkegaard, Sartre, Heidegger

Sören Kierkegaard is, like Nietzsche, one of the progenitors of Existentialism, a philosophy that rejects the rationalistic and systematic claims of Idealism in favour of reflection on the lived experience of the individual. Although Kierkegaard's works do not add up to an

ordered philosophical system, they manifest a high degree of psychological insight. They are archaeological excavations, so to speak, into
the structure and the functions of the individual's psyche. Unlike
Schopenhauer, who conceived of art as a privileged insight into the
order of things, and unlike Nietzsche, who conceived of art as a vital
experience and a creative force, Kierkegaard subsumed the artistic
into the aesthetic, and identified aesthetic experience with a particular
existential stage in man's life.

His main treatment of aesthetic problems is to be found in
Either/Or (1843). This is a fundamental Kierkegaardian work, since it
outlines the total map of existential experience which, he argues,
unfolds through a progressive movement of self-realisation towards
authenticity. This existential journey consists of three fundamental
stages: the aesthetic, the ethical and the religious. In the aesthetic stage,
the individual lives his experiences as a spectator, an observer who is not
yet committed. In the ethical stage, the individual commits himself to
social duties and hence to active participation in the shaping of the
human world. In the religious stage, the individual, conscious of the
vanity of existence and of existential finitude, abandons worldly
concerns and seeks authenticity, as an individual, in faith or in the
abandonment to the call of Otherness.

It is quite clear, even in this brief outline, that art and aesthetic
experience are considered to be the lowest stage of this existential
journey. In fact, if the individual remains caught within the aesthetic
stage, he loses himself in aestheticism. This is because aesthetic experience, in Kierkegaard's view, is not concerned just with questions of
beauty and art, but involves a whole way of being, an existential disposition towards reality in all its aspects: beauty, love, thought, action,
affective and emotional states, ways of interacting with the world,
ways of conceiving and expressing sexuality. In fact, Kierkegaard's
discussion of the aesthetic metamorphoses into a complete analysis of
lived experience, a mode of aesthetic existence complete with its inner
contradictions and final despair. The aesthetic hero, in Kierkegaard's
view, is Don Juan, and he devotes an entire section of *Either/Or* to
Mozart's *Don Giovanni*. Here he describes the aesthetic life, not with
reference to truth and the Absolute, but rather to the finitude and
insufficiency of human existence. In particular it is one of the ways,
though an unsatisfactory way, of dealing with otherness. The beauty
of art and music is seen by Kierkegaard as a lure, a means to avoid
commitment, a refusal to make choices, an escape from lived experience
or *engagement*. In the aesthetic life reality is observed and consumed
in cheerful self-gratification and narcissism, and is thus characterised
by an inauthentic disposition of superficiality, amorality, laziness and

mystification. It is a fragmented and eccentric life, destined finally to end in solitude, disillusionment, alienation, melancholy and nausea. It is not hard to find, in Kierkegaard's negative phenomenology of aesthetic experience, an echo of Plato's warnings against the sirens of art and beauty. Kierkegaard warns against the danger of turning life into art, so that the search for authentic ethical and religious experience deviates into aesthetic contemplation and sensual gratification. As with Plato, however, there was a positive appraisal of the aesthetic concealed within the negative. For art, even if it involves a deviation from authenticity, has as its inspiration the desire to overcome mortality and finitude, by inventing different worlds from the one that we have inherited. This conception of art as possibility and creative projection was inherited by Kierkegaard's existentialist successors.

Sartre and Heidegger both manifest some of the characteristics of the existentialist movement, though in different ways and in different degrees, and without really identifying with it in either case. It is in fact misleading to think of existentialism as a 'movement'. Its very emphasis on individual existence and experience meant that it never generated a homogeneous philosophical school nor a set of common suppositions. As a result, there is no such thing as an existentialist aesthetics, but only a number of individual contributions by various thinkers who were touched by the existentialist spirit.

Jean-Paul Sartre was a novelist and dramatist as well as a philosopher, so he was particularly interested in literature. In *What is Literature?* (1948), however, he distinguished between literature and poetry. To be precise, he distinguished between literature and art, but he included poetry in the category of art. Poetry is art because of the way in which it handles words. Words are the substance of poetry, a material or stuff whose density, weight and texture are shaped and structured as a painter might smear his paint upon a canvas. A poem is a thing, and it has all of the opacity and autonomy of things.

Literature, in contrast, is both a revelation of truth and a project for change. Literature, first of all, names things, and to name things is to lift them out of obscurity and make them objects of consciousness. Whatever is without a name might as well not exist, for its existence remains outside the sphere of what we know and what constitutes the world for us. Naming produces the world, or the world in so far as the world is what we consciously exist in, and is the object of our knowledge and desire, and the arena of our lives.

Thus, naming also affects our behaviour. Once a thing is named it can no longer be ignored; or if it is ignored that in itself is a stance taken towards it. All our actions are actions in the world – that is, ways of fixing, altering and maintaining the relations between ourselves and the world. So to name things is to alter subtly the world we live in, our relations to it, and our behaviour in respect of it.

Literature, in short, is both a revelation and, in consequence, a project for transforming the world. Yet Sartre did not mean that literature was a weapon to be employed for the purposes of propaganda, edification or political ends. He was not at all minded to agree with Stalin's infamous remark that writers are engineers of the human soul. He knew that writers who collaborated in occupied France soon fell silent, for in using their work as a means to an end they came to lose their way and then their voice. The proper role of literature is, rather, to free people from the constrictions of the familiar and the habitual. Naming things releases people. It creates and projects new possible worlds, including imaginary worlds, so that its readers can cast off their customary mental shackles and become aware of their infinite potential. A literature that tries to persuade, to bend its readers to the writer's will, ceases to be literature. A literature that frees its readers by opening their minds to possibilities is fulfilling its proper role. It is therefore one of the paths to personal authenticity, to existential freedom, and a way to bridge the gulfs of solitude that divide people from one another.

One of the truly great philosophers of the twentieth century was Martin Heidegger. Heidegger dealt with the problems of art in several of his works, particularly in those dealing with language, and in his essays on Hölderlin. His most important work on aesthetics was *The Origin of the Work of Art* (1936). In this essay he repeats his conviction – already explored in *Being and Time* (1927) – that human beings have a distinctive mode of existence which he calls *Dasein* or *Being-in-the-world*. He means by this that, when we start to become conscious of the kind of beings that we are, we realise that we are situated in a world, and a world, moreover, that is constantly in movement from the past into the future. It is not a static world of objects, but a dynamic world of happenings and events, and it is in this kind of world that we have to make sense of our existence.

The happenings and events in which we are situated are, furthermore, fundamentally linguistic in character. That is, they are known to us through the medium of language and of meanings of all kinds. Language and meaning themselves, however, must have some kind of foundation. And this foundation is art. Art, ultimately, is the ground upon which human existence rests, in all its historical and ontological variety. Art does not merely express and reveal truth, but is the ground upon which truth itself depends. Art therefore constitutes us as the kind of beings that we are. It is not a frivolous ornament in the world, but a means whereby the world is constituted. As one commentator puts it:

> In Heidegger's conception of the ontologically grounding power of art, we encounter a thesis already present in modern aesthetics from its inception, namely the Kantian thesis according to which the work of art is a gratuitous event, not deducible from the laws of existence, and therefore the production of genius. In the Kantian tradition, especially in neo-Kantianism, the gratuitousness of art had come to signify the insubstantiality and lack of the aesthetic dimension (as aestheticism, for instance in Kierkegaard), removed from the deep concern with truth and falsity, good and evil. In Heidegger, on the contrary, the gratuitousness of art stands to signify its historical happening as authentic event of novelty. (Dufrenne and Formaggio 1981, I, p. 338)

This is the sense in which art is creative: it creates the ever moving and changing world in which we are situated. Art, that is, is essentially original. It produces and discloses the realm of possibilities. Every work of art, according to Heidegger, is a novel event, which never ceases to be novel, which is never completely exhausted by interpretations. Long after its original creation it continues to generate new possibilities. It does this in part because of its material properties, for everything material is deeply enigmatic and ambiguous. Art shares this ambiguity with technology, which is fundamental to the character of contemporary culture.

In Heidegger's philosophy we find what is perhaps the last expression of the great German tradition of systematic philosophy.

Conclusion

We have now come to the end of our historical survey. Our exploration of the possibilities of artistic production and artistic experience will no longer come from an examination of past generations of thinkers, but from entering into a dialogue with the arts themselves. This we will prosecute in the chapters to follow.

We conclude, all the same, by indicating the general theoretical framework within which contemporary discussions of art take place. One of the foundation stones for the framework is the Hegelian view that art is in some kind of penultimate state, that it is approaching, and has long been approaching, an ending or closure. The very institution of art is in doubt. This is often expressed by means of the word 'crisis': art in crisis, art exposed to critical question, art deprived of its reason for being. Many aesthetic theories have the appearance of desperate attempts to stave off this crisis. The formalists retreated to a sort of minimalist austerity, discarding artistic wisdom, knowledge and insight, in the hope that there was an autonomous realm in which art could remain inviolate and from which it could never be ousted. Nineteenth-century positivists, and Darwinists of every period, have tried to save art by finding for it some kind of utilitarian or survival value. Logical positivists in the twentieth century pushed art into the sphere of pure feeling, on the ground that its claims to knowledge were entirely spurious and demolished by the advances of science. Art criticism increasingly sought to analyse the techniques and formal structures of art, leaving the analysis of its social and historical significance to the sociologist and the art historian. Structuralism concentrated upon artistic syntax, and found meaning only in the self-referential interrelations of signs. A few despairing souls tried nominalism yet again, and claimed that art is whatever is called art by an artworld establishment.

Concomitantly with these desperate theoretical remedies, the practice of art itself underwent momentous changes, which were most apparent in the early decades of the twentieth century. These changes were in part the product of a new sensibility, but in part also a reaction to the crisis in the arts that afflicted the artists' philosopher cousins. Avant-garde art typically sought to explore the very structure of the artefact that it was in the process of making. It was dazzled and seduced by the alchemy of the artistic process. Structure became, to some extent, an end in itself, not a means to explore the depths of the human heart. The greatest artists, of course, continued to do both.

Perhaps the main energy underlying the avant-garde arose from a sense that art really is in crisis, and a consequent belief that art should question itself, just as it was being questioned in society at large. Thus, art came constantly to seek the overthrow of other art – the art of the past, the art of the orthodox and the conservative, arts that bowed to convention or expectation. Art came to seek constant innovation. Revolution became its very lifeblood, and almost seemed to define the perennial role of art in the life of mankind.

This led, in the end, to the limits of experimentation, to incomprehension, elitism and massive social alienation. Art approached dangerously close to silence, which is the ultimate, the final, rebellion of art against art. Inevitably, in reaction to this, a new sensibility with a new set of aspirations arose, and this has been given the name 'Postmodernism'. Initially in architecture and literature, but increasingly in all the arts, it came to be thought that, instead of rebelling against the past, art should explore the past. It should revisit and exploit past styles, past solutions. In architecture this led to a new syncretism and eclecticism. In literature it led to intertextual play between past and present. With the general postmodern retrieval of art, instead of its abolition, there has been a reawakened sense of pleasure, a recognition that the 'reader' is important, that a return to what is already known is a way of overcoming the mass alienation from high art that is so characteristic of our time and our culture.

We make no direct comment upon these recent developments, except to note that intertextuality and eclecticism, and a return to the past, are not new phenomena in the history of the arts.

6 The Arts

Introduction

What is art? What is a work of art? At the very least it is a sign of human presence, just as surely as a footprint in the sand. Art is made by human beings; works of art are 'artefacts'. But how do we tell what is made and what isn't? How do we distinguish art from nature? Both, after all, have meaning. I casually lift a stone, and glance at it. My friend happens to glance at it as well and says, 'That's a fossil'. I look in amazement, and there it is: a white segmented line, a petrified creature, embedded in the stone. My friend knows how to 'read' the stone, and now I can read it too. My friend is a geographer. He begins to explain and interpret the landscape to me, its history and significance which are written in every contour, and now I come, little by little, to see its meaning as I never saw it before.

But there is a difference between the meaning that everything has, just because it is part of an intelligible and rule-governed universe, and a meaning which is introduced into the world by the hand of a human being. As my friend interprets the landscape to me I realise that part of its meaning relates to slow and massive geological and climatic changes and events, but that another part relates to the work of untold generations of men and women. A log of wood can be 'read' as an object that is made of oak and is of a certain age and species, but when the log is taken home and used as a garden seat it is lifted out of nature and becomes a part of culture. Its new meaning is a product of human intelligence and imagination, and is no longer part of the natural order of things. It is this purposiveness, this invention of meaning, that determines the artefactual.

All artefacts are artistic to some degree, even a log of wood used as a garden seat. Everything from a spoon to an aeroplane, a spool of thread to a cathedral, a single gesture to a football match, can be described and evaluated in terms of its aesthetic character, as well as in terms of its use. In fact we constantly do this. When we choose a particular colour of paint for the kitchen, or a tie to go with a jacket, or a certain way of arranging the furniture, these actions incorporate aesthetic judgements. They aim to achieve a certain kind of 'rightness' which is neither utilitarian nor ethical, but which is a constant and inalienable feature of our everyday lives. We are all, innately and necessarily, aesthetic animals.

Artefacts are produced for many reasons. Often the reasons are utilitarian, as with tools or vehicles or houses or clothing. Sometimes they are political, as with flags, marches and sit-ins. Sometimes they are religious, as with churches, liturgies or processions. Sometimes they are commemorative, as with mausoleums and cenotaphs. Often several of these reasons combine in a single artefact. But another reason is to produce something that is aesthetically valuable, something 'beautiful'. When this reason is a particularly important one, or even the only reason, we are accustomed to call the artefacts in question 'works of art'. As we noted in the first chapter, it is not only works of art that have an aesthetically valuable character. Every artefact can be described and evaluated aesthetically. But tradition determines that, for the past few centuries at any rate, we have reserved the terms 'art' and 'work of art' for those artefacts whose aesthetic value is particularly evident, or which were manufactured with their aesthetic value particularly, or exclusively, in mind; or whose aesthetic character we choose to emphasise for historical or cultural reasons.

Languages of Art

At least two important intellectual movements in the second half of the twentieth century, structuralism and semiotics, have made it acceptable to think of art as a sort of language. Works of art are objects with meaning, and it is reasonable to suppose that natural language, which we use every day to express and communicate meaning, has therefore many instructive analogies with art.

A language is, in the first instance, a system of signs. The word 'system' signifies that there is an organisation of the signs, that there is a set of rules which preside over the way that the signs are arranged. The term 'sign' refers to something that stands for something else. The signs that constitute a natural language can most conveniently be regarded as words, although words themselves have a complex inner structure that is highly organised and requires the recognition of other constituents of languages, such as phonemes and morphemes.

If we now draw an analogy between language and art, we can start to think of the forms and genres of art as 'languages'. Music, for instance, has sounds as its signs, and the rules of composition as its code, its grammar. In the same way, painting is a language of volume and mass, and architecture is a language of space, mass and volume. This analogy between art and language emphasises one other significant feature of art, namely that forms of art have a historical dimension. That is, they change and develop; they are influenced by the cultures from which they emerge; they adapt to technical changes and to the changing sensibilities of particular ages and cultures. Art is *fundamentally* historical.

The assimilation, or partial assimilation, of art to language is therefore a fruitful development in contemporary art theory. At the very least it reminds us that artworks are signs rather than mere objects, that they are rule-governed, and that they have a symbiotic relation to human history and culture.

Systems of the Fine Arts

Problems of Classification

The arts seem to be systematic in another way. They seem to fall naturally into certain categories. There are visual arts, such as painting and sculpture. There are literary arts, such as poetry and novels. There are musical arts, such as song and instrumental music. But very little reflection is needed to show that this way of classifying the arts generates a host of problems. Too many arts cross the boundaries. Drama is visual as well as verbal, and opera is musical on top of that. The visual arts tend nowadays to disrupt the traditional categories in ways that are sometimes thought to be shocking and irrational. Dance does not fit easily into any category. There are other significant arts such as glass-making, pottery or fashion, and industrial arts such as printing, graphic design and industrial design. Architecture and town-planning seem to question the very idea of distinguishing between what is art and what is not.

Part of the problem is that, since all that we make or do has something of an artistic character, our use of the phrase 'the arts' is a product of history, of cultural fashion, and has no agreed logical or psychological basis. None the less, the desire to classify art into its different kinds is a very ancient one. The Greeks listed seven arts (although we must recall, yet again, that the Greek word *téchne*, usually translated as 'art', connoted skill or craft of any kind): grammar, rhetoric, dialectic, arithmetic, geometry, music and astronomy. These were further sub-divided, in medieval times, into two subsets: the first three were called the *trivium*, and the remaining four were the *quadrivium*. The latter were thought to be connected with physical labour and the manipu-lation of materials. Thus, the fine arts in the modern sense would have been akin to the members of the *quadrivium*, which were also called 'mechanical arts'.

The ancient world has also handed down to us a different way of classifying the arts. In the *Poetics*, Aristotle used the word 'poetry' – from the Greek *poieín*, to do or make – to refer to a group of art forms comprising music, literature, drama and dance. All of these arts, in Aristotle's view, shared two common properties. They represented 'people in action' (*Poetics* 1447b); and they all made use of one or more of three artistic media: words, musical sounds, and bodily action and gesture. He appeared to think that visual art, or painting at least, belonged to a different category, even though it had important similarities to poetry. Some centuries later, Horace expressed this similarity in the memorable phrase *ut pictura poesis*.

Lessing, Hegel, Schopenhauer

Something of an Aristotelian spirit survived, though in a different form, in one of the most influential of all the systems of the arts. This was expounded in Gotthold Lessing's famous *Laocoön* (1766), a book inspired by reflections upon an antique sculpture of Laocoön and his sons struggling with serpents, first described by Pliny, which had been rediscovered in Italy in 1506. Lessing argued that all art could be divided into two kinds: arts of space, and arts of time.

> Painting employs in its imitations quite different means or signs than poetry – the former figures and colours in space, the latter sounds in time. But the signs used must have a definite relation to the thing signified. It follows that signs arranged together side by side can express only subjects which, or the various parts of which, also exist side by side; whilst signs which succeed each other can express only subjects which, or the various parts of which, succeed each other. (Lessing [1766] (1930), § 16)

Lessing thus established a distinction, which was to prove remark-ably long-lasting, between arts which were variously described as spatial or static or plastic on the one hand, and temporal or dynamic or kinetic on the other. To this there came to be added yet another way of categorising the arts, based upon the view that they could be arranged in a hierarchy, and expounded most notably by Hegel and Schopenhauer.

We saw in the last chapter that Hegel distinguished three *forms* of art – the symbolic, the classical and the romantic – which differed from one another in the degree to which the Ideal was or was not expressed in a material artistic form. But Hegel also distinguished five *kinds* of art: architecture, sculpture, painting, music and poetry.

Architecture, in the Hegelian system, was the kind of art which most perfectly epitomises symbolic art. For, although it is cognate with and points towards the Ideal, it remains fundamentally material and external to the Ideal realm. Architecture does symbolise or signify the Ideal, but always as something inalienably different from its own essentially material nature.

Classical art is most perfectly epitomised in sculpture, which completely captures and articulates the Ideal in material form. The material of which it consists does not merely point to or stand for the Ideal, but is the Ideal become matter. It is matter spiritualised, and spirit transmuted into material substance. Because of its spiritual character, the shapes of sculpture have a sort of 'abstract spatiality'. In sculpture, Hegel writes,

> the inward and the spiritual for the first time appear in their eternal peace and essential self-sufficiency. To this peace and unity with itself there corresponds an external shape which also persists in this unity and peace. This is shape according to its *abstract spatiality*. (Hegel [1842] (1975), I, p. 85)

As Lessing might have put it, sculpture, like architecture, is an art of space.

In romantic art the Ideal manifests itself, not as something transmuted into matter, but in its own true inward and subjective nature. Thus the form of this kind of art is less weightily material and more evanescent and spiritual. One such art is painting. Here, matter is reduced to pure surface, and has lost the volume and mass of sculpture and architecture alike. Painting is, as Hegel puts it, 'visibility inherently subjectivised and posited as ideal' (Hegel [1842] (1975), I, p. 87).

Music is even less material, and more penetrated with subjectivity. Its sensuous body is temporal rather than spatial, and it thus 'releases the Ideal, as it were, from its entanglement with matter' (Hegel [1842] (1975), I, p. 88). Music is half way between 'the spiritual sensuousness of painting and the abstract spirituality of poetry' (Hegel [1842] (1975), I, p. 88), for poetry is the most perfect of the romantic arts and highest of all the arts. In poetry, sound is at its least sensuous, for it

serves merely as a sign. It loses its own intrinsic value and merely
signifies or indicates the realm of the spirit. The true element of poetry
is the imagination, not the external matter of the words. It is at this
point that art reaches its upper limit, for poetry can easily yield to
prose, where imagination is replaced by thought, poetry by philosophy,
and we have come to the end of art.

In this way Hegel takes Lessing's spatial and temporal arts and
arranges them in a hierarchical order: architecture, the most material
of the spatial arts, is at the bottom of the hierarchy; and poetry, the
most spiritual of the temporal arts, is at the top.

Schopenhauer devised a different hierarchy of the arts. The ultimate
reality, for Schopenhauer, is Will. But Will objectifies itself, so far as
human cognition is concerned, in Platonic essences or Ideas. For Plato
art represented particular things rather than Ideas. For Schopenhauer
art strives instead to express Ideas, and different arts succeed in this
endeavour in differing degrees.

Architecture, he says, is the 'lowest' art. For, although it gives distinctness to Ideas such as gravity, cohesion, rigidity and hardness, it is
a utilitarian art which achieves only the lowest grade of cognitive
objectivity. Schopenhauer considers the other arts in turn, analysing in
each case the extent to which they express Ideas in their true objectivity and free the human consciousness from subordination to Will.
He places painting above architecture, and then, in ascending order,
sculpture, poetry and the other literary arts, and finally music, a universal language which is a 'copy of the will itself, whose objectivity
the Ideas are' (Schopenhauer [1818] (1886), I, p. 333). There are also
hierarchies within each of the arts. Paintings of the human figure, for
instance, are higher than landscape paintings, and tragedy is the highest
form of literature. He has little time for grand opera, which he
describes, in his cantankerous manner, as 'an unmusical invention
for the benefit of unmusical minds' (Schopenhauer [1851] (1974), II,
p. 433).

The Twentieth Century: Croce to Lalo

Hegel and Schopenhauer were only two of the vast number of nineteenth-century philosophers and critics who attempted to construct
classifications of the arts. The twentieth century has been less concerned with this issue. At the beginning of the century, Croce attacked
the whole idea of classifying the arts with a vigour and conviction that
was to have a lasting influence (Croce 1902, pp. 436–49). Even as he
wrote his *Aesthetic* the visual arts, already a hotbed of cultural rebellion,
and ably assisted by writers, were preparing to shock and outrage
people by attempts to undermine the traditional boundaries: dada,

surrealism, experimental typography, concrete poetry, performance art, happenings, conceptual art. The impulses underlying these kinds of artistic works are still powerful. Postmodernism, despite or because of its desire to exploit the art of the past in an eclectic and syncretic fashion, is also impatient with the lines traditionally drawn among the different art forms.

Yet the impulse to classify the arts has not disappeared, and the twentieth century has produced its own systems. One of these, Alain's *Système des beaux-arts* (1926), is based upon a distinction between 'social' and 'solitary' art forms. Social arts have to do with collective, rather than individual, experience. They are designed to be shared, and must be shared if they are to realise their true nature. The arts of clothing, dance and rhetoric are collective arts. An art is solitary either because it can be completed fully by an artist working on his own – the art of pottery, for instance – or because it can be enjoyed by an individual on his own, as is the case with the art of prose. Most of the traditional art forms can manifest themselves both as solitary and as collective arts.

Alain's system of the arts is open to question, but not the least of its merits is that it abandons the distinction between the fine arts and the 'minor' arts. Thus he associates the art of dance with the arts of etiquette, acrobatics, fencing and equitation. He associates etiquette with tailoring and jewellery. He connects architecture with the art of the garden.

Alain believed that his system of the arts was compatible with the traditional distinction, derived from Lessing, between dynamic and static arts. Others have attempted to supersede or abandon it. Etienne Souriau (1947, pp. 73–113) conceded that our perceptions of artworks can be described as either spatial or temporal: spatial in the case of painting, for instance, and temporal in the case of music. But perception, he argues, is no guide to the ontology of art. The supposed arts of space – architecture, painting, sculpture – persist through time, and reveal themselves through time. A building, for example, discloses different aspects of itself at different times of day and in different seasons of the year. Music – supposedly a temporal art – occupies space as well as time. Its sounds come from a particular direction and are dispersed in space, and music discloses different aspects of itself depending on where one is standing or sitting, and depending on the kind of space – a room, a concert hall, an amphitheatre – that it occupies.

It is thus a mistake, according to Souriau, to classify the arts on the basis of sense perception. Rather, one should classify them on the basis of 'sensible *qualia*'. There are seven of these: lines, volumes, colours, luminosities, movements, articulate sounds and musical sounds. Each of these can be employed either in non-representational art (arts of the first degree or 'primary art'), or in representational art (arts of the second degree or 'secondary art'). This schema therefore generates a list of fourteen types of art.

It is a clever and interesting schema, but it is not quite as neat as one would like. Souriau himself discusses some of its ragged edges. Theatre is an art form that crosses several boundaries, for it includes, at the very least, music, poetry, mime and dance. The 'minor' arts are also transgressors. Pottery, for example, involves elements of design, painting and even sculpture. Souriau could just as easily have drawn attention to boundary problems within the schema. Painting involves lines as well as colours, and arguably luminosity as well. Cinema is just as transgressive as theatre. The art of song involves both articulate and musical sounds. Souriau is not indifferent to these problems, but he thinks that he has found a framework that at least provides the conceptual resources for describing all art forms in terms of representation and sensible qualia.

This argument against the inheritance of Lessing has been developed with unusual elegance and sophistication by Mikel Dufrenne (1973, pp. 239–329). Dufrenne argues that the spatial and temporal qualities of works of art are not the space and time *within which* art objects are located, but rather the temporality and spatiality which are *constitutive* of art objects. It is not the astronomer's space and time, but the space and time which are constituents of the forms of lived experience. As Heidegger demonstrated, time is a form of the interiority, the subjectivity, of the human person. Dufrenne follows Kant in adding to this the form of space. Spatiality and temporality are equally involved in our identification of ourselves to ourselves and in our manner of opening ourselves to the world and to others. And, just as there is a solidarity of space and time in the subject, so too they are inextricably interfused in the object. This is why, Dufrenne continues, we find the same three structural categories – harmony, rhythm and melody – present in all of the arts: not only in an allegedly 'temporal' art like music, but also in an allegedly 'spatial' art like painting.

Maurice Nédoncelle devised a system of the arts based entirely upon the human senses, specifically the senses of movement, sight and hearing (Nédoncelle 1963). Tactile-muscular arts include sport, athletics and dance. The main arts of vision are architecture, sculpture and painting. The arts of hearing are music and literature. The arts of theatre and cinema are 'synthetic' because they involve all three of the senses mentioned.

Some elements of this system are debatable. Is it really enough, for instance, to describe literature as an art of hearing? Is mime not a silent form of theatre? What is the role of the intellect, of the emotions, of the imagination? Also, the system is incomplete because it pays little attention to the 'minor' arts. An interesting subsidiary question, arising from this, is whether there are arts of taste and smell. Nédoncelle inclines to the ancient and medieval view that they are not, since these senses are too closely connected with sensuous and sexual pleasures. However, the same could be said of the tactile-muscular arts. And in any case, there are those who would argue that cooking, wine, perfume-making, erotic rituals and lovemaking can be aesthetic practices and experiences in the full sense of the word.

Charles Lalo is a case in point (Lalo 1951). Lalo devised what he called a 'structural' classification of the arts. The basis of the classification was a list of seven 'sectors' in which artistic structures are manifested: hearing, vision, movement, action, construction, language and sensuality. This list seems to have a purely empirical, not a logical or conceptual, character. In each of the seven sectors, some artistic structures are 'superstructures'. This means that all of the elements involved in the arts in that sector are present in the structures. In the arts of hearing, the superstructures make use of pitch, loudness, timbre, tempo and any other elements that can be used in these arts. Orchestral and choral works are examples of musical superstructures. Other structures are produced by a kind of 'abstraction', in which some musical elements are used but others not. Piano music is an example, also chamber music and music for percussion. Finally, some structures are produced by a 'contamination' of musical elements, which means that they are mixed with extraneous items: programme music, songs, dance music, martial music and the like.

This threefold division of structures – that is, superstructures, abstracted structures and contaminated structures – is pursued through all seven of the listed sectors; and there are other refinements and subdivisions that we do not propose to mention here. In the end it becomes a rather dense and complex system, which works better for some sectors than it does for others. It is better for music, for instance, than it is for literature. But one of its advantages is that it allows space for all of the arts, including the minor arts. Another advantage is that it allows the inclusion (rightly or wrongly) of the 'arts of sensuality': of courtship, lovemaking, food, perfume. There is much to be said for a schema that enables us to distinguish, on aesthetic grounds, between a good meal and a hamburger.

A Last Word on Classification

The most exhaustive study of the classification of the arts must be Thomas Munro's *The Arts and Their Interrelations* (1967). Not only does he list and paraphrase a large number of classification systems – many more than we have touched on here – but he examines the whole question from several different points of view. The philosopher's approach to classification will differ from the Museum curator's, the educator's or the librarian's; and all are influenced and modified by the concepts of art, craft and industry that are current at the time. Munro also points out that the method of classification will vary according to the standpoint adopted. A classification from the standpoint of the artistic medium, for instance, will differ from a classification from the standpoint of the skills and processes used in the manufacture of artworks.

Munro's own classification, in which he attempts to synthesise all standpoints, is based upon a sixfold division: visual arts, auditory arts, arts of verbal composition, arts of public performance, lower-sense arts and arts of personal appearance. Within each of these there are several further divisions and subdivisions. The lower-sense arts include the art of tobacco-making (and 'other plant preparations for smoking'). The arts of personal appearance include plastic surgery.

It might be tempting to suppose that classifications of the arts are something of a sterile exercise, or, at least, that they throw little light upon art as a human activity. This would be a serious mistake. Classification and understanding go hand in hand, and revolutions in human thought often occur when an old classification gives way to a new one. Newtonian physics, for instance, made it possible to place the falling of an apple to the ground, and the rising and setting of the moon, in the same category, where before they had been thought to be entirely separate and independent phenomena. Classification of the arts is not to be taken lightly, and those classifications which lead us to consider the artistic aspects of tattooing, sport or food cannot help but throw new light on this most complex and astonishing of human activities.

Entering Worlds of Art

Whatever about the theoretical interest of the problem of classification, it does not require a solution here. Aristotle, himself an inveterate classifier, was not particularly concerned about the various lines, traditions and boundaries that separate the arts. He noted in the *Poetics* that drama is an art that combines the features of other arts into an organic whole, since it utilises all of the artistic media simultaneously. In our own time we see that the cinema, the dominant art form of the age, amalgamates several of the other arts into a new and complex unity.

The arts that nowadays stand out, as it were, from the others, the arts that occupy the high ground in our artistic culture, have been determined by history and tradition. There are, and have been, cultures without drama, without architecture, without painting. But our culture is one in which, for more than two and a half millennia, certain art forms happen to have played important roles in expressing and shaping the minds and sensibilities of the people whose culture it is. We make no apology, therefore, for presenting our introduction to art in accordance with European tradition. We shall devote a chapter to each of the following: literature; the dramatic arts; music; the visual arts. This may seem excessively orthodox, and to suffer from a sort of logical arbitrariness, but it does answer to the character of the culture that we and our readers share.

We conclude this chapter with some methodological points. We mentioned earlier that philosophical aesthetics should not be confused either with the history of art, the history of art forms, or with criticism or the history of criticism. But at the same time, philosophy of art cannot ignore the contributions of historical and critical discourse about art, just as it cannot be prosecuted without knowledge of, and reference to, artistic techniques and structures. Furthermore, Croce's claim that philosophical aesthetics is not just a part or branch of philosophy, but the whole of philosophy, is not without foundation. We have seen how aesthetics implies a knowledge of the history of ideas in general, and also of the various branches of philosophy such as epistemology, anthropology, metaphysics, the philosophies of language, history, science and so on. No one nowadays can lay claim to universal knowledge or learning, but we shall adopt a Socratic disposition towards historians, critics and philosophers in general, by interrogating and interpreting them as and when the need arises.

Finally, we shall engage with contemporary debates about the arts, but shall have no qualms about introducing theories and practices of the past as well. We make no apologies for amalgamating the synchronic and the diachronic dimensions of art, and of the philosophy of art, as seamlessly as we can. The notion that the responses to art and the reflections upon art of past generations are no longer 'relevant' has no place in our thinking.

7   The Art of Literature

Poetry is language in a state of crisis.
(Mallarmé)

Introduction

The first problem that we run into is the word 'literature' itself, an English word which, unfortunately, has acquired several meanings. In one sense it refers to all verbal material of any kind: we talk of oral literature, French literature, advertising literature, tourist literature, scientific literature and so on. In another sense it refers to a subset of verbal material, namely, the kind of written (and, sometimes, oral) matter that is taught in schools and studied in university departments, is given literary prizes, and receives grants from Arts Councils and Foundations. In this second sense it is an evaluative term, for it connotes verbal material which has a high degree of aesthetic value, and includes poetry, novels, short stories, essays long and short, historical works by such writers as Thucydides, Livy and Gibbon, and even philosophical works by Plato and Lucretius. In a third sense 'literature' refers to works of fiction, irrespective of their aesthetic value but excluding 'factual' works of history or philosophy or science – with poetry treated as a sort of honorary fiction irrespective of its content and character. A further complication arises in connection with drama. Drama is studied in university literature departments, but it is studied as literature rather than as theatre. And yet within literature departments it is common enough to hear people talking about 'literature and drama': a recognition that they are different arts.

We will cut through this verbal jungle in the following way. We will consider literature in the second of the above senses, as all written or oral verbal constructions – we may as well use the fashionable word 'texts' – which have a high degree of aesthetic value: texts, that is, whose aesthetic value is an essential rather than an accidental property. But we will exclude drama from the category of literature, and treat it separately later on.

Literary Kinds

European literature, which is our concern here, means literature written in European languages. Nowadays, it includes literature written in many non-European countries and continents, such as India, the Americas, parts of Africa, and Australasia. It has an immensely long history – from the Old Testament up to our own times – but its roots are lost in prehistory. The earliest extant Hebrew poetry can be dated to the eleventh century BC, and Homer's works derive from oral poems already in existence before the eighth century BC.

Hebrew poetry, and biblical literature in general, came to have a significant impact on European literature because of the rise of Christianity. It was the Greeks, however, who invented many of the forms of literature with which we are still familiar. Epic seems to have developed independently in many languages, but Hesiod (eighth century BC) provided us with the earliest Georgic, Sappho (seventh century BC) the earliest lyrics, and Pindar (sixth–fifth century BC) the earliest odes. The Greeks also invented the novel, in or about the first century AD. (The Latin novel appeared at the same time.) One other notable Greek literary form, currently unfashionable, was the epigram. Satire was primarily Roman, although one form of satire is named after the Greek writer Menippus (third century BC).

Words such as 'ode', 'lyric', 'novel', 'epic' inevitably point to the vexed question of literary genres. There have been many ingenious attempts to devise systems of genres (see Hernadi 1972), none of which have won general acceptance, and few of which are even known outside the specialist circles which take an interest in the matter. It seems impossible to determine a conceptual basis for genre distinctions, because they so often belong to different conceptual categories. 'Narrative' is a mode of representation; 'sonnet' is a form of verse; 'elegy' refers to content; 'epithalamium' gets its name from an occasion; 'epigram' has to do with size. It is small wonder that Croce rejected the whole idea of genres, which he referred to as 'empty phantasies' (Croce 1902, p. 42). He considered that every work of art was too individual, too unique, to belong to an artistic type. 'Every true work of art', he wrote, 'has violated an established genre' (Croce 1902, p. 41). Literature, in this view, is just too complex and various to sustain a comprehensive classification into a finite set of mutually exclusive varieties.

However, the history and vocabulary of genre criticism and genre theory are not without value. The vocabulary, in fact, has become indispensable. If we are to talk about literature at all we must use, or devise, such terms as short story, heroic couplet, ballad, epistolary novel, satire, essay. The function of these terms is not to install literary artefacts in special, logically distinct compartments. It is rather to give names to relationships among different works which illuminate or explain their character and properties. Literary works of art are not isolated texts surrounded on all sides by empty space. They constitute a vast and complex network – an entire verbal and aesthetic culture – such that when we enter it at any point we are drawn into a multidimensional web of endless interconnections. 'Genre' terms are the signposts in this web, and it is a web that transcends languages, time and geography.

Some genre terms have such a large extension that they are serviceable as names for very broad classes of literature: epic, novel, essay, for instance. But when defined in these very broad senses – long narrative in verse, long narrative in prose, short meditations on various topics – we see that they convey little information about the works that fall under them. Their main use is in literary history, where it makes sense to talk about the medieval epic or the nineteenth-century novel. As historical categories, moreover, they enable us to grasp something of the fluctuations and destinies of literature in Europe over the centuries. They enable us to talk of the rise of the novel or the death of tragedy, and give birth to questions about the relations between literature and the socio-economic ideas and conditions in which they are embedded.

Genre theory may be, as Croce said, an empty phantasy. But genre language is often a midwife for the inventiveness and the ingenuity of the intellectual culture that literature has gathered around itself (see Fowler 1982).

Literature and Language

Literature is a verbal art. There are other verbal arts, such as drama and song, but literature consists of language alone. Not even the bravest among us should attempt to define 'language'; but at least we can distinguish between the two principal methodologies for studying language which have emerged in the twentieth century. One of these is associated with Ferdinand de Saussure (Saussure [1916] (1974); see Bredin 1984b). The other is more traditional in character, though a tradition radically transformed by Noam Chomsky and his many followers (see Chomsky 1965).

At the heart of Saussure's methodological system is his belief that the identity of a verbal sign is determined by its relations with other signs, not by its own intrinsic properties. There are two kinds of such relations. Paradigmatic relations obtain among verbal signs which have some sort of similarity with one another. Thus, {tea, coffee, cocoa, hot chocolate . . . } is a paradigmatic set. So is {sick, sickens, sickly, sickness . . . }. Syntagmatic relations obtain among verbal signs whenever they are picked out of their paradigmatic sets and combined into intelligible strings, such as 'Cocoa is comforting when you feel sick'. The main sorts of syntagmatic relations are grammatical relations and logical relations. Each verbal sign's identity, according to Saussure, is determined partly by its relations to other signs within the paradigmatic sets to which it belongs, and partly by its relations to other signs within the syntagmatic string in which it is being used.

It can be seen that in Saussurean linguistics the basic building blocks of language are texts rather than signs. Signs have properties that derive from their relations to other signs in the language to which they belong. They then acquire further properties when they are selected and combined with other signs in a text. But the properties that words already have, before they are incorporated into a particular text, are derived from the part that they have played in previous texts. Signs therefore derive all of their properties from texts. Instead of texts being defined as structures of signs, signs are defined as constituents of texts.

Another feature of Saussurean linguistics is that no account is taken of reference. Paradigmatic and syntagmatic relations subsist entirely within language itself, without any reference to non-linguistic reality. Thus language is investigated as the bearer of meaning, of sense, irrespective of its referential adequacy, descriptive force or truth-value.

Literary theorists who come from a background of Saussurean linguistics (and many of the most interesting do) tend, in consequence, to neglect or ignore the question of truth in literature. They also seek to define literature in terms of properties internal to literary texts themselves, rather than in terms of the connections that those texts have to the socio-historical circumstances from which they emerge, to the beliefs and understanding of their readers, or to the world that we all inhabit. We shall encounter some of these literary theorists in the next section.

Traditional linguistics, as reformed by Chomsky, distinguishes among various 'levels' of language, each of which is studied by a discipline that is to some extent independent of the others. There is no general agreement on how many levels there are, but for convenience we can list at least four. One of these consists of the sounds made when a language is spoken, and which are studied in Phonetics and Phonology. A second level is the grammar of a language, which is sometimes subdivided into Morphology (the study of internal word structures) and Syntax (the study of word sequences). A third level is meaning, which is studied under the heading of Semantics. A fourth level is texts or discourse, studied in Text Linguistics or Discourse Analysis.

This kind of linguistics has produced no distinctive theory of literature. However, in a perfected Chomskyan linguistics all of the disciplines just mentioned would lose their independence and flow seamlessly into one another. For, despite the distinctiveness of the levels, language is believed to constitute an integrated structure from top to bottom. So far as literary theory is concerned, this would lead to a conception of literary texts in which all of the properties of the text constitute a single harmonic structure. We shall refer to this possibility again in the final section of this chapter.

Chomskyan linguistics, like Saussurean linguistics, is largely indifferent to the issue of verbal reference. Neither of these two leading methodologies of language study lends itself to discussion of a central question in the philosophy of literature: the question of literature and truth.

The Literary and the Non-literary

Several determined attempts have been made during the twentieth century to establish what it is that distinguishes literary texts from other verbal texts. Most of them have been unsuccessful, because they have tried to argue that there is something distinctive about the *language* used in literary texts. A group of thinkers known as the Russian Formalists (for example, Shklovsky [1917] (1965)), and their intellectual successors in the Linguistic Circle of Prague or Prague Structuralists (for example, Mukarovsky [1932] (1964)), held that literary language is language which deviates significantly from the language of everyday conventional usage. They claimed that the best method for producing literary deviations is 'foregrounding', which means giving special prominence to one aspect of language and pushing its other aspects into the background. For instance, we could foreground the sound of words through alliteration or rhyme. Or we could foreground syntax by employing an unusual word order, or by means of figures such as antithesis or syllepsis.

The purpose of foregrounding, or any other way of deviating from conventional language, is to stir up the readers' thought-processes. There is conventional thinking as well as conventional language, and deviations from convention in one produce deviations from convention in the other. Striking and novel language expresses and communicates striking and novel ways of perceiving and thinking about the world. Literature therefore 'defamiliarises' things and 'deautomatises' our responses to them.

This is a very plausible description of how literature works, but unfortunately it fails to distinguish literary from non-literary texts. In the first place, many non-literary texts also defamiliarise things and deautomatise our responses to them. Good art criticism has that effect. So has a report on a famine in a foreign country. *The Communist Manifesto* and *The Second Sex* have effected radical changes in the outlook of hundreds of thousands of people. And if we want really striking examples of defamiliarisation we need look no further than Copernicus, Newton and Einstein. In the second place, literature does not always change our outlook on things, but may, instead, confirm our outlook and our beliefs. Pope said that in poetry we find 'what oft was thought but ne'er so well expressed', and a great deal of literature is in fact of this kind. It supports and confirms the great universal truths of the human condition, instead of challenging and replacing them.

Another attempt to define literature in terms of its language was influenced by a philosophical movement known as Logical Positivism. Its most determined exponent in literary theory was I. A. Richards, a poet and literary critic of considerable distinction. In *Principles of Literary Criticism* (1926), Richards distinguished between two uses of language, the referential use and the expressive use.

A statement may be used for the sake of the *reference*, true or false, which it causes. This is the *scientific* use of language. But it may also be used for the sake of the effects in emotion and attitude produced by the reference it occasions. This is the *emotive* use of language. The distinction once clearly grasped is simple. We may either use words for the sake of the references they promote, or we may use them for the sake of the attitudes and emotions which ensue. Many arrangements of words evoke attitudes without any reference being required *en route*. They operate like musical phrases. But usually references are involved *as conditions* for, or *stages in*, the ensuing development of attitudes, yet it is still the attitudes not the references which are important. It matters not at all in such cases whether the references are true or false. Their sole function is to bring about and support the attitudes which are the further response. The questioning, verificatory way of handling them is irrelevant, and in a competent reader is not allowed to interfere. (Richards 1926, pp. 267–8)

Richards was here repeating a standard Logical Positivist view: that meaningful assertions can be verified or falsified by empirical methods such as observation and experiment; and, further, that assertions which cannot be thus verified or falsified are meaningless. Meaningless language (in this sense of 'meaningless') can none the less have other uses and values. For instance it can stir people up by making them feel sad or happy or emotional in some other way. Literature is couched in this sort of expressive, emotion-arousing language. According to Richards, literature has the further valuable role of bringing our feelings into harmonious alignment with one another, and thus of making us feel happier and more fulfilled.

This is a very restrictive conception of literature, and there are so many counter-examples that it gained few adherents outside the Logical Positivists themselves. The suggestion that literature has nothing to do with truth, and has only an incidental reference to the world that we live in, cannot explain satire and caricature, nor the fact that we learn about people and about life from novels and plays; nor can it explain the literary character of essays, criticism, journalism, history, philosophy and science. Furthermore, there are texts which can arouse strong emotion in us – a report of a famine, for instance – without necessarily being literature. Finally, the idea that language can be *either* referential *or* emotive is difficult to understand or accept, since the two functions nearly always go together. Language makes us experience emotions *because of* what it says. Reference and emotion are inextricably entwined.

A third attempt to pin down the essential nature of literature is associated with Roland Barthes (Barthes 1977) and Michel Foucault (Foucault 1984), both of whom took the view that there are two kinds of texts: authored texts and authorless texts, and that literary works are authorless texts.

If we conflate the thinking of Barthes and Foucault, the distinction between the authored and the authorless is as follows. An authored text, first, is a text whose authorship is an essential factor in our interpretation of it. Knowing that it is written by Shakespeare, say, or by Bacon, affects the way in which we read and understand it. We relate the text to other texts by the same author, and also to the author's period, contemporaries, predecessors, influences and the like. An authored text is part of the history of a society and a culture. It is also a trace of and a memorial to a particular individual – but an individual as defined and determined by an entire spectrum of circumstances, including the other texts that he or she has produced. Foucault argued (with some justification) that texts and authors define one another. The famous author whom we identify as 'Shakespeare' or 'Wordsworth' is a construct determined by the corpus of texts that we ascribe to him. But at the same time we define the texts as those characteristic of a particular author: they are not just any old texts but 'Wordsworthian' or 'Shakespearean' texts.

Literary works, according to Barthes and Foucault, should be read as texts without authors. The phrase connected with this view is 'the death of the author'. It is not clear whether this means that the only correct way of reading literary texts is to read them as authorless; or whether we are coming to read them as authorless nowadays because that is the way our literary culture is developing. Barthes seems inclined to the former view, Foucault to the latter. When we read a text as an authorless text, we experience it, not as emerging from a particular culture and historical moment, but as something 'eternally present'. It exists, always, here and now, and is not a voice speaking to us from the past or from a distance. Therefore we do not seek to discover its pre-established 'correct' meaning – the meaning, for instance, that it had for its author, or for the readers of its own time and place. Instead, its meaning is whatever meaning it has for my own understanding here and now. This may vary throughout my own life, and vary among different readers, but every interpretation is equally legitimate. Literary meaning is really determined by its readers, not by its authors.

There is another consequence of killing off the author. Let us take a sentence from *Ulysses*, about a moment in the life of Leopold Bloom: 'Kidneys were in his mind as he moved about the kitchen softly, right-ing her breakfast things on the humpy tray.' What are these words about? To what do they refer? Obviously not to anything in the 'real' world. It might be said that they refer to a man, his thoughts, his movements, activities and location, as imagined by James Joyce. But if James Joyce, the author, is then cut out of the picture, we can no longer say that the words refer to figments of Joyce's imagination. According to Barthes's theory of literary discourse, the referents of the words in *Ulysses* are, instead, whatever might be picked out by alternative words with a similar meaning. For instance, we might says that 'kitchen' refers to whatever is also referred to by the words 'room where food is cooked'. Then the word 'room' refers to whatever is also referred to by the words 'part of a house enclosed by walls, floor and ceiling', and 'house' refers to whatever is also referred to by the words 'building designed for human habitation'. Obviously we can go on like this indefinitely. We never, according to this line of thinking, get to the point where we pass beyond words to things. We never encounter the referent itself, only further meanings, in an endless chain of meanings (an endless 'semiosis' as it is called). The referent itself is endlessly 'deferred' as we find ourselves continuously enmeshed in the meanings of the words whose referent it is supposed to be.

It is worth noting, in passing, that if this theory of literary discourse were applied to all discourse, it would become a version of epistemo-logical Idealism – that is, the belief that the objects of consciousness are, not things themselves, but our mental representations of things.

Imagine that each of our minds is enclosed in a gilded cage, filled with and bounded by wondrous things: sights and sounds, tastes and smells, ideas and beliefs and memories. But we have no way of knowing whether there is anything outside the cage that corresponds to what is within it. It is not just that I cannot get out of the cage; rather, my mind *is* the cage. Now, imagine that what fills and defines the cage is language, not just verbal language but also the languages of music and vision, of activities and gestures, of mathematics and maps. This is the picture that begins to emerge from the later writings of Barthes, and which has come to maturity in some parts of the movement known as postmodernism.

The theory of the death of the author is sometimes motivated by this more general, postmodernist theory of knowledge and consciousness. Sometimes, instead, it is simply meant to distinguish between literary discourse and non-literary discourse. In either case it is explained in the same way, as follows. Literary language is filled with referentiality: that is, it always *appears* to be 'about' something, something non-linguistic. But when we try to pin down the reference we find that it is never there, it is always endlessly deferred. All we ever encounter is more and more meanings. Ultimately we cannot escape from words to things. The language may strike us as being referential language, but there is nothing outside of it that it actually refers to. It is, ultimately, 'self-referential'.

This striking, and currently very widespread, theory of literature does not make every heart beat with joy. It is quite a radical thing to detach a literary work of art from its cultural and historical roots – according to some an impossibility, since the very language in which it is written is heavy with the weight of history and resonant with the accents of place. Where would Shakespeare be without Warwickshire and London, or Dante without Firenze, and both without the humanism of late medieval and Renaissance Europe?

Another problem is the claim that all interpretations of literature are products of the reader, and all equally legitimate. It is not just that this is intuitively questionable, but it also leads to a radical privacy of literary experience. The social and dialectical character of literary criticism, literary history and literary scholarship would vanish, or at least would lack legitimation. The pedagogy and dialectic of literature, the sense of revelation and discovery that comes with repeated reading and discussion, would be an illusion. The slow penetration into a poem that is memorised and remembered would be nothing but a sequence of isolated and contingent moments. The *objectivity* of literature would be lost.

There are some for whom this conception of literary experience is perfectly acceptable. The image of the exquisite literary moment, the unique and irrecoverable epiphany, the instant of personal realisation and fulfilment that literature can bring, is rooted deeply in our cultural imagination. Yet there is a different and an older literary tradition: friends and neighbours gathered to hear the tale, carousers in the meadhall, the audience in the market square. There are no private reveries here, but laughter in the crowd, the touch of bodies, the clink of pennies on the ground (see Bredin 1986).

Finally, with the death of the author comes the death of truth. A referential language that does not refer, whose meaning is a function of how it is interpreted by its readers, is a language to which the categories of truth and falsehood do not apply. This consequence, this radical disjunction of the literary and the truthful, is a commonplace of the twentieth century. I. A. Richards and all the Logical Positivists, many structuralists (Roman Jakobson for instance), most poststructuralists (the later Barthes, Derrida), and postmodernists (Baudrillard) either deny that literature has a truth-value, or simply ignore the matter altogether as if it were of no account.

The question of literature and truth emerged at the very beginnings of literary theory, in Plato and Aristotle, and its importance has always been taken for granted, until the twentieth century. Truth in literature has sometimes been underestimated, as when Locke claimed that many poets' works could, if rewritten in plain language, be 'contained in a nutshell' (Locke [1690] (1975), III.xi.26). Sometimes it has been overestimated, as when Wordsworth wrote in his *Preface* that poetry 'is the breath and finer spirit of all knowledge'. But no one doubted that it was an important question, and that the truthfulness or otherwise of a literary work was a significant part of its value. Next, therefore, we will look at this vital, though not everywhere fashionable issue, and we will start by looking at the different kinds of truth that are to be found in literary works of art.

Literature and Truth

The first kind of truth consists in true accounts of historical events and of real persons and places and physical facts. It is to be found in literary works such as *War and Peace*, Shakespeare's history plays, Wordsworth's *Preface*, some aspects of *Ulysses*, many passages in *Moby-Dick*. We can learn a great deal about whales from *Moby-Dick*, and a great deal about the Napoleonic wars from *War and Peace*. James Joyce was notorious for ensuring that he got the topography of Dublin exactly right. This kind of truth is conspicuous in some literary works, and present to some extent in many, though not all. It is greatly enjoyed by modern readers, and readers can also become irritated if they happen to know that the author has got some historical or geographical detail wrong. Both the enjoyment and the irritation appear to be peculiar to the sensibilities of readers in the past couple of centuries – although they have not, for the most part, had any influence on literary judgements: we do not mind, and do not think the worse of Shakespeare or Keats, if a clock strikes anachronistically in *Julius Caesar*, or if it was not in fact stout Cortez who first gazed on the Pacific.

At least two interesting questions arise from this kind of truth in literary works. One is heuristic: how can we tell whether a particular text is factual or fictional? If I read an account of a criminal trial, for instance, can I tell whether it is a trial that really took place, or a trial imagined by the writer? Or: how do I tell the difference between a first-person novel and an autobiography?

In some cases there may be internal clues, such as elements of the fantastic or improbable, or even internal linguistic clues. Käte Hamburger has studied the latter in great detail in *The Logic of Literature* (1973). Take the following passages: (1) But in the morning she had to trim the tree. Tomorrow was Christmas. (2) Still today, when she closed her eyes, she saw before her the expression on his face (Hamburger 1973, p. 72). The unusual combinations of tenses – 'tomorrow' with 'was', 'today' with 'closed' – are enough to alert the *experienced* reader, who sees right away that these are characteristic of the narrative style of fictions. Notice, however, that it is likely to be an experienced reader who responds to linguistic clues of this kind. That is, the differences between factual and fictional linguistic styles have to be learned. They are not self-evident features of discourse. Furthermore, they are contingent upon custom and usage. Today's narrative styles may be quite different from tomorrow's. It is notorious, for instance, that the styles employed in reportage and in fiction constantly impinge upon one another. Ernest Hemingway and Graham Greene illustrate this very well, and James Joyce exploited the mannerisms of newspaper reporting to comic effect in the Aeolus section of *Ulysses*.

A less comfortable consideration is that, in some cases, certain banal external factors may determine whether a text is taken as fact or fiction by its readers. If we read a work by Edith Wharton we are inclined to take it as a novel because we know that she is a novelist. But if we open *A Backword Glance* the blurb on the back of the book has already conveniently told us that it is her autobiography; and, in any case, we have found it in the biography section of a bookshop or a library.

A second question is not so much heuristic as ontological. What is 'fiction' anyway? We know that this is a question of some importance, since we apply quite different criteria of value to fiction and non-fiction. A striking clock is a serious mistake in a history of Julius Caesar, but not in Shakespeare's play about him. We know also that it is not enough to claim that fiction is invented whereas history or journalism is not. For Shakespeare's *Julius Caesar* is about 'real' people and 'real' events, yet it is still a fiction, not a documentary.

Both the heuristic and the ontological questions are matters of some political and historical importance. Human beings are not endowed with an instinctive knowledge of the difference between fact and fiction. This is why characters in soap operas – the fictional characters, not the actors – are sent birthday presents and Christmas cards by members of the public. A harmless enough lunacy, perhaps. But what if the fiction should be about a conspiracy of Catholics, Jews and Freemasons to set up a world government through the United Nations in order to undermine true Christianity and bastardise the white race? History is filled with fictions disseminated as facts. It is not just a matter of telling people lies – telling them, for example, that a Great Leader is alive when in fact he is clinically dead. The influential lies are almost always narratives – of Popish plots, *Reichstag* fires, or whatever – and that is to say that they are fictions. They are fictions that lie, and their being fictions and their being lies are different things. The natural inability of people to tell the difference between the factual and the fictional is not a minor oddity, but something that can be of crucial significance in human affairs.

The problem of fictions arises not just in connection with literature, but also with drama, and with any art form, such as painting, or sculpture, that can be representational. This is as good a place as any to consider the nature of fictions in general, so it is to this topic that we turn in the next section.

Fiction

There is quite an extensive literature on the nature of fictions (note, in passing, the sense of the word 'literature' here), but a great deal of it has to do with an ontological problem, namely, what kind of entities fictions are. What is their mode of being? They are in some sense non-existent entities. But how, then, can we think and talk about them, come to know more about them and understand them better, and, in general, entertain them as objects of consciousness? This is a problem mainly for philosophers, since fictions provoke intriguing questions, about meaning and reference, about the concepts of existence and being, the actual and the possible. One of the most interesting of the

philosophers who have examined these questions was Alexius
Meinong (see Parsons 1975).

For anyone who is interested primarily in the philosophy of art,
however, there is another, more pertinent question. This has to do
with the phenomenology of the experience of fiction: that is, the manner in which fictions are present in our consciousness. Consider the
following questions: if a clock strikes in Shakespeare's *Julius Caesar*,
why does this not matter? If we were to discover that, because of a
monstrous conspiracy of historians, Tolstoy's descriptions of
Napoleon's campaigns in *War and Peace* were totally false, why is it
that this would have no effect on our estimate that it is one of the
world's great novels? Why, in short, does the distinction between
what is actual and what is imagined *not matter* in those forms of
literature which we describe as 'fictions'?

The most effective answer to this question can be found in Jean-
Paul Sartre's *The Psychology of Imagination* (1940); or rather, it can
be constructed on the basis of some of Sartre's ideas in that work.
Sartre writes that, 'Every consciousness posits its object, but each does
so in its own way' (Sartre 1940, p. 11). The words 'posits its object'
refer to the existential judgement that is included within every state of
consciousness – a judgement, that is, about the existential status of its
object. The state of consciousness that we call 'perception', for instance,
includes the existential judgement 'This object that I am perceiving
really exists'. If it were to turn out subsequently that the object didn't
exist, I would then say that it hadn't been perception in the first place,
but a mirage or an illusion or a dream-image or something else like
that. Genuine perception 'posits its object' as an actually existing
object.

Sartre goes on:

> The image also includes an act of belief, or a positing action. This
> act can assume four forms and no more: it can posit the object as
> non-existent, or as absent, or as existing elsewhere; it can also
> 'neutralise' itself, that is, not posit its object as existing. (Sartre
> 1940, p. 11)

Sartre is talking here about imagination, not perception, and he believes
that the imaginative consciousness posits its object as 'nothingness'.
But there are four kinds of nothingness, which are listed in the passage
just quoted. The first kind is non-existence: for instance, I might
entertain an image of a centaur, perhaps a very clear and detailed
image, in the full knowledge that there isn't such a creature. The
second kind of nothingness is absence: for instance, I might entertain

an image of my dead child, in such a way that it is the sheer absence of the child from my life that dominates my consciousness. The third kind of nothingness is existence elsewhere: for instance, I might entertain an image of my dead child in heaven – busy, perfect and fulfilled, though still not here for me; a child who cannot be seen or heard, smelled or touched, but who none the less exists elsewhere.

The fourth kind of nothingness occurs whenever the imaginative consciousness simply doesn't posit its object as existing. That is, the consciousness refrains from making any existential judgement. The consciousness, as Sartre puts it, 'neutralises' itself. It is easy to see how this can be taken as the mode of consciousness that we adopt towards literary, dramatic and any other kind of fictions. The phrase 'suspension of disbelief' – often used to describe our experiences of fiction – is very unsatisfactory, because it can be taken to mean that I temporarily play at believing, or pretend to believe, in the existence of fictional persons and events. But it is extremely rare to meet anyone who claims to have had the experience of pretending for a few hours to believe in the existence of Don Quixote, Falstaff, Candide or King Kong. What happens instead is that we make no existential judgement whatsoever. We simply set to one side the question of whether they exist or not. This is why actual and imagined persons, places and things can be mingled higgledy-piggledy in fictional works. This is why an atheist can read *Divina Commedia* or *Paradise Lost* in perfect equanimity, and why we are not in the least put out by talking animals in *Animal Farm*. This is also why a play about Winston Churchill and a documentary about Winston Churchill have quite different kinds of truth-value, and why an autobiography and a first-person novel are read and understood in quite different ways, even if the first-person novel has close parallels with the author's own life.

The term 'fiction' must therefore be used with some care. In one sense it refers to any content of consciousness that does not represent anything actual. In another and quite different sense it refers to any symbolic representation (verbal, dramatic, pictorial, etc.) of objects whose existential character is a matter of indifference. Of course, it is quite possible that people will get it wrong. I might very well read a first-person novel as an autobiography, or think that there really was a man called Robinson Crusoe who was once marooned on a desert island. This will just be my mistake, comparable in many ways to rushing on to the stage to save Desdemona from being strangled.

It is also possible that this account of fictions could be taken to justify the conclusion that literary truth or falsehood is a matter of indifference also – that, in the case of literary fictions at any rate, truth-value is not the point, and that we can safely leave this whole issue to one side. But as we shall shortly see, any such attempt to detach literature from its truth-value would be mistaken.

Realism

In 'Literature and Truth' we discussed one kind of truth in literature: true accounts of historical events and of real persons and places and physical facts. A second kind of truth is sometimes called 'realism' or 'naturalism'. This is what is meant when someone remarks that James Joyce had a good ear for speech, because the way in which his characters talk can be heard in Dublin to this day. D. H. Lawrence is often thought, by young people, to have captured with miraculous perfection their sensitivities, desires, fears, joys and sorrows. Truth in this sense refers to a resemblance between the way in which a writer represents things and the way in which we, the readers, experience things in our everyday lives. Such representations are then called 'truthful' or 'true to life'.

Realism is, like the first kind of truth, characteristic of modern prose fiction. Even a modernist device like stream of consciousness is ultimately, perhaps especially, at the service of realism. But it is also arguable that realism is a feature of all narrative mimesis. The *Odyssey*, for all its exotic locations and adventures, is memorable also for the hardheaded realism of its characters. Dante travels in his imagination through circles of Hell, but pays punctilious respect to the realities of human psychology. The universal pleasure that people get from stories seems to require that they resonate with the lives and experiences of their readers, however magical or improbable the incidents related might be.

We also know, however, that the sensibilities of human beings vary from culture to culture, and from period to period. It follows that a narrative that is felt to be realistic in one age and place might seem less so in another. Realism, that is, is a relative rather than a fixed quality. Here is how Walter Scott describes Captain Porteous's state of resentment and anger because of a fancied slight to his authority.

His step was irregular, his voice hollow and broken, his countenance pale, his eyes staring and wild, his speech imperfect and confused, and his whole appearance so disordered, that many remarked he seemed to be *fey*, a Scottish expression, meaning the state of those who are driven on to their impending fate by the strong impulse of some irresistable necessity. (*The Heart of Mid-Lothian*)

Scott was, and is, a major novelist, but he wrote in the manner of his own time and place. This passage must at the time (1818) have seemed a reasonable description of a person suffering from pique, but nowadays it appears mannered and unintentionally comical. It is perhaps interesting to note that the description corresponds very closely with the style of acting current in the eighteenth- and early nineteenth-century theatre.

No one has studied the many versions of literary representation more exhaustively than Erich Auerbach in *Mimesis* (1946), a monumental work which examines the history of literary mimesis from *Genesis* up to Proust. Auerbach repeatedly and vividly brings out yet another important motive in literary descriptions, that they are designed to play a role in the larger economy of narrative. They are seldom included just for their own sake (unless, perhaps, in second-rate literature where they are used to create 'local colour'). Two passages quoted by Auerbach will illustrate this point. One is the opening of Chrétien de Troyes's *Yvain*.

> It happened seven years ago that, lonely as a countryman, I was making my way in search of adventures, fully armed as a knight should be, when I came upon a road leading off to the right into a thick forest. The road there was very bad, full of briars and thorns. In spite of the trouble and inconvenience, I followed the road and path. Almost the entire day I spent thus riding until I emerged from the forest of Broceliande.

As Auerbach points out, this is written in a flowing, naturalistic style, full of circumstantial details: seven years ago, a road to the right, briars and thorns. But these details are not in fact as naturalistic as they seem. To a twelfth-century reader or listener a road to the right signified the road of virtue. This is why it was full of briars and thorns; a road to the left would have been the road of vice, and therefore pleasant and easy. We now realise that the knight was 'fully armed', not just with physical weapons, but with spiritual defences against temptation. And the period of seven years is not meant to be taken literally, but to indicate, like the phrase 'once upon a time', that the story takes place in the indefinite realm of fairytale and romance.

All of the 'naturalistic' elements, in short, are exploited in the service of other elements in the story: its status as a romance, the character of the hero, the moral significance of the action. Realism in good literature is not adventitious, but intertwines with the larger purposes of the writer. Another passage which illustrates this comes from *Madame Bovary*.

> But it was above all at mealtimes that she could bear it no longer, in

that little room on the ground floor, with the smoking stove, the creaking door, the oozing walls, the damp floortiles; all the bitterness of life seemed to be served to her on her plate and, with the steam from the boiled beef, there arose from the depths of her soul other exhalations as it were of disgust. Charles was a slow eater; she would nibble a few hazel-nuts, or else, leaning on her elbow, would amuse herself making marks on the oilcloth with the point of her table-knife.

What is striking in this passage is how carefully selective Flaubert is in the details that he chooses to mention. No verbal description is ever exhaustive. We could devote ten pages to describing a matchbox and still fail to describe it completely. Descriptions have to be selective, and the details that a writer selects, as well as the details he does not select, are determined by the purpose which the description serves. Every detail about Emma Bovary's mealtimes – smoking stove, damp floortiles, boiled beef, oilcloth on the table – has been picked out in order to reflect and convey her mental state. It is also curiously atemporal, since they can hardly have eaten boiled beef every day, the chimney must have been swept occasionally, and the oozing walls must have dried up in summertime. When examined carefully, it is much less like straight reporting than it seems, and is more emblematic than realistic. Its main purpose is to drive the narrative forward by establishing the motives and the mental energies upon which later, climactic events in the novel will hinge.

It is this structural, emblematic function of literary description that prevents it from losing its force when it becomes dated – that is, when the average reader's sensibility is no longer in tune with the manner of representation that the writer has adopted. There is another factor, however, which may determine whether a reader finds a verbal representation realistic or not. This factor is the reader's sexual identity. Feminist criticism has made it clear that a passage which seems realistic to a male reader may not seem so to a female reader, and vice versa. Molly Bloom's soliloquy usually seems realistic to men, but much less so to women (this is how men would experience being women if they were women, but not how actual women experience being women). Mr Rochester and St John Rivers, men who are depicted entirely from Jane Eyre's point of view, sometimes strike the male reader as slightly false.

Realism, then, is not something that a work of literature has or hasn't, but denotes rather a property related to the experience of literature (what is called in the jargon a relational rather than an exhibited property). What is objectively present in literary works is representations – descriptions – of persons, places and things, in which certain features of the described objects are singled out for mention, and other features omitted. If a representation presents its object in a manner that is similar to the manner in which a reader experiences such an object in everyday life, the reader feels that it is 'realistic'. To call a description realistic is therefore analogous to calling it amusing: it refers to its potentiality for provoking a certain response. Whether the potentiality is realised depends upon contingency and chance.

The Aristotelian Theory of Truth

The next kind of truth in literature takes us back, initially, to Plato's attack upon poetry in his *Republic*. Plato is often misrepresented in this regard, as a severe and puritanical censor who wanted to bowdlerise or even abolish literature. In fact he defended poetry's role in education, and argued that it was a necessity in the preparation of young minds for the onset of reason. It was different for rational adults. For them, poetry – and not just poetry, but all forms of representation – was virtually useless as a means of articulating and communicating truth; and, in addition, it encouraged its readers or listeners to wallow in emotion. It simply could not rival philosophy – that is, systematic and rational thought, based upon accurate observation – as a method for investigating the world and discovering truth. At most it represented the external and contingent appearances of things, not their underlying and universal nature. Just as a picture of a Gothic arch shows what it looks like but not the stresses and forces that hold it together, so too, in literature, we find descriptions of particular men and women and their words and actions on particular occasions, but nothing about the universal characteristics of human beings, or the universal motives and energies that produce and explain human behaviour.

Aristotle disagreed with this account of literature, as we can see in the following famous passage from his *Poetics*.

It is not the poet's function to relate actual events, but the kinds of things that might occur and are possible in terms of probability or necessity. The difference between the historian and the poet is not the difference between using verse or prose; Herodotus's work could be versified and would be just as much a kind of history in verse as it is in prose. No, the difference is this: that the one relates actual events, the other the kinds of things that might occur. Consequently, poetry is more philosophical and more elevated than history, since poetry relates more of the universal, while history relates particulars.

'Universal' means the kinds of things which it suits a certain kind of person to say or do, in terms of probability or necessity. (1451a–b)

Two things emerge from this passage. The first is that Aristotle agrees with some of what Plato had said. He agrees that literary representations do represent particular persons, places and things. That is, a writer depicts Jane Eyre or Leopold Bloom, not some universal 'woman' or 'man'. Literature, lyric and narrative literature at any rate, is alive with the sensations and textures of concrete particulars, and this is essential to its excitement and power.

The second thing, however, is that these literary particulars embody universal truths about human psychology: 'the kinds of things which it suits a certain kind of person to say or do'. For Plato, the representation of particulars was the end of the matter. It was the purpose and point of poetry. For Aristotle, there was an ulterior goal: the presentation, in a literary rather than a philosophical mode, of a certain kind of universal truth. Literary representations, however, do not *state* but rather *exemplify*, these universal truths. For instance, we might say, 'Jealousy often blinds people to the truth, warps their judgement, and can produce violent behaviour'. This is an abstract statement about human beings, a 'universal truth' of a certain kind. Shakespeare, however, expresses the same truth (and of course many other truths about human beings) by writing *Othello*. Shakespeare does not state the truths, but *shows them in action* in the lives of people.

The Aristotelian theory of literary truth has been the one most favoured throughout the history of European thought upon the subject. If it has a fault, it is that it does not do justice to the kind of universal truths that are simply stated, not instantiated in a narrative or a character. These truths are perhaps more characteristic of poetry than of narrative or dramatic fictions. Here, for instance, is William Blake:

> Abstinence sows sand all over
> The ruddy limbs and flaming hair,
> But Desire Gratified
> Plants fruits of life and beauty there.

And from Rilke's first *Duino Elegy*:

> For Beauty's nothing
> but beginning of Terror we're still just able to bear,
> and why we adore it so is because it serenely
> disdains to destroy us, Every angel is terrible.

These are statements, albeit very complex statements, of facts, albeit very complex facts, and are straightforwardly true or false, in whole or in part. Some even more obvious examples are the essays of Robert Louis Stevenson or Francis Bacon. These are works of literature whose truth is an essential property, whose truth is often stated in propositional form, and whose truth is necessary to both their identity and their value.

The Values of Literature

Truth is one of the principal values in terms of which we pass judgement upon people and their actions and artefacts, and it is now time finally to consider the value, or values, of literature. We have distinguished four kinds of literary truth: (1) true (accurate) descriptions of actual persons, places and things; (2) a manner of representing things (factual or fictional) which is very similar to the manner in which things are experienced in everyday life by a particular readership; (3) representations of things in such a way that they exemplify universal truths about human nature and human behaviour; (4) statements of universal truths.

The first and second of these (discussed earlier in this chapter, in 'Literature and Truth' and 'Realism' respectively) are useful rather than valuable. The first is clearly of use to writers. Tolstoy and Joyce, for instance, appear to have needed a strong framework of actual place and actual history to support their fictions. This is how their imaginations worked. Readers, too, are drawn into these fictional worlds all the more easily because of the meanings and purposes conferred upon actualities that they are already familiar with. The second kind of truth is also useful in confirming the outlook and the values of readers. It validates their modes of experience by reproducing them in narrative and description, and articulates for them their understanding of themselves and their world.

But neither of these kinds of truth, however useful and enjoyable, is constitutive of literary value. Literature without them is just as good as literature with them. Or, to put it in another way, they are values that are specific to some literary works but not to all.

The third and fourth kinds of truth are a different matter. In a sense they are both of the same kind, namely, universal truths about human beings and the human condition. But they are distinguishable in that they are different ways of articulating these universal truths – by plain statement in one case, by exemplification in action and life in the other. Essays, philosophy, history and similar works can possess the former; novels, epic, short stories and similar works can possess the latter. Poetry can possess either or both.

The articulation of universal truths is, we wish to claim, one of the principal values of literature. It supplies an infallible criterion for assessing and comparing literary works with one another. Sentimentality and stereotyping, for instance – both species of falsehood – are signs of mediocrity; whereas good works of literature involve discoveries and revelations about those regions of human experience that are most central to, but also most resistant to, our understanding of ourselves.

There is also another kind of literary value, one that refers us back to the levels of language which are distinguished from one another in traditional linguistics ('Literature and Language'). In everyday speech, we tend to use words in a very utilitarian fashion, which is to say that we tend not to take much notice of them apart from their meaning. If I am given street directions I may follow them perfectly well without remembering or thinking of the exact words in which the directions were couched. I can summarise Descartes's theory of mind and body without using a single word taken from Descartes's own works. I can take notes on the content of a lecture or an interview, but entirely in my own words, not the words actually uttered. There is an important kind of usage, therefore, in which words are *merely* a vehicle for thought, in which we 'pass through' language to its meaning, and retain the latter even as we discard the former.

Literary discourse is not at all like this. Instead, it involves a usage in which all of the different levels of language – the phonetic, syntactic, semantic and discursive – are so thoroughly integrated that we cannot consider any one of them in isolation from the others. This is why we cannot paraphrase or translate poetry. If the words change, everything changes. This is why a poet will search for weeks or months, or half a lifetime, for the 'right' word – a word that has exactly the right meaning, fits in with the grammar, matches the character of the words used elsewhere in the poem, and has exactly the right sound. All four levels match and echo one another in an integrated totality.

This total integration of levels has always been known about by literary critics, who explore such aspects of literature as sound echoing sense, the correspondence of syntax and meaning, patterns of imagery which reflect a central theme, *mise en abîme*, structural linkages that bind works together, and, in general, all of the factors that produce what Aristotle called unity and wholeness (*Poetics* 1451a). Any text that possesses these factors possesses, for that reason and to that extent, some degree of literary value.

Mediocre literature can be skimmed. We read it mainly in order to find out what happens next. In the same way, we read a newspaper to find out what is happening in the world, irrespective of how well or badly it is written. But we cannot skim Jane Austen. We cannot skim Milton. We cannot skim Francis Bacon or Montaigne. In good literature words matter, and so too does structure, order, grammar and the manifold internal interconnections and the multi-levelled reciprocities that good literature possesses.

We hold, therefore, that there are two main values in terms of which we can pass judgements upon works of literature: truth, and textual integrity. These are values that all of them must possess to some degree, if they are to be called 'literature' in the evaluative sense. Individual works or categories of work may also possess other values. A humorous work is or is not amusing. A satirical work is either effective or ineffective. A didactic work enlightens or fails to do so. A religious work is inspirational or otherwise. Other values again – political, hortatory, informative, historical, persuasive, rhetorical, commemorative, as well as entertainment value – abound in the endless panorama of the world's literatures. But these are values shared among literary and non-literary texts alike. The values that we single out as distinctive of works of literature – truth and linguistic integrity, truth articulated in a language whose levels are bounds integrally together – define literature, for all its internal varieties, as a single art.

8   The Dramatic Arts

These our actors,
As I foretold you, were all spirits, and
Are melted into air, into thin air.
(Shakespeare)

Introduction

The use of the human body as an artistic medium is of great antiquity. One of the earliest representations of dance – the *Leopard Dancers*, painted on a wall found in Çatal Hüyük in Turkey – has been dated to 6000 BC. But the phenomenon must be much older than that. There is no known society in which the human body is not exploited at least in dance and ritual, and artistic uses of the body seem to proliferate as societies grow larger and more complex. The Euro-American culture that currently dominates the councils of the world has produced the following: a huge variety of dance forms, from breakdancing to ball-room to ballet; sports such as gymnastics, skating and diving; military displays and tattoos; acrobatics; mime of various sorts (Heads of State inspecting a guard of honour, curtseying and bowing, clowns); pro-cessions and parades, both religious and secular; etiquette, from table-manners to lovemaking; ice-shows, striptease and circuses; and then the obvious ones: plays, operas, film and television, each of which has itself several sub-varieties and genres.

What is common to all of these is that the human body, rather than pigment, sound or stone, is an artistic medium. Many of them involve other artistic media as well as the body, and a few of them employ virtually the entire spectrum of artistic media. Stage-plays make use of scenery, costume, words, light and music, as well as gestures and movements; and the same is true of film, although film consists of representations of bodies rather than actual bodies. Stage-plays – which we will take as the paradigm of drama – and films are the two most important kinds of dramatic art. This is due partly to the very variety and complexity of artistic media that we have just alluded to.

It is due also to the central and defining role that they play in European culture: drama throughout the history of that culture, and film in the present century. But for reasons of space we will concentrate, in what follows, on stage drama alone.

The Uniqueness of Drama

Plays are not always stage-plays. They have been, and are, performed in streets, fields, churches, pubs and private houses; and radio plays, which use aural representations of bodies, are performed in studios. None the less, it is striking that drama is the only art, throughout most of our history, that has generated forms of architecture designed specifically for it, whether it be Greek and Roman amphitheatres, opera houses or theatres as we know them today. Nothing could illustrate more acutely how closely drama is entwined with the heart and nerves of European culture. The other forms of artistic architecture – museums, galleries, concert halls – are of comparatively recent vintage. Even libraries are not designed specifically for the literary arts, but for books; and a library is, in any case, just a building with pigeon-holes or shelves. A library is a kind of warehouse; a theatre is more like a church, in which the audience, the play, the players, the technicians, are compelled by the building itself to assume certain spatial, intellectual and emotional relations to one another. Drama is essentially a social art. This accounts in part for its power and persistence over the centuries.

History of Drama

Drama has developed into a fully-fledged, sophisticated art form in a number of the world's cultures – Europe, Japan, China, India – but our concern here will be with European drama alone. In Europe, drama began as a Mediterranean art, which eventually spread across the rest of the continent. It started, like most of European culture, in Greece, perhaps with dithyrambic odes sung in honour of Dionysos. These may have developed in such a way that a number of odes were sung in sequence, interspersed with lines spoken by individuals. But the point at which this was transformed into a dramatic narrative, into an enacted story, is lost and irrecoverable. It was that transformation, that collective paradigm shift in the Greek psyche, that gave birth to drama. The genius of the transformation was matched almost at once by the unparalleled genius of its practitioners – Aeschylus, Sophocles, Euripedes, Aristophanes – as if the millennia without drama burst suddenly like a dam released into these human vessels.

Drama occupied an important place in the Greco-Roman world. In

Rome and the Latin West, it never came to have the religious and civic importance that it enjoyed in the Greek sphere of influence. But wherever the Roman Empire put down its roots, an amphitheatre usually followed. In Rome, however, there was also hostility. It is sometimes thought that pagan Greece and Rome were favourable to the theatre, whereas puritanical Christians like St Augustine were against it. The reality was more complex. Stoic moralists, such as Seneca and Marcus Aurelius, tended to despise the theatre as a frivolous distraction from the serious things in life. The Emperor Tiberius expelled all actors from Italy because of their alleged licentiousness. The acting profession was, in fact, an object of opprobrium and even of legal discrimination in the Roman world for many centuries. The supposed association of the stage with loose morals is a very ancient one, and Augustine's denunciation of the theatre (*City of God* II.8–14) was not so much anti-pagan as a new variation on an anti-theatre tradition of long standing.

In the end, it was barbarian invasions rather than Christian asceticism that brought about the demise of drama in the Latin West, although it is possible that it survived at least as an orally transmitted art in Italy. What did not disappear was what might be called the spirit of drama, which re-emerged very early in medieval times, both in folk drama and in ecclesiastical or liturgical drama. The latter, naturally enough, is the better documented. One authority (Chambers 1903, II, pp. 14–15) dates the rebirth of European drama to a dramatic rendering of an Easter Sequence, with detailed stage directions, devised by a Bishop of Winchester in the tenth century. In the same century a Benedictine Abbess, Roswitha or Hroswitha, wrote six plays in Latin for her nuns (Hrotsvit of Gandersheim 1966). Miracle plays, mystery plays, passion plays, morality plays: the divisions of the genres are uncertain, but all of them dramatised the central narratives and mysteries of Christianity, much as the Greeks had dramatised their own mythology. Folk drama had its roots rather in the semi-pagan traditions of the peasantry.

Modern secular drama began in Spain and Italy, a consequence of the accelerating classical revival that culminated in the Renaissance, but Italy proved to be more influential, and Ferrara was for a time the main centre of the theatrical Renaissance. Here it was that one of the earliest vernacular comedies, Ariosto's *La Cassaria*, was staged in 1508; and here it was that the first modern, purpose-built theatre was constructed, in the 1530s (though it lasted for only a year, as it burned down in 1533). Many other permanent theatres were built in other Italian cities, and the influential architect and painter Sebastiano Serlio wrote about the construction of theatres, stage effects and scenery, in the second Book of his *L'Architettura* (1545). Above all, Italy produced three playwrights of genius – Ariosto, Aretino, and Machiavelli – and early stage designers included such artists as Raphael and Andrea del Sarto.

By the end of the sixteenth century, drama was fully reinstated as a European art form. It consolidated its place, then and in the century that followed, by an unprecedented flowering of dramatic genius that seemed to know no bounds: Elizabethan and Jacobean drama in England, Corneille, Racine and Molière in France, Lope de Vega and Calderón in Spain. Despite these geniuses, however, European drama had to overcome one final obstacle. Puritanism in England closed the theatres for a time, and, despite the eccentric brilliance of Restoration comedy, an important thread of continuity was broken. Jansenism in France had a less radical influence, but it none the less inspired Racine to give up writing plays for twelve years.

These problems notwithstanding, the art of stage drama kept its place at the heart of Europe's artistic culture, and the eighteenth century produced its own galaxy of theatrical genius: Lessing, Schiller and Goethe in Germany, Alfieri and Goldoni in Italy, Goldsmith and Sheridan in England, Voltaire and Beaumarchais in France. The early nineteenth century was something of a fallow period in European theatre, but towards the end of the century Ibsen and Chekhov galvanised and transformed the literary and theatrical worlds by the naturalistic forms of drama that they pioneered.

Drama throughout the twentieth century has been extraordinarily eclectic and experimental. It is deeply embedded also in most educational systems, and has even come to be regarded as a form of therapy in prisons and hospitals. It has assumed different forms, and acquired new techniques of presentation, in radio, film and television. In stage drama, there has been a growing consensus that it is not just a literary art, but a syncretic art that involves the co-operation of multiple artistic skills. When the history of twentieth-century drama is written in the future it will not be, as in the past, a history of playwrights, but a history also of actors, directors and designers.

Dramatic Media

Eight different artistic media are involved, or can be involved, in stage drama in the late twentieth century: the human body, language, music, scenery, costume, lighting, theatre architecture, audience. This large number of media requires in turn a large number, and large variety, of people to contribute their knowledge and skill: technicians, designers,

producers, directors, investors, bankers, insurance brokers, seam-
stresses, shoemakers, painters, electricians, carpenters, cleaners, ticket-
sellers, reviewers, even the bus and taxi drivers who take the actors
and the audience to and from the theatre. Every performance of a
stage-play is a logistical triumph, and a witness to the complexity and
efficiency of developed societies.

Dramas can exist quite well without this complexity of medium
and skill. All that is needed is an actor or two, a space, a script (even
an improvised one will do), and an audience, and the towers and
palaces of the world can be conjured out of thin air (see Brook 1968).
But the fact of the matter in the twentieth century is that minimalist
stagings like this are comparatively rare. The great theatrical showcases
of Europe and elsewhere are wizards' dens of clever technology.

The Human Body

The dramatic media, both severally and collectively, generate a wide
spectrum of artistic properties and values. But the human body is
fundamental in all drama, and its artistic and aesthetic qualities arise
from its physical beauty, its movements and its speech. We are inclined
nowadays to parsimony in our judgements of human beauty, but it
was not always so. Hegel observed that, for the Greeks and the classical world in general, the human body was a perfect marriage of matter and spirit. This ontological perfection was also important in
medieval times, when the body was considered to be the vesture and the
image of the soul, and, as God's creation, to be innately and necessarily
beautiful. Human kind were the most perfect of the animals, not just
because they possessed reason, but because they had the most beautiful bodies; and after death these bodies, designed as they were for
eternal life, were resurrected and glorified.

A sort of secular glorification of the body occurred in the
Renaissance, when something like the classical attitude was revived for
a time. But before long a new element arose, which, following Foucault,
we may call a progressive sexualisation of the body (see Foucault
1990). As Foucault tells it, from the seventeenth century to our own
time the human body has come to be regarded more and more as seat
and instrument of sexuality. This has entangled it within a complex
web of debate, evaluation and controls – social, domestic, educational,
medical – so that nowadays the sexual body is just as much an object
of political concern as the opinions which the owners of the bodies
might hold or express. Another factor, not discussed by Foucault, is
the commercialisation of our images of the body throughout the
twentieth century. Our conceptions of the beauty and worth of
bodies are strongly influenced by fashions and trends which are

deliberately and consciously created by the imperatives of marketing and consumerism.

Despite the cultural conditions that shape our outlook at the present time, despite the current restrictive paradigms of human beauty, and its heavy suppression by sexuality, our instinctive pleasure and wonder at the human body has not entirely vanished. It emerges, for instance, whenever babies and young children reawaken our astonishment at the sheer existence and presence of living human bodies. This sense of wonder is also awakened by the living, breathing bodies that inhabit the stage before our eyes and embark upon the creation of an imaginary world. Stage bodies do not, of course, assume statuesque poses in front of us. They move about, make gestures, adopt a variety of facial expressions; and, above all, they speak.

Gesture

Bodily posture and movement constitute a fascinating and still imperfectly understood form of human communication and bonding. Some studies of it occur in the context of language learning by children, where, no doubt, it plays an important role. But there is great interest also in the language or semiotics of gesture, and a substantial body of literature on it (see bibliographies in Bremmer and Roodenburg 1991, and Calbris 1990). In the case of drama, however, the gestures made by actors are unique, because they are gestures which represent other gestures. When Paul Robeson, playing the part of Othello, points to something on the stage, it is not Paul Robeson pointing, but Paul Robeson acting the part of Othello pointing. All actors' gestures are metagestures.

The study of gesture was important in the ancient world, because of the importance of rhetoric and the practice of teaching and learning the art of oratory. Quintilian, in Book Eleven of his *Institutio oratoria* (XI.3.65–183) devoted most of his attention to gestures appropriate to oratory. But he also gives us a few tantalising glimpses of actorial conventions in first-century Greco-Roman theatre. In one passage he compared the acting styles of two comic actors, Demetrius and Stratocles. Each was particularly suited to certain kinds of roles, partly because of the timbre of their voices, and partly because of the movements that they employed:

Demetrius showed unique gifts in the movement of his hands, in his power to charm his audience by the long-drawn sweetness of his exclamations, the skill with which he would make his dress seem to puff out with wind as he walked, and the expressive movements of the right side which he sometimes introduced . . . On the other

hand, Stratocles' *forte* lay in his nimbleness and rapidity of movement, in his laugh . . . and finally, even in the way in which he sank
his neck into his shoulders. (XI.3.179–80)

In the eighteenth century (and well into the nineteenth) actors
learned and deployed a repertory of gestures, each appropriate to the
words being spoken. There were recognised gestures for all of the
common emotions – grief, surprise, aversion, shame, welcome – and
also for differing rhetorical situations, such as beginning or ending a
speech. The audience, far from condemning this acting style as artificial, expected it and took pleasure in it. They knew what each of the
movements and gestures meant, and were able to judge how appropriately they matched the words they accompanied. Gesture signified
verbal meaning, rather than personality. As one authority puts it:

> The fundamental technique of 18th century acting was the use of a
> vocabulary of basic gestures, each of which had an individual
> meaning known to all in advance. Because each of the basic gestures
> had an individual meaning and is of short duration, the action tended
> to be matched to the short phrase rather than to whole passages.
> One acted by the word rather than by the paragraph or by the
> pervading emotion. (Barnett 1987, p. 18)

The aesthetic qualities produced by actorial gestures are of two
kinds. One is the innate beauty of bodily movement itself. Just as the
human body has an innate beauty to which we instinctively respond,
so too have its movements. In drama, however, this is strongly over-
laid by the semantic force of the movements, which have the specific
function of enacting a narrative, whether by complementing spoken
words or by occupying the interstices between the words. Their main
aesthetic value, therefore, rests upon the degree of perfection with
which they succeed in this function.

What is meant by success here is difficult to define, but can be seen
in the differences between an amateur and a professional actor. In the
case of a good professional actor, his gestures and the meaning of his
gestures flow seamlessly into one another, and the more fully they
achieve this seamless character the more perfect the acting. The audience
do not consciously have to interpret the meaning – to pass, as it were,
from gesture to meaning as if they were two things. Instead, the gestures
fully embody and so fully convey whatever the narrative requires.
The movements and gestures of actors are a kind of onomatopoeia of
the body.

Speech

There is a kind of verbal onomatopoeia which may be called 'exemplary onomatopoeia' (see Bredin 1996). This occurs whenever the sound of a word or phrase instantiates a property associated with the meaning of the word. For instance, the sound of the word 'slothful' instantiates the property *slow* that is one of the properties of slothfulness. The sound of 'nimble' instantiates the property *quick* that is one of the properties of nimbleness.

If we now imagine all the acoustic resources of language exploited towards the goal of exemplary onomatopoeia, we approach the ideal of the actor's speech. This is speech understood, not as a mere articulation of dictionary meaning, but speech as gesture, speech as the enactment of meaning.

Speakers articulate meaning in two ways. One way is simply to follow the phonological rules of the language being spoken; that is, to pronounce the words correctly. 'Soap' is not pronounced like 'soup', still less like 'fish' or 'technicolor'. Native speakers of a language internalise these rules very early in life and, with the exception of a few unfamiliar words, apply them without difficulty for the rest of their lives. However, most languages, and certainly all European languages, have phonetic variants connected with region and culture. The word 'iron', for instance, is pronounced 'ion' in parts of southern England, 'eye-irn' in parts of Scotland, and 'eye-rn' in parts of western Ireland. These kinds of variations can be used by actors to mimic the region, and, often enough, the occupations and even the social class of their characters; and audiences become adept at interpreting accents in the appropriate ways. Accent is not the only clue to character, of course, but it can point the audience in the direction of a character type: Southern redneck, Yorkshire farmer, retired Brigadier, cowboy, prostitute, intellectual. The use of accent in this manner was exploited by Aristophanes to poke fun at the Spartans, and the device may well be as old as drama itself.

The second way in which speakers articulate their meaning is through properties of language known as prosodic features: pitch, loudness and tempo. These features have a major role to play in the production of meaning. There is a narrow, technical sense of the word 'meaning' in which these features of speech would not count as features of verbal meaning; and for some purposes – examining the logical validity of an argument, for instance – this narrow sense of meaning is perfectly adequate. However, the verbal interchanges of everyday life, and verbal interchanges on the stage, necessitate a much richer and more complicated concept of meaning, and this is the concept that we are using here.

One other feature of semantic importance in spoken language is the timbre of the speaker's voice. Timbre is something that people are born with, for it is determined by the physical structure of the vocal organs. It is what we recognise when we recognise someone's voice on the telephone or around the corner. Without such recognition, radio plays would be impossible.

Actors can alter the timbre of their voices to some extent, for instance when a man acts the part of a woman, or an adult assumes the voice of a child. But for the most part they exploit timbre in the interests of creating and projecting character. Good actors are very versatile and can play a wide range of parts. None the less there is good casting and bad casting, which depend not just upon physique and presence, but also upon voice timbre. Edith Evans exaggerated the natural timbre of her voice in order to make herself an unrivalled Lady Bracknell. When silent movies were ousted by the talkies, some hitherto famous names vanished from the screen because their voices turned out to be shrill and unsuitable.

This briefest of glimpses at the phonology of language has at least shown how complex and varied are the acoustic resources that actors employ in the enactment of narrative. The aesthetic qualities that actorial speech engenders are equally complex. There is, as always, an innate beauty in voice itself: the human voice excites the human ear by its mere presence just as the human body excites the eye; though as well as this, some voices are more attractive than others. Voices can have a charisma of their own, so that we sometimes will sit and listen to them no matter what is being said.

In drama, however, the main aesthetic quality of speech relates to the perfection with which it matches the other dramatic elements that accompany it. It has to match character for a start; that is, its various features should embody and express occupational and personality traits such as timidity, aggressiveness, optimism, anxiety, confidence, egotism and so on. Voice must also match the meaning of the words: angry words are spoken angrily; an interrogative voice is different from an assertive one; a meditative voice is not suitable for challenging someone to a duel. Voice, finally, should match the logic of the narrative. When Macbeth says, 'If it were done when 'tis done, then 'twere well it were done quickly', his voice should convey, not just the decisiveness of a man who is about to commit murder, but a man who knows, at some deep level of his psyche, that he is embarking on the path to his own death.

Costume

Actors' bodies on the stage are clothed bodies. Even stage nudity, it has been well said, is a form of clothing. The clothing, moreover, has a more theatrical, less literary, character than the words or even the movements of the actors. The playwright is master of the words, the story, the appearance or disappearance of characters on stage, all of which affect in turn the spatial relations and movements of the cast. Costume is out of the playwright's reach, for it begins where words end. Costume is spectacle.

This visual, spectacular element in drama produces its own aesthetic challenges and imperatives. A painter balances masses and colours on a flat surface. The bits in the corners of his picture (to put it crudely) must fit together with the bits in the middle and at the sides and with one another. On the stage (again to put it crudely) the coloured bits, the masses and the shapes, as actors' bodies move to and fro and interweave continually, are like a new picture every second, but arranged in three dimensions instead of two. The costumes – their colours, patterns, shapes, the way they flow and change as their wearers move around – must somehow continue to dispose themselves appropriately in every circumstance. The aesthetic and so the artistic challenge is immense. Stage costume is one of the most demanding of the visual arts.

The second thing about costume is that it tends to differentiate itself from the everyday clothing worn by the audience. Long robes, tunics, garments of fantastic richness, head-dresses and wigs, makeup (also a kind of clothing), tights and skirts, robes and gowns: these are worn, not for warmth or to engage in the business of life, but to be looked at. 'Ordinary' clothing is also worn, of course, but it is ordinary clothing that makes a point. The aproned housewife, the twinset and pearls, the fancy waistcoat, the business suit, the pince-nez, the jeans, hairstyles, the scar on the face – all are emblematic, bearers of information. They are signifiers, designed to denote gender, age, character type, social class, occupation.

And yet, the amount of information conveyed by costume is relatively small. Throughout much of the history of drama it has been minimal: a mask to convey anger, the colour of a robe to signify an old man, a patchwork garment to show that its wearer is a Fool, a turban to indicate someone from the East, keys as a mark of St Peter, splendid robes to clothe a king, a helmet for a soldier. It is only 'contemporary' clothing that can be interpreted more fully by its audience, because the audience is familiar with what Roland Barthes has called the vestimentary code (Barthes 1985). Historically accurate clothing on stage did not become a fashion until the nineteenth century, but it has never conveyed more information to an audience than the period and perhaps the country in which the play is set. A fourteenth-century dress need only look approximately right. The length or width of the sleeves, its colour, its binding and decoration, bother us not at all, for we are not familiar with and do not care about a meticulously exact reproduction of the vestimentary code of the fourteenth century.

The poverty of costume as a signifier points to a third general point about costume, connected with the nature of drama. It is an elementary, or rather an obvious, point. A performance of a drama takes place in real time and space (the time measured by the clock on the wall, the space occupied by the bus driving past the door of the theatre); but the drama of which it is a performance takes place in its own time and space. Thus, we might say that the duration of a performance of a drama is three and a half hours, but that the duration of the drama is three years; that the performance takes place in the Abbey Theatre, but the action of the play occurs in Rome and Egypt.

This is why the historical, geographical and vestimentary meanings of costume are relatively unimportant. The only imperative is that costume should be compatible with the character wearing it in a very general, conventional way – a woman in woman's clothing, a soldier in uniform – but after that the play is, as it were, for all time. Lady Macbeth is that woman in front of us here and now, and in a hundred years' time she will still be that woman in front of us here and now. We do not experience her as a historical figure perceived retrospectively through the centuries. For successive generations of playgoers she is eternally present. Julius Caesar was stabbed, once in history, in the Theatre of Pompey. Shakespeare's Julius Caesar is stabbed, for all time, in the Senate House.

Twentieth-century designers, who often try to create a visual analogue of the themes and the atmosphere of a play, are correct. It does not matter whether Lady Macbeth is in Elizabethan dress, or Scottish dress, or in royal robes. Any of these might do. But so too would a dress of our own time, or a costume related to no time, place, country or culture. Her deeds and thoughts relate to all times and places.

The artistic qualities of costume are thus of two kinds. First, the costumes must be so designed that they convey, by way of visual analogy, the general character and theme of the dramatic action. Secondly, they must continue to act as visual analogy throughout the constant visual changes brought about by the gestures and movements of the actors. It should be added that this does not necessarily mean a constant visual harmony on stage. In some cases the visual effect might be one of dissonance, unrest or anarchy.

If costume fulfils both of these requirements it will also be aesthetically successful. There is a third requirement, which we come to straightaway. This is, that costume should marry with the scenery.

Scenery

Scenery appeared almost as soon as there was a stage to put it on. The back-scene of the early Athenian stage was painted with columns and pediments to look like a palace or a temple. Shortly afterwards – Aristotle ascribes the innovation to Sophocles – painted screens were introduced which could represent rocks, trees, the sea, or whatever might be needed. Vitruvius, writing in the first century BC, spoke of devices called *periáktoi*. These were triangular structures, with each face painted differently, which revolved to bring about quick changes of scenery (*De Architectura*, V.6.8). By Vitruvius' time, scenery painting had achieved a high degree of sophistication, including the use of perspective.

Scenery goes hand in hand with theatres. Drama that is staged in other places – streets, marketplaces, churches – does without. This was often the case with medieval theatre. However, sometimes Mystery plays were staged by itinerant groups of players in wagons (known as *pageants*), the inner surfaces of which were painted or decorated to produce the effect of scenery.

Scenery on the modern stage began with the Italian Renaissance. Vitruvius had written about theatre architecture and scenery together, in Book V of *De Architectura*, and after the revival of interest in this great work in 1414 he came to have as great an influence on theatre as he had on architecture in general. Scenery was influenced also by the reinvention of perspective drawing. Baldassare Peruzzi (1481–1537) was the first Renaissance artist to design and use perspectival scenery, in 1514. Peruzzi's pupil, Sebastiano Serlio, inspired by Peruzzi and Vitruvius alike, gave an illustrated explanation of perspective and stage design in his *L'Architettura*, which was published in various stages between 1537 and 1547, and was widely translated and studied in the decades that followed. This book, and the Italian designers who followed its precepts, dominated European theatre for two centuries.

Early Renaissance scenery aimed to reproduce on stage the illusion of a street or a rural setting, receding from the audience into the distance, in accordance with the laws of perspective. This was achieved by arranging flat screens on both sides of the stage, painted over with pictures – of buildings, trees, rocks or whatever – the pictures becoming smaller as the screens succeeded one another towards the back of the stage, where there was a back-screen. The vanishing point (where all the 'horizontal' lines meet) was situated in the centre, some distance behind the back-screen.

This arrangement was not without its problems. One was that the full perspective effect could be obtained only by someone standing or sitting at the central axis of the auditorium. Another was that, if an actor were to walk to the back of the stage, he would tower over what were supposed to be the tall buildings to his right and left.

The second problem was solved easily enough. The actors simply did not walk through the scenery, but performed on the part of the stage in front of it. For all that it had real physical depth, the scenery served only as a visual background to the action. The first problem was not solved for a century and a half, when Ferdinando Bibiena (1657–1743) developed what is called multipoint perspective on the stage. In this system, several vanishing points are employed for different parts of the scenery. The effect is more 'realistic' for persons throughout the auditorium, no matter where they are seated. It also enabled actors to begin using the scenic part of the stage as well as the front part.

The whole period from the sixteenth century to the late nineteenth century was devoted to creating better and more realistic illusions on the stage. The nature of the illusion was to convey to the audience visual impressions similar to what they might experience outside the theatre in the 'real' world. A lot of very clever machinery was devised for this purpose, and many ingenious ways of producing special effects, such as mist or storm or being underwater. As well as this, however – superimposed upon the extreme realism of field, mountain, street or palace – more glamorous effects were employed as well. Choirs of angels could float on high, or nymphs arise from the earth. Actors could vanish and reappear as if by magic. Entire scenes could change in the twinkling of an eye. Audiences came to be dazzled by the sheer ingenuity of stage technology. Sadler's Wells had a water tank installed beneath the stage, so that its producers could stage a sea battle if they felt so inclined. Another development, dating from the 1830s, was the 'box set', which in many cases could be described as three walls of a room, the fourth side of which had been removed so that the audience could look into the room and see what was going on.

Not surprisingly, this extreme realism eventually produced a reaction, though not until the very end of the nineteenth century. One of the impulses behind this reaction came from the literary movement known as Symbolism, which considered that mood and emotion could be achieved directly through the music and imagery of words rather than indirectly through the wooden precision of naturalistic description. Another influence was the writings of a Swiss designer, Adolphe Appia (1862–1928), who advocated a theatre in which scenery, light and costume would form a seamless complement to the mood and atmosphere of the play.

Throughout the twentieth century various other factors have influenced stage design: Expressionism (a complex movement, one of whose elements was the urge to express mood accurately even if the descriptive content had to be distorted to do so), the cinema and, perhaps above all, the availability of new materials, such as fibreglass, plywood, light metal alloys, new adhesives. Fashions have swung unpredictably between the urge to empty the stage of all save the actors and a few props, and the urge to create striking, emblematic scenic structures which symbolise the theme and brood over the human actors who play it out: scenery as another, inanimate, actor.

When we reflect upon the role of scenery in European theatre, we are struck by a number of things. One is the sheer ubiquity of scenery. In all the periods and places where drama has flourished, only the Elizabethan theatre seems to have taken little interest in it. Ever since drama was established permanently in European civilisation, from the Renaissance onwards, the role of scenery has become ever more important and complex. The second thing is that scenery is actually unnecessary. As Aristotle observed in the *Poetics*, spectacle is inessential to tragedy. And in our own century, some directors have reduced it to a minimum or dispensed with it altogether. These two things point to a third: that the urge to use scenery arises, like the urge to use special costumes, from a desire to go beyond the words, to produce a theatrical event in which the play is given a visual, not just a verbal, articulation. If gesture is a kind of onomatopoeia of the body, scenery is a kind of onomatopoeia for the eyes.

It is this desire to produce visual analogues of plays that has driven the creation of scenery from the very start. It has never been necessary to show an audience, visually, where the action was taking place. The Greeks and the Romans already knew the place of the action, just from the acting and the words. The temples and palaces painted on the back-scene were not signifiers of a place, but signifiers of a context. Palaces symbolised the aristocratic persons whose destinies were played out in tragedy. Temples symbolised the relations of humankind to the gods and to Fate. Palaces and temples were one and the same in the painted scene: not geographical at all, but visual emblems of the social arena in which tragedy had its home.

Vitruvius saw this very clearly in Book V of *De Architectura* (as did Sebastiano Serlio, following Vitruvius, in the sixteenth century). Vitruvius (*De Architectura*, V.6.8) distinguished three distinct kinds of scenery for three kinds of plays: the tragic, the comic and the satyric (a burlesque involving a mythical hero and a chorus of satyrs). Tragic scenery was of royal palaces, comic scenery of private houses and satyric scenery of rural landscapes. In each case, the scenery symbolised a category of human activity, not a place in which the activity occurred. If the intention had been to represent places the back-scene would have had to change – one for Thebes, a different one for Delphi, and so on. It is precisely their permanent, static nature that reveals their symbolic, rather than descriptive, role.

The huge and ingenious efforts to produce an ever greater realism on stage, from the sixteenth to the nineteenth centuries, were ultimately driven by the same motive. At first sight the goal of realist scenery appears to be the construction of a space as similar as possible to the place in which the action is set. But a drawingroom or a kitchen on a stage, especially one whose fourth wall is missing, is not at all like the drawingrooms and kitchens of the audience. The difference, the foundation of all the other differences, is an ontological one. A stage drawingroom is never one particular, unique drawingroom, but 'a' drawingroom, 'some' drawingroom. It has a general, not a particular, reference. The stage set is a sign of a drawingroom; it is not, but rather stands for, a drawingroom. It is a sign through and through. It signifies the kind of place in which the action occurs: drawingroom action, not kitchen action. The drive for perfect realism was never a drive to perfectly reproduce a place, but to perfectly create a sign of a kind of place. The underlying belief was that perfect realism would produce the perfect sign.

What is the signified of scenery? In part it is the spatiality of human activity. Even actions that occur in the inner spaces of the mind are actions also of a body, and bodies inhabit space. Scenery re-creates that space by being a sign of it. It may also give the space a character – domestic, political, martial, storm-driven – or instead it may establish the space in a way that visually matches the action abstractly or expressionistically. The more completely it does this, and the more completely it combines with the costumes and the choreography of the actors, the more completely it realises the aesthetic possibilities of stage drama.

There is another aesthetic value of scenery. Whenever opera setpieces are staged in the great Italian opera houses – say the Grand March in *Aida* – the curtain rises on an empty stage. If the audience approves of the scenery, it applauds. The audience's instinct here is a sure one. Stage scenery can be its own reward, simply as a spectacle and as a technical triumph. For a moment, before the stage fills with crowded action, the audiences react to it purely as a work of visual art.

Lighting

Lighting has become a distinctive feature of drama in modern times, from the early Renaissance onwards. In classical and medieval times, natural light was the only light available, with whatever variations chance or the time of day might bring; although we cannot be sure to what extent light may have been exploited in the churches and cathedrals of the Middle Ages.

Stage lighting was the handmaid of architecture, since theatres with roofs made it not only necessary but, in consequence, a new source of stage effects. Theatre people were alert to its possibilities early in the sixteenth century, and experimented with back-lighting, reflectors, darkening and colour. Footlights and side-lighting were in use early in the seventeenth century, and by the eighteenth century had become practically universal. The two main sources of light during these centuries were oil lamps and candles. Huge chandeliers provided a general, overall light in theatres, and lamps were used on the stage. Reflectors of tin or tinsel, and mirrors, enhanced the lamplight, and strategic positioning of the lamps, together with movable covers, provided for special effects such as darkening or brightening. Colour was produced by shining light through coloured liquids, coloured paper or laquered glass.

Technological developments in lighting, when they came, happened quickly, and the Industrial Revolution brought about the introduction, first, of gaslight in theatres, then limelight and finally electric light. The brightness of limelight made it possible to create spotlights, which were eventually to become the main kind of lights in use upon the stage. The contemporary spotlight is a wondrous affair, equipped with colour filters which produce a multitude of tints; lenses and shutters that enable it to emit a beam of any shape; dimmers to control the brightness of the beam; cut-outs and movable drums that can throw shadows of leaves or clouds upon the stage. Computer technology, finally, now makes it possible to key an entire lighting programme into a single console.

Electric lighting, in short, has enabled stage lighting to come of age. It has simplified the production of stage effects that had been difficult before, and created possibilities of entirely new kinds of effects. Stage lighting design is now a complex and sophisticated art form in its own right.

Still, whatever about the technology, we are entitled to reflect on whether the fundamentals of stage lighting have really changed since they were introduced in the sixteenth century. The first, and indispensable, function of theatre lighting is a utilitarian one, namely, to enable the audience to see the actors and the stage. This is still the foundation of everything else. The practice of darkening the auditorium during performances had the goal of improving visibility, not, as is sometimes claimed, to increase the psychological distance between the space occupied by the actors and the space occupied by the audience.

The utilitarian role of lighting did, however, quickly engender various artistic functions. For instance, the action of the play may sometimes require that some actors, and some parts of the stage, are more visible than others; and this is brought about by lighting and by the interactions between lighting and colour. Another artistic function, one which was practised from the earliest times, is to produce through lighting visual effects analogous to the mood of the action upon the stage. Colour and brightness are the two main instruments for doing this. A dark and sombre stage is different from a bright and cheerful one; a yellow light has a different effect from a blue light. These are elementary examples, but they do point towards the subtleties of atmosphere that lighting can produce or reinforce. Theatre lighting is in one way freer from limitation than film lighting, for it does not have to contend with film emulsions. But both theatre and film lighting must contend with another significant restriction: the interactions between light and colour. There is no use in producing a dark and sombre effect by the play of light upon the scenery, if in so doing the costumes are rendered almost invisible; or if a garment worn by a grief-stricken character shines out with gay florescence. The very richness of the possibilities in contemporary stage lighting has made the interrelations of scenery, costume, makeup and narrative action extremely complex. This is the artistic challenge, and where the artistic expertise of the lighting designer is tested.

One last artistic element in stage lighting has to do with the character of the scenery. One of Adolphe Appia's dissatisfactions with the scenery of his own day was that it was flat, whereas actors are three-dimensional. It is now the standard assumption that everything on the stage should be three-dimensional, unless flatness is required as a special effect. Lighting is one of the ways to produce three-dimensionality; for even a three-dimensional object can look flat if it is not carefully lit, and a painted surface can be given extra depth by clever lighting. Lighting can also be used to create scenery. A scene in a forest, for instance, does not have to rely on cut-outs of trees. Instead, lighting alone can be used to project the effect of moving leaves upon the set.

The aesthetic value of lighting is, yet again, twofold. One is the sheer beauty of light in itself. It is worth referring once more to the medievals, who were sharply aware of the intense aesthetic pleasure given by light, and often used it as a metaphor for reason, creativity and divine power. A second aesthetic value of stage lighting arises from its consonance with other elements in drama: visual elements like costume, scenery and gesture, and narrative elements such as mood and action. It is this kind of integration of the component parts of drama that draws us ever closer to the classical concept of beauty as harmony.

Theatre Buildings

We remarked earlier that drama is the only art form which, from the very beginning, produced an architecture specifically designed for it. Drama can be performed without a theatre, but the historical and actual fact of the matter is that European drama is usually staged in theatres, and its history is in part a history of its architecture. Drama and theatres influence one another reciprocally. The theatre's design is determined, naturally enough, by the fact that dramas are going to be performed in it before an audience; but the ways in which dramas are written and performed are also affected by the kind of theatres in which they are going to be staged.

The history of European theatre building is in some respects simple enough: open-air semicircular theatres in Greece and Rome, and roofed rectangular theatres from the Renaissance onwards. There were many variations on these, and some exceptions. Early Greek theatres were usually constructed on hillsides, but Hellenistic and Roman theatres were usually special buildings, open at the top, with raked semicircular seating and awnings overhead. Early Renaissance theatres copied the Roman style, with the addition of a roof, but soon developed into a horseshoe shape, with tiers of boxes attached to the walls. Elizabethan playhouses, however, were circular, with tiers of galleries, because they were derived from the structure of inn-yards. By the late seventeenth century, the standard theatre everywhere was a rectangular building with a stage at one end and an auditorium consisting of a space at ground level – the parterre, subsequently named the pit, and then the stalls – and boxes and galleries projecting from the side and rear walls. Richard Wagner designed a new kind of theatre, the Festspielhaus, which opened in Bayreuth in 1876. The raked seating was, as in the ancient world, arranged in a fan shape, so that everyone had a direct view of the stage. This was to have a lasting influence on theatre design, although not on a large scale until the twentieth century. It is currently fashionable to break the seating up into separate blocks, each projecting from a steeply raked auditorium floor, though still arranged contiguously in a semicircle above and around the stage.

All theatres, whatever their design, require a minimum of two things: a space for the actors (the stage) and a space for the audience (the auditorium). The relation between these two spaces is governed by two further requirements: that the audience can see the play, and that the audience can hear the play.

The latter two requirements are easily stated but less easily achieved. The best arrangement for good sight lines is the original Greek one: steeply raked seating arranged in a curve and looking down upon the stage. But a problem that is ultimately insuperable, in this or any other seating arrangement, is that people seated at the back just do not see things as well as those seated at the front. The same problem arises with sound. Voice amplification can help to some extent – the electronic amplification of our own time, perhaps some kind of megaphone effect in Greek masks – but amplification, if it is too evident, becomes excessively artificial and deforms the character of live theatre.

The problem of theatre acoustics is a very ancient one. One of the difficulties in classical theatre was that the human voice, with no walls or ceiling to reflect it, could easily get carried away in the open air. Vitruvius gives detailed instructions, in *De Architectura*, on how to produce extra resonance, by positioning inverted bronze or earthenware jars throughout the auditorium. He warned also against raking the seats too steeply, for the sound waves should not strike against seats as against an obstacle but instead pass smoothly from front to back. It is clear, from the amount of space Vitruvius gave to the matter, that acoustics were a serious problem in classical theatre design (*De Architectura* V.3, 5, 6, 8).

Acoustics were not a problem in modern theatres, until, in the twentieth century, a new style of building was adopted. In this style, the ornate interiors of traditional theatres – draperies, wood panelling, intricate plasterwork – were replaced by clean modern lines and smooth plaster walls. The actors' voices bounce, echo and reverberate in such interiors, and so the modern science of acoustics came into being. On the whole it is a successful science, or has become so because of painful experience. Yet the traditional problem – that people at the back of the theatre do not hear as well as people at the front – still remains.

These visual and acoustic disparities, among people seated in different parts of the auditorium, have created particular artistic problems for actors and designers. All actors learn how to project their voices. But projection involves a degree of extra loudness. This means that speech is delivered in a manner that would be unnatural in everyday life. Intimate conversations on stage, even whispers, are only comparatively less loud than shouts of anger or fear. Also, the actors must for the most part face front, or nearly front, so that their voices carry as far as possible. The technical skills required to speak and move in these unnatural ways, while none the less conveying a feeling of naturalness to the audience, are very considerable. In fact, the audience in the end must collaborate; it has to be familiar with the conventions of the stage, and willing to accept them without protest.

The visual artistry needed to deal with audience distance is also very considerable, and quite complex. Ideally, the visual impressions created by acting, costume, scenery and lighting should be fully available to people in the back row. Because of this, stage acting is large-scale acting. Film acting is small-scale acting, because the large size of cinematic images confers significance on the merest twitch of an eyebrow. If a stage actor pockets a bunch of keys that he is not supposed to have, he will ostentatiously spot them on a table, stand still, glance furtively around to see whether anyone is looking, step to the table, pick up the keys, throw them into the air and catch them, thrust them into his pocket, look around again, and then go on to do something else. All stage acting is like this – larger than life, replete with gestures whose meaning can be deciphered a hundred feet away.

Costume and scenery also have to avoid features that are too subtle. The buttons on a suit or dress, the cut of a pocket, the exact matching of a pattern, count for little. The effect of clothing depends rather upon overall shape, structure and colour. It is like scenery used to dress the body. Scenery itself operates on the same relatively large-scale, easily visible way. This is why a film of a stage play, unless it is done very cleverly, can be oddly disappointing. The acting can seem like overacting, the scenery plain, the costumes stereotyped. What works at a distance from the stage does not easily work in close-up.

Audience

Many forms of art can be practised and experienced by artists themselves, without reference to anyone else. Paintings, sculptures, poems and novels can be finished and complete even if no one sees or reads them. No doubt their creators want money and fame, and so require an audience. But Emily Dickinson's poetry would be undiminished even if no one had read it. Performance arts might seem to be different, and there is some value in the comparison between a script and a score. But a quartet of musicians can play music together, or a choir sing together, just for the pleasure of it, without ever wanting or needing an audience.

It is difficult to imagine actors coming together and staging a play, not in order to perform it for an audience, but just for the pleasure they get from it themselves. An audience is a necessity for stage drama, not a desirable option. The relation of a performance to an audience is intrinsic to its nature. Live drama is essentially, not accidentally, a social art form.

It follows that audiences are themselves an artistic constituent of stage drama – not in the same way as scenery, costume or gesture, but necessary none the less. An audience takes part in a drama, and must possess the skill to do so. It is a skill that can be exercised only if the rules and conventions of dramatic performance have been internalised.

There is a passage in *Tom Jones* which describes the reactions of Mr Partridge, who had never seen a play, to a performance of *Hamlet*. During the grave-digger scene Mr Partridge exclaims aloud:

> 'I never saw in my life a worse grave-digger. I had a sexton, when I was a clerk, that should have dug three graves while he is digging one. The fellow handles a spade as if it was the first time he had ever had one in his hand. Ay, ay, you may sing. You had rather sing than work, I believe.'

Mr Partridge, who had not internalised the rules, did not have the skill to be a member of the audience. Audience skill is overtly manifested in various ways: applause, silence, an intake of breath, cries of shock or surprise; and, in the case of comedy, laughter. There is a constant dialectic between actors and an audience, which can influence timing and rhythm upon the stage. Sometimes the dialectic can be verbalised, for instance when an actor directly addresses the audience, or the audience at a pantomime shouts back at the actors or sings along with them.

There are occasional debates about whether a theatre audience should or should not be drawn into the action of a play. One view is that the actors occupy their own space and time – an imaginary space and time – and the audience are situated in a different, 'real' space and time. In this view, the audience are interested observers of the stage action, but ultimately detached from it. If an actor directly addresses the audience, this is a temporary aberration: the actor emerges for a moment into 'real' space-time before retreating again into the stage illusion. The other view is that the barriers between action and audience should be broken down as far as possible, that the audience should feel drawn into the play almost, though not quite, as if they were taking part in it themselves. They will thus experience it more intensely and immediately, and find it more 'relevant' in their own lives.

Both of these views are wrong. The space-time of the actors, and the space-time of the audience, are certainly different. But the space-time of the audience is not the same as the space-time of the street outside the theatre either. The noise of a helicopter roaring above a theatre will disrupt the illusion of a play; the collapse of an item of scenery, or coughing by the audience, will not. The members of the audience are not actors on the stage, but they are actors none the less (see Brook 1968, pp. 27–31). They must act the part of an audience. If an actor on stage addresses them directly this is still part of the total illusion. It is actors and audience together who finally and completely bring plays into existence. When the play ends, and people emerge into the street to look for buses, trains and taxis, they lay aside their roles. When I meet my actor friend in the theatre bar for a drink afterwards, we now meet as ordinary people. He has ceased to act before me on the stage, and I have ceased to act as a member of his audience.

Language and Representation

Stories can be told in several different ways. The story of Cinderella can be told in a ballet, in mime, in an opera, in a stage-play, in a film with human actors, in a cartoon film, in a television play, in a strip cartoon or in a storybook. All of these are different ways of presenting and communicating the story; or, we might also say, different ways in which the story of Cinderella is 'represented'. Or finally, we can say instead that they employ different systems of signifiers, though with a common signified.

Some of the signifiers are verbal or partly verbal, and these can in turn be subdivided into a narrative type and a dramatic type. There is a vast literature on the nature and complexities of narrative, although the unrivalled masterpiece of narrative theory is Gérard Genette's *Narrative Discourse* (1972).

A curious omission in many discussions of narrative, including Genette's, is a proper treatment of oral storytelling. In oral narrative, words are supplemented by signifiers which have some affinities with the art of the actor: the aural properties of speech, facial expressions, corporeal presence, an audience. Many of the conventions of written narrative – punctuation, lineation, indentation, paragraphing – are simply clumsy substitutes for what the human voice can achieve effortlessly. Writing has, of course, produced its own distinctive characteristics and genres. The novel, unlike the epic, could hardly emerge in a pre-literate society. But narrative storytelling always retains indelible traces of the oral. Stories have a sound as well as a plot.

Aristotle used the verb *apaggélo* (report or relate) for narrative representation, and the verb *dráo* (do or accomplish) for dramatic representation (*Poetics* 1449b). *Mimesis* was a generic term for both. He gave a list of six constituents of dramatic representation: plot, character, diction, thought, spectacle and song (*melopoiía*). All of these, including spectacle, are rooted in the language scripted by the playwright. Drama is in part a literary art form, although the language of the playwright has quite a different role from its role in narrative. Narrative language tells a story; dramatic language is a blueprint for telling a story (see Pfister 1988, pp. 103–59).

What is present in narrative, and missing in drama, is the representation, by means of countless linguistic devices, of the narrative logic that binds the story together. A narrative is a structure, but a script is a list. All scripts are Humean, for the only indication of causality is the order in which the list of speeches is written. Sequence is converted into causality by the producer, the actors, the designers. It is interesting, in this connection, to read Bernard Shaw. Some of Shaw's earliest plays were published in book form before they had been performed on the stage; and, as a result, they came equipped with interwoven comments and elaborate stage directions. He kept this up for the rest of his life. The script of *Pygmalion*, for instance, reads like a novel *manqué*. There are detailed instructions about movements, gestures, facial expressions, vocal pitch, costume, even about wallpaper, furniture and pictures – everything, in short, that the play requires over and above the spoken words.

Even Shaw conceded that these supernumerary instructions involved a sort of trespassing; for, unlike the spoken words, they are printed in italics. They are an abstraction from theatrical practice. What Shaw could not escape was the severe difficulty, faced by all playwrights, of conveying the inner thoughts and feelings of the characters. Speech in drama is mostly public speech, addressed to another character as part of a dialogue. It is performative language in a sense, since it is language as a form of action, language that creates and sustains a plot. Apart from the soliloquy, actors rarely stand alone, uttering words that express their inner thoughts. Their inner lives have to be observed or guessed at indirectly. There is a similar difficulty, though a lesser one, in narrative, which uses various methods for articulating the inner life. Some typical examples are:

> 'Have you got it?' he cried eagerly.
> Tears flowed down his cheeks.
> He was unable to move a muscle.
> He had been pacing up and down for half an hour.

Stream of consciousness is another such device, although one that is heavily dependent on convention, for what actually occurs in the human consciousness is very unlike a stream of words. In detective stories, the detective's inner thoughts are often represented by a tidy, well-thought-out set of reflections upon the circumstances of the crime, converted into improbably tidy, well-structured paragraphs of grammatical sentences.

The problem for the playwright is even more acute, for he must rely on the dense thicket of gestural, phonological and visual signifiers, created in a performance, to supplement the force of his words. Words, none the less, are the ultimate authority for performances, and the playwright's genius is ultimately a verbal genius. The speeches written by playwrights, and direct speech written by novelists, are closely akin. Both can capture the way in which a few inconsequential sentences articulate a personality and a situation:

> 'The Signora had no business to do it', said Miss Bartlett, 'no business at all. She promised us south rooms with a view close together, instead of which here are north rooms, here are north rooms, looking into a courtyard, and a long way apart. Oh, Lucy!' (*A Room with a View*)

The cleverness of this little speech, which are the opening lines of E. M. Forster's novel, and which could be used directly in a dramatisation, reminds us also that drama and literature are in constant communication with one another. Narrative techniques have always been influenced by those of the dramatist; and, in our own time, by the cinema.

Conclusion

The number and variety of the dramatic arts is so huge that it is not easy to formulate a single value, or set of values, that they all share. Literary, pictorial, aural, intellectual, musical and tactile values jostle about through and across their endless variations. The artistic skills that are employed in the service of these values encompass the entire range of artistic skills from all of the arts. If architecture was the all-encompassing art of the Middle Ages, the dramatic arts are the all-encompassing arts of the twentieth century.

Many of the dramatic arts are representational, however, and this brings them within the scope of Aristotle's theory of truth, discussed in the last chapter. Plays, even more than the literary arts, are vehicles for the exhibiting of universal truths about the human condition, and their value can be judged by the significance and universality of the truths that they embody.

In the case of literature we referred also to the verbal integrity of literary texts, the way in which the phonological, syntactic, semantic and discursive levels in texts flow seamlessly into one another. This criterion of value applies also to the language of drama. In addition, though, there are other 'levels' in drama, to which much of this chapter has been devoted, and the synchronisation of these levels constitutes a huge extension to the elements that have to be drawn together by the artistic skills displayed in performance.

The second criterion of value, therefore, in literature and the dramatic arts alike, is what the Greeks called 'harmony'. The Greek word *harmonía* comes from a root which refers to joinery. In Attic Greek it was often used in connection with shipbuilding. This is what the Pythagoreans had in mind when they defined beauty as harmony. They meant a fitting together of parts so as to produce an ontological perfection – a thing that was what it ought to be, a ship that sailed, a temple that glorified the gods, music that soothed and restored, or stirred to action. So too with the dramatic arts. Because of their internal complexity they demonstrate, perhaps more vividly than any of the other arts, the need for harmony and the universality of the Pythagorean aesthetic. Truth and harmony are yet again, as they have always been, the most fundamental values in the representational arts.

9   Music

The fathers were in the desert,
but the desert was not in them,
and this is music.
(Franz Kafka)

Introduction

Music, despite its cultural diversities and complexities, is practised by all human races, and is arguably the most universal of all the arts. Its origins are shrouded in the past, but we can offer some educated guesses and hypotheses about its beginnings. The rhythmic patterns that we can discern in all music, no matter how simple, suggest that music may have been born from the co-ordinated movements of the body in dance. The earliest musical works, so to speak, would have been produced by percussion instruments and the silent dancing body. Melody may have developed from the unavoidable difference in pitch between percussion instruments. Melodic articulation is also present in the inflections of our voice. So we can guess that music existed from the moment that our ancestors learned to communicate by speech, learned to co-ordinate their bodily movements, and abandoned themselves to the pleasure of dancing accompanied by the rhythmic beat of percussion instruments, or even the simple clapping of hands.

The Specificity of Music

It is only in recent centuries – approximately since the late Renaissance, and certainly since the seventeenth century – that music came to be thought of as an autonomous art form. We now define it simply as the art of sounds: the invention, formal organisation, manipulation and production of sounds, aimed at achieving an aesthetic effect. Sounds are audible phenomena generated by a vibrating body, carried through the air as acoustic waves, and received by our eardrums which in turn, vibrating with the length and shape of the acoustic waves, send information to the brain. Music therefore addresses itself – in so far as it is material and sensuously perceptible – primarily to the sense of hearing. Through our hearing we experience inwardly a sense of movement, duration, organised sequence, rhythmic and metrical scansion, and quasi-spatial intervals among pitched sounds.

In ancient times music was deemed to possess mysterious and magical powers. It was, after all, intangible and invisible. The mythical Orpheus could tame the wildness of nature by his music. The song of the Sirens could captivate and mesmerise the sailors that came within reach of their voices. These myths, and many others as well, embodied the belief that music was profoundly, and in some sense irresistably, moving.

Even in our own times, it is commonly held that music is exceptionally expressive, stirring and meaningful. Even in its instrumental forms, when divorced from the voice and from texts, and deprived of mimetic or descriptive intentions, music still succeeds in triggering powerful emotional responses. Also, more than any other art form, more even than language, music appears to be intuitively and universally communicative, almost regardless of its time and place of origin. We seem to respond to musical messages in a more immediate, less culturally bound way, than is the case with the other forms of art.

There are at least two reasons for this. First, music is strongly linked with our biological and metabolic processes. It is well known that our bodies and bodily processes have a rhythmic character. The heart beats, and the lungs expand and contract. Other metabolic processes are regulated by temporal sequences, successive stages of tension and relaxation, bursts and withdrawals of energy. We can venture to say that music is primarily and fundamentally informed by our biological structure and our biorhythms. Musical messages may somehow reproduce, in their internal organisation, the dynamics of our bodily pulsations.

A second reason may be found in the unique nature of music, whose invisible and untouchable sounds both envelop and penetrate us. When listening to music we are immersed in the flow of sonorous events, events which we experience as totally introjected within our minds, with an intense degree of immediacy and directness.

A Survey of the History of Music

The word 'music' derives from the Greek *Mousa*: the Muse, which is the generic name given to each of the mythical beings who presided over, promoted and inspired the various arts. In Greek antiquity, music was not thought of as a fully autonomous art form. It belonged rather with poetry and dance, and formed, together with them, what the Greeks called *choreía*, from the word *chóros*, a group dance. These three conjoined arts were considered to be inseparable. The triune choreia constituted a category of expressive art, which was distinct from the category of constructive art, the group which included architecture, sculpture and painting. The close association of music with poetry and dance, and the expressive quality which they collectively possessed, explains the antonomastic name given to 'music', the privileged art of the Muses. This is clearly illustrated in a well-known passage in Plato's *Phaedo* (60d–61b). Shortly before his death, we are told, Socrates wrote a poem in honour of Apollo, and versified some of Aesop's fables. Asked why he has done this, he replied that he was following an instruction given to him in repeated dreams: to 'compose and practise music'. For the ancient Greeks, and for centuries after, the functional autonomy of musical sounds, their independence from the word, was simply unknown.

It may be that songs in archaic Greece were not accompanied by instruments. For, according to one story, it was the poet and musician Archilochus who introduced, in the seventh century BC, the practice of unison doubling of sung melodies with string instruments such as the lyre, the cythera, the trigonon, the magadis, or the wind instrument known as the aulos, ancestor of the oboe. This seems to have remained the Greek practice for many centuries: unison, and monody. They did not practise either harmony or polyphony. And they did not conceive of an independent instrumental music.

The beginnings of music as we now understand it were not to occur for many centuries. One reason for this was that, until the ninth century AD, musical practice and musical theory were kept completely separate. Its practitioners cultivated the traditional skills of producing sounds to accompany poetic recitation and dance. Its theorists speculated on the numerical laws, the metaphysical foundations, and the cosmological properties of musical proportions. It was the Pythagoreans who, in the fifth century BC, had founded musical theory of this philosophical and mathematical kind.

The Roman world and the Middle Ages inherited and adopted the musical theory of the Greeks. Music was important as an instrument of worship in Christianity. Vocal music, in particular, developed to a high degree of beauty and sophistication, which we can still enjoy in the wealth of liturgical singing known as Gregorian chant. But for all its beauty, church music remained monodic and melodic, and for the most part vocal. Just as for the ancient Greeks, music was used to enhance the poetic diction of religious texts, and to adorn religious rituals with sound.

For many centuries it was only rarely that music was written down, and the techniques for doing so were very approximate and simple. Singers just learned melodies by heart. Sacred music was written down from the fourth century onward, but initially by means of a simple notation consisting of series of letters of the alphabet which indicated the pitch. Much later, around the tenth century, there appeared more sophisticated signs known as 'neums'. These were superscripted above the line of words, and indicated groups of notes, their relative pitch, and the way to carry the voice or to phrase the melody. It is a form of notation also known as 'cheiromatic', for it represented, in a sort of pictorial manner, the movements of the conducting hand (*cheír*, in Greek). It helped to codify and preserve the traditions and practices of liturgical singing.

But once music began to be written down, it became possible to elaborate and develop the written musical texts. Just as the art of writing words facilitated development in natural languages, and then in logical and philosophical thought, so the writing of music was one of the conditions for the emergence of polyphony.

From the ninth century onwards, the organ was played in churches. Although quite a primitive instrument at the start, it was a significant step towards making music with more than one melody. The birth of polyphony has also been traced to the practice, in the British Isles, of accompanying songs with quite sophisticated harps. An English manuscript of the tenth century carries a prayer with two superimposed lines of alphabetic notation, and this, it has been suggested, indicates the appearance of an incipient polyphony and harmony. In the case of secular music, the practice of gymel (twin), was also well established. This consisted in a sung melody with two other voices singing at intervals of two thirds below the melody. In the tenth century, Hucbald of Saint Amand outlined six formulas for the accompaniment of a principal melody with parallel fourths and fifths. Finally, in a French treatise of the eleventh century we find a reference to the practice of descant – that is, singing an accompanying melody above the principal line or melody.

An important contribution to these developments was made by Guido d'Arezzo, in the eleventh century. Before him, neums were written on a stave system of three lines, in three different colours to indicate the pitch: red for F, black for A, yellow for C. Guido added a fourth stave. He also introduced an important innovation in melodic structure. Before him, melodies were constructed by exploiting combinations of four notes (known as a tetrachord). Guido expanded this to a six-note matrix (known as a hexachord). This opened the way to other innovations: polyphony, improvements in traditional instruments and the invention of new musical instruments, a merging of song with instrumental accompaniment; and, in the end, the birth of a purely instrumental music. By the time all of this had happened, the marriage of musical theory and practice, initiated in the ninth century, was permanently established.

Very simple forms of polyphonic composition had begun to appear in the ninth and tenth centuries. In the fourteenth century monody was finally abandoned, except for liturgical plainchant. A school of musicians in Florence founded a movement known Ars Nova, whose aim was to develop new elements already present in secular music, and to find a new musical language that could express the emerging spiritual and cultural sensibility that was soon to flourish in the Renaissance. Ars Nova set out to invent new kinds of melody, and to adopt and develop more popular material. It set to music texts based on classical literature, and it invented the ancestors of melodrama and opera, in the form of dramatic works acted and sung by two or three voices, with an instrumental accompaniment. The consistent use of more than one voice, coupled with a small orchestral ensemble, finally established the practice of polyphony.

However, a more solid and scientific foundation for polyphony was established by Flemish composers, also in the fourteenth century. The new forms invented by Ars Nova were lacking in rigour and homogeneity, and the Italians composed lyrical works in a rather free and loose style. The Flemish adopted more rigid and mathematical laws, and initially they concentrated on compositions for interacting singing voices only, without instrumental accompaniment. This style of singing came to be known as singing *a cappella*. They increased the number of voices or parts to four, thus giving final shape to what has ever since been the standard for choral composition. They also laid the foundations for the future development of harmony. In their polyphonic works they employed the techniques of counterpoint: the interrelation of all the parts according to increasingly sophisticated relations of note to note, point against point. This practice, of composing for voices according to the laws of counterpoint, had the further consequence of fostering the development of organ music and of the organ as an instrument.

The contrapuntal skills of some composers were soon to reach a high degree of virtuosity. There are extant compositions for thirty-six parts! Elaborate and complex works such as these were called *musica artificiosa*: excessive, overwrought and extravagant. A century later, in the atmosphere generated by the Protestant Reformation and the Catholic Counter-Reformation, a need was felt to restore clarity to church music. Lassus and Palestrina, among others, loomed large in this musical landscape. Palestrina above all succeeded in giving discipline and simplicity to his sacred music. He often borrowed melodies from Gregorian chant, or wrote melodies inspired by it – though with some interesting exceptions where, undetected by the Church authorities, he adopted popular love-songs. The vocal diction was clear, the words intelligible, and the music perfectly matched the general meaning and feeling of the words.

The fifteenth and sixteenth centuries also witnessed an impressive proliferation of musical treatises, and the birth of comprehensive scientific theories of music. In some sense, it was the beginning of music as we understand it now. In 1547 Henricus Glareanus published his treatise *Dodekachordon*. In this work he analysed all of the ancient musical modes, still employed by his contemporaries, which were based upon tetrachords and hexachords. He discovered that all of them could be reduced to two fundamental modes, and these correspond to what we now know as the two tonalities or tonal sequences in a given octave: major and minor. It was a discovery which led eventually to the adoption of the diatonic system, based on the octave as its basic nucleus, and it also simplified very considerably the practice of composition and the structure of musical instruments.

At the same time, new kinds and genres of music began to appear, and new instruments were contrived and developed. After the organ there appeared the harpsichord, which in turn was to lead to the piano. The lute, forerunner of the guitar, came from the Spanish viluela. Wind instruments became more specialised, and came to be clearly distinguished into woods and brass. Towards the end of the sixteenth century, in Florence, a group of musicians established the famous Camerata dei Bardi. They exploited the potentiality of profane genres, such as the madrigal, to invent the melodrama, the ancestor of modern opera. A melodrama is a drama set to music. In it, the singing voice is freed from the constrictions of polyphony, and from counterpoint. It flows freely and expressively, telling stories based upon classical literature, accompanied and sustained by orchestral instruments played according to the new diatonic system of tonal music.

This new music, our modern diatonic system, was finally forged by Monteverdi. He constructed larger chords, such as the seventh, and exploited the use of dissonance to produce a state of acoustic tension. This, in turn, inaugurated a new era in the history of music, grounded on the laws of harmony. In melodrama the melody, carried by the voice, was still seen as more important than harmony, but with Monteverdi music came to be understood as harmonic both in theory and in practice. This allowed the flourishing of instrumental and symphonic music, as well as the development of the oratorio, the cantata, chamber music, the concerto and finally opera.

At this point in the history of music, we encounter the extraordinary genius of Johann Sebastian Bach. His music is a synthesis of poly-phonic counterpoint with a diatonic language, a harmonic sensibility and melodic emancipation. To Bach we also owe the almost universal dissemination of the temperatura, or equal temperament tuning: the final determination of the intervals among the twelve tones that make up the diatonic scale or octave. It was to illustrate the merits and potentialities of the tempered scale that Bach composed his *Well-Tempered Clavier*, in two volumes, each containing twenty-four preludes and fugues. Each prelude, followed by a fugue, is written in a different key based on each of the twelve tones of the diatonic scale, exploiting the major and minor variations in each key.

The adoption of the harmonic and diatonic system found its cul-mination – and the beginning of its end – in Wagner. Before him, diatonic tonal composition was structured as a sequence of modulations which started with a tonic chord, progressed by way of a dialectical dynamic of dissonances and consonances, and returned to or resolved into the initial chord as the final resolution. Wagner, however (among others), expanded the realm of harmonic modulations, the changes from chord to chord, so that they don't quite seem to resolve into the fundamental tonic. Large chords tend to produce unresolved har-monies, which in turn produce more unresolved harmonies, and the consequence is a musical universe in restless and continuous expansion. A certain kind of cohesion, determined by harmonic gravitation around the fundamental tonic, is partially lost.

In Wagner's music, the expanding energies of harmonic modulations overpower and weaken the tonic-centred configuration. Dissonant tension prevails over consonant rest. Wagner's style initiated a lin-guistic transformation in music, which was to culminate – through the Impressionists and Gustav Mahler among others – in the early expressionistic works of Arnold Schönberg, and in so-called 'atonal' composition. This abandonment of tonal gravitation was the final consequence of the Wagnerian revolution. In atonal composition – a more accurate name would be 'free tonal' – the work privileges frag-mentation over synthesis and unification. Dissonance prevails over the traditional harmonic-diatonic consonance. The anchoring centrality of tonality and the tonic chord is lost. Without gravitational centres, the musical work approaches the condition of chaos, and borders on uncoordinated noise.

Schönberg avoided this final danger by devising a new manner of sound organisation, founded on his theory of dodecaphony or twelve-tone composition: 'composition with twelve sounds which are only in relation to each other', to quote his own definition. The cen-trality of the tonic is finally and completely abandoned. Each sound in the twelve-tone scale is endowed with the same value, so much so that in a rigorous dodecaphonic composition no individual sound can be repeated before all the other eleven have been articulated. The nucleus and starting-point of a composition is the 'series': the sequence of all twelve sounds of the scale. These generate further transformations. The technique is the same as that of counterpoint. The method is rigidly geometric. The audible result is sequences and clusters of disquieting dissonances.

We must also mention the experiments of the Futurists, who toyed with the production and manipulation of sounds, and noises, by means of what are, by our standards, quite primitive electronic devices. Their rather unconvincing compositions, which often are no more than mechanical noise, inspired the later composers of *musique concrète*. This consists mainly in recording and manipulating natural sounds and noises, and in the collage of these in order to produce the finished work. Of course, the sounds made by traditional musical instruments could also be used. We have, in other words, something like the musical equivalent of Marcel Duchamp's 'readymades'.

The improvement and refinement of electronic devices, and the invention and development of synthesisers, have given birth to the virtually limitless possibilities of electronic music. We are inclined to associate synthesisers with pop musicians, but the greatest exponent of avant-garde electronic music is Karl Heinz Stockhausen, so far the leading figure in this new kind of musical language. The avant-garde has by now been superseded by postmodernism. In order to avoid the last outcome of musical experimentation – silence – music has returned, as have so many forms of art, to its tradition. Composers have, for the time being at any rate, tried to say something new which yet refers to the musical tradition to which we belong. The results are more comforting to listeners. As in other forms of art, the pleasure of aesthetic fruition has become a legitimate goal for the artist. Music is retrieving the pleasure of listening.

The Elements of Music

The raw material of music is the sounds which are produced by particular vibrations of physical bodies. Prior to the avant-garde movements of recent times, musical sounds were identified as a limited set of artificially produced physical vibrations contained within a minimum and maximum number of vibrations per second. The vibrations had to be regular and continuous. Any other kind of sound, which did not meet these requirements, was regarded as noise.

This notion of musical sound has become obsolete, due to the musical innovations and inventions of the twentieth century. Nowadays we are content to describe musical sounds as sounds which possess, from the acoustic and psychological point of view, the quality of pitch. These 'notes' are, then, the raw material of music. They are to music what phonemes are to language and to poetry. In the language of music, sounds are organised in accordance with four structural grids, which are the basic elements of musical discourse: rhythm, melody, harmony (in a broad sense that includes counterpoint) and timbre.

Musical rhythm is an order in the sequence and distribution of intensities or accentuations, and of the duration of sounds. Rhythm elaborates the metrical structure of musical discourse, producing thereby the tempo of a piece and the experience in the listener of an organised time sequence. Even very primitive percussion music rests on this most fundamental element of musical organisation. Its origin is clearly connected, as we have said, with our inner biological experiences of tension and relaxation.

Different composers and different kinds of music exploit the rhythmic element in varying degrees. It is not very prominent in plainchant, or in contrapuntal polyphony, but it is strongly evident in Baroque and in eighteenth century works. In our own times, almost all of the works by Stravinsky tend to foreground rhythm over other aspects of composition. Jazz, of course, places strong emphasis on the improvisation and elaboration of rhythmic figures. It is perhaps worth noting that composers often show a preference for one or other of the four elements of music.

Melody is a temporal sequence of individual sounds connected as in a syntactical discourse. A melody, that is, is loosely analogous to a sentence. It has a beginning, a development with internal inflections, and an end. In fact, there may well have been some association between the origins of melody and human speech: consider how, if we are to be comprehensible in speech, we must introduce differentiation, accent, inflections to the voice. In this way we modulate our diction from 'mono-tony' to a sort of melody. Musical melodies emulate the human voice at least in adopting the principle of tension and relaxation. It is melody that, in general, we identify and follow most readily in a piece of music. It still carries within it its origins in the vocal, and this may explain why we are so readily charmed by it.

Polyphony arises from the interaction of several melodies, organised in accordance with principles of repetition and variation. Harmony is a vertical combination and contemporaneous coexistence of melodies and sounds. Harmony consists of what are called 'chords'. In the Middle Ages and the early Renaissance, chords were played on very simple organs, and on the lute, in support of the singing voice.

When harmony emerged, it did so accidentally. Polyphony involved the overlapping of voices in a manner determined by the structuring codes and conventions of counterpoint. Harmony resulted from this inevitably but, as it were, unintentionally. Gradually, composers began to seek harmonic progressions for their own sake, not just as an accidental consequence of polyphony. The laws of harmony were eventually systematised by Jean Philippe Rameau in his *Traité de l'harmonie réduite à ses principes naturels* (1722), and *La génération harmonique* (1737) Harmony was now quite independent of contrapuntal combinations of notes, and was developed for its internal potentialities, whether or not it was employed in support of melody (as in melodrama and opera). When we come to Wagner, we find that harmony is dominant: music is a progression from chord to chord, or from one cluster of chords to another. The melodic lines are absorbed into the harmony. Even the singing voice – and this is evident in Mahler even more than in Wagner – is treated as if it were another instrument of the orchestra, another part of the harmonic tapestry.

The fourth ingredient of musical discourse is timbre, or colour. Different instruments have their characteristic qualities and colours: deep and warm, high-pitched and sharp, gentle and mellifluous, strong and resonant, clean and bright, dramatic and vibrating. This is not a question of pitch. It has to do rather with harmonic vibrations, with the structure, complexity and shape of the acoustic waves. This is timbre or colour. To use another analogy, timbre is exploited by composers in a manner similar to the painter's use of the tonalities of colours and their mixtures on the palette. Since Romanticism, orchestral and chamber music in particular have exploited the colours of the instruments, aided in this by improvements in the instruments themselves. The characteristic 'voices' of the instruments are an important factor in triggering affective responses in the listener.

In general we tend not to pay sufficient attention to harmonic progressions and the harmonic mixture of colours. But we do easily identify the timbre of instruments, especially when they carry the melodic lines or themes of a composition. Stravinsky again comes to mind, because of his colourful orchestrations. A less ambitious, but eloquent, example is Prokofiev's *Peter and the Wolf*, which was designed precisely to illustrate the identities and peculiarities of various instruments. We may think also of Mussorgsky's *Pictures at an Exhibition*, in the orchestration by Ravel. And, of course, Ravel himself with Debussy and all the Impressionists are also cases in point. Their compositions, many of them designed to suggest imaginary visual landscapes, again illustrate the fact that different composers exploit different elements of musical discourse.

In conclusion, we must mention the most unnoticed, discreet and inconspicuous, yet very powerful, ingredient of music. This is silence! Silence is the stage and background from which sounds emerge and into which they fade away. But silence is not just a background. It is also the connective tissue and the deep structure that links and separates all the individual sonorous events. Silence, finally, is the inner stage where we, as listeners, re-enact the musical narrative. Here we absorb, reconstruct and elaborate the piece of music. Here we respond to and resonate with the musical messages. This is perhaps the motive underlying John Cage's *4'33"*, which is precisely a piece of silence lasting exactly four minutes and thirty-three seconds.

A Brief Survey of the Theory of Music

Antiquity and the Middle Ages

So far as we are aware, the Pythag-oreans were the first to observe and to formulate the acoustic laws governing the relation between the length of a vibrating string and the pitch of the sound that it produces. The Pythagoreans also believed that the universe as a whole is governed by the laws of number. Music therefore encapsulated the harmony of the universe, and existed on the cosmic level as the music of the spheres (see James 1995). Further, if the cosmos is a harmony, so too is the soul. Music was therefore congenial to the soul, and could restore order to the soul, and through it to the body. In the School of Pythagoras, music was thus understood in the light of metaphysical, mathematical and moral considerations.

These same considerations and concerns are to be found also in Plato. Plato, however, distinguished between music which educates the mind and establishes harmony in the soul, and music which gives us only sensuous pleasure. It is the latter sense that he had in mind when he said that 'there is an ancient disagreement between philosophy and music' (*Republic* 607a). Elsewhere, however, Plato used a concept of music more akin to Pythagorean harmony. This is why he wrote in the *Phaedo* that 'philosophy is the highest kind of music' (61a). In this context, music is understood as an object of knowledge, and a kind of knowledge. In this sense, music, beauty and truth coincide.

Aristotle also shared the idea that music was a source of spiritual harmony and moral education. But he did not condemn its power to give us sensuous pleasure. Like all of the arts, one of its essential functions was that of giving pleasure, and this pleasure was an essential element of its aesthetic worth. Even for Aristotle, however, the pleasure was envisaged as the pleasure of listening to it, not the pleasure of practising it oneself. Throughout antiquity and the Middle Ages, the belief stubbornly persisted that the physical execution of music was a manual activity, inferior to the activity of listening to it, and of theoretical reflection upon it.

Still, the writings of Aristotle and his school, particularly those of Aristoxenus and Theophrastus, and later Cleonides, were marked by an interest in the nature of musical perception, and in the faculties that preside over musical judgements. They can therefore be regarded as the founders of the aesthetics of music, and of the psychology of musical experience.

But it was Platonism, and Neoplatonism, that dominated in the centuries that followed. Plotinus wrote that 'music, and music in the world of sense, is made by the music prior to this world' (*Enneads* V.8.1). This mystical conception of music was echoed in the writings of the Church Fathers. John Chrysostom and Jerome wrote of an inward, spiritual music of the heart, through which we sing to God. Augustine defined music as *scientia bene modulandi* (the science of modulating well), which meant, ultimately, proceeding in accordance with the laws of number (*De musica*, Book I). Augustine was well aware of the sensuous pleasure of music, but he considered that music as a form of knowledge – knowledge of the rules of harmony and proportion – was greatly superior.

A similar distinction was to be found in Boethius' influential treatise *De institutione musicae*. If we are really to understand music, he asserted, we must reflect rationally upon its nature, rather than just experience it sensuously. Boethius, however, provided a novel distinction of music into three kinds: *musica mundana*, the harmony of the cosmos as a whole; *musica humana*, the harmony within the human soul; and *musica instrumentalis*, the art of music as we now understand it. The last of these played only a minor part in musical theory until the end of the first millennium.

At the beginning of the new millennium there appeared the first treatises intended for pedagogical purposes, and, therefore, the first hints of an aesthetic analysis of music focusing on the concrete sonorous phenomena. Significant advances followed also from the increased practice of writing music, and from the contributions of Guido d'Arezzo. By the thirteenth century music was almost completely emancipated, and the opposition between theory and practice had been overcome. Johannes de Garlandia (the Younger), in his treatise *Introductio musicae*, distinguished between three types of music: *musica plana*, which denoted Gregorian chant; *musica mensurabilis*, which referred to the incipient polyphony; and *musica instrumentalis*, which referred to the production of sounds by means of instruments. This classification was far removed from the abstract and theological considerations of the preceding centuries.

The Renaissance

With the cynicism of retrospection, we can say that the new music, and new ideas about music, had finally arrived when they were condemned by Pope John XXII in a Papal Bull of 1322. But the Bull had little effect. The development of musical practices and theories carried on, regardless of the papal intervention. On the level of theory, a significant figure in the story of music aesthetics was Johannes Tinctoris, author of the first dictionary of music (*Terminorum musicae diffinitorium*, c. 1495), whose definitions of terms consistently made reference to the effects of music upon the listener. He clearly thought of music as the art of producing sonorous events whose object lay in the pleasure of listening to them. After Tinctoris – as before him – musicologists (as we would now call them) devoted their efforts almost entirely to the technical and psychological problems in musical theory.

Another important figure was the Swiss monk and humanist Henricus Glareanus. His main achievement, in his *Dodekachordon* (1547), was a revised system of the musical modes. But he also made an interesting distinction between the polyphonists (*Symphonetae*) and the melodists (*Phonasci*). The former, he said, borrowed musical themes and elaborated upon them. The latter were genuine musicians who invented their melodies. This somewhat severe attitude towards polyphony was symptomatic of the emergence of a new music, a music of clear melodies which enhanced, instead of obscuring, words and meaning.

Glareanus's ideas were developed very significantly by Gioseffo Zarlino, one of the most influential theorists of the Renaissance. Zarlino undertook a systematic analysis of the structure of musical intervals, and of their aesthetic properties and expressive values. He concluded that musical pitch and the intervals between tones were grounded upon natural laws. He carried out pioneering studies on harmonic resonances, and anticipated subsequent theories of Rameau. He argued that the perfect major chord exists in nature, while the minor chord is produced artificially. Finally, he also paid considerable attention – after Tinctoris, and in a similar vein – to the problem of meaning and expression in music.

Zarlino's ideas were adopted by the members of the Camerata dei Bardi, who were also dissatisfied with polyphony. Vincenzo Galilei (father of Galileo Galilei) believed that music must express feelings and produce feelings in us; that monody was more natural than, and thus superior to, polyphony; and that every interval and every chord corresponds to a particular affective state. Not everyone criticised polyphony. Giovanni Maria Artusi sprang to its defence. Artusi was also a forerunner of formalist aesthetics, in that he rejected the view

that music expressed feeling or aroused feeling. Music, he held, possessed its value quite independently of its effects upon our sensibility
(*Artusi* 1600–3).

The Modern Era

The seventeenth century witnessed not only the birth of modern
philosophy, but the birth also of modern music. In particular, it laid
the foundations for a clear understanding of the autonomy of music
as an art form, an understanding that was to be finally achieved, on the
theoretical level, in the eighteenth century.

A number of factors contributed to this development. One was a
debate about the relative merits of poetry and music, which led to
investigations of both natural and musical languages, and to a realisation that the language of music was *sui generis*. Another, ironically
enough, arose from efforts to condemn purely instrumental music on
the ground that it was inferior in 'musicality' to melodrama. The
notion of musicality carried with it, naturally enough, the idea of
musical autonomy. A third factor was a debate about the differences
between Italian and French melodrama. This debate, which took place
in the years 1702 to 1704, between Raguenet and Lecerf de la Viéville,
produced the claim that, while French melodrama was poetically
superior, Italian melodrama was musically superior. A final factor was
the emergence, in the eighteenth century, of a philosophical aesthetics
which asserted the autonomy of art in general, and, of course, music in
particular. It was an aesthetics associated with such names as Shaftes-
bury and Hutcheson in England, and Batteaux and Dubos in France.

By far the most significant theorist, however, was Jean Philippe
Rameau, who was the founder of modern musical theory. Rameau
definitively codified the laws of harmony in his *Traité de l'harmonie
réduite à ses principes naturels* (1722). He held music to be a science
with clearly defined rules. These rules ought to derive from evident
principles and these principles could not be found without the aid of
mathematics. Music, in this perspective, was amenable to mathematical
analysis. But this did not mean that the cognitive and theoretical
aspects of music were given precedence over its practical aspects. Both
kinds of aspect were symbiotically interactive. Rameau gave birth to
the explicit presumption that musical theory and practice feed one
another and are mutually supportive.

The main focus of this work was something already adumbrated in
Zarlino: the principles of harmonic resonance. Rameau worked out
that each sound in the diatonic scale, each note, contains secondary
sounds or 'harmonics'. Each note, when sounded, sets off sympathetic
vibrations in other notes, so that it is actually a complex group of
sounds. It was a discovery that was to have particular significance in the

theory and practice of avant-garde music in our own time. For Rameau, however, it meant that musical harmony is grounded in nature, and delights us for that reason. Furthermore, it appeared to have the character of a universal language, governed by mathematical principles. Melody, in contrast, was a more casual and arbitrary phenomenon, not easily amenable to scientific investigation. Rameau believed that harmony is the most fundamental element in music: historically, structurally and logically prior to melody, and even to rhythm.

Rameau's investigations carried the implication that music is not a language of feeling, and for this reason it met with great resistance from many of his contemporaries. Foremost among these were the Encyclopedists, and in particular Jean-Jacques Rousseau, whose numerous articles in the *Encyclopédie* were later collected in his *Dictionnaire de musique* (1767). Rousseau considered that melody and harmony were quite distinct, and even opposed to one another; and furthermore, that harmony was an artificial invention of the reason. It is not always clear that he fully understood the nature of harmony, and he may have been thinking of polyphony instead. It is ironic to note that, in the Age of Reason, he should condemn something for being an invention of reason. But Rousseau believed that nature was the source of song and melody, and that this was to be preferred because of its simplicity and spontaneous expression of feeling. It was the first indication of Romanticism in the philosophy of music.

Rousseau (and Diderot, whose ideas were somewhat similar) not only anticipated Romanticism, but echoed some of the intuitions about music already formulated by Giambattista Vico. Vico suggested that music, together with poetry, was the expression of our ancestors' deepest passions. Music preceded language, and abstract thought, and was the earliest means for articulating and disclosing the inner nature of the human mind: 'Men burst into song when they experience strong emotions, particularly those of sorrow and happiness' (Vico 1982, p. 247). Music, he believed, was the first language of all.

Romanticism, Idealism and Postromanticism

We must refer very briefly to Kant. In the *Critique of Judgment*, Kant argued that poetry was first and highest of the arts. If the arts are considered from the point of view of their charm (*Reiz*) and their relation to the emotions, then music comes closest to poetry. If, however, we consider the arts from the cognitive and intellectual point of view, music is last among the fine arts, 'because it only plays with feelings and emotions' (First Part, § 53).

With this assertion, Kant turned his back on the numerous investigations into the rational and mathematical character of music that had appeared in the two centuries preceding him. And he also fell into the trap of trying to establish a hierarchy among the arts, an attempt which, like all those that were to follow, was based on the dubious assumption that all of the arts can be explained and analysed from one single point of view. However, his commitment to an emotive conception of music related to the Romantic sensibility which was then in the process of formation. The apparent lack of conceptual meaning in music, seen as a weakness in previous centuries, became for the Romantics its greatest strength. For music seemed to them to articulate the deep and ambiguous nature of things which could not be captured in verbal or scientific concepts. For many of the Romantics, therefore, music was the highest form of art.

The nineteenth century was extraordinarily prolific in the philosophy of music. Here we will consider only a few of the principal figures: Hegel, Schopenhauer, Wagner and Nietzsche, with some references to others in passing.

Hegel took from Schelling the axiom that music, though a material phenomenon, was an articulation of the temporal rhythm and order of existence. Sounds, he noted, have a quality of quasi-immateriality. They do not stand before us in the manner of external objects, but are interiorised and experienced in the manner of a pure inwardness. Their sensuously perceptible form is metamorphosed into sentiment. Music is in fact an unfolding of truth, a manifestation of the Absolute in the form of feeling, as an inner sentiment structured in the temporal mode of the human consciousness. Music is given to us in time, not in space, and this is why it is akin to the structure and essence of the mind. For, as Hegel put it, 'the subject is in time, and time is the being of the subject' (Hegel [1842] (1975), II, p. 908).

Music, then, does not express particular feelings, but rather reveals to the mind its own essence and identity: 'For music takes as its subject-matter the subjective inner life itself.' This seems to ascribe to music a role that matches the importance and centrality of human consciousness. But in fact Hegel's position was more complex and ambiguous. Music, he said, was superior to the other arts in so far as it was the farthest removed from materiality. But it was also the lowest art because of its lack of any ideational content.

Schopenhauer, the arch-enemy of Hegel, took music more seriously than any of his predecessors. Arch-enemy or not, he was close to the spirit of Hegel when he said that music is a universal language which expresses, not any particular sentiment, but the essence of sentiment.

[Music] does not therefore express this or that particular and definite joy, this or that sorrow, or pain, or horror, or delight, or merriment, or peace of mind; but joy, sorrow, pain, horror, delight, merriment, peace of mind themselves, and therefore without their motives. (Schopenhauer [1818] (1886) I, § 52)

Schopenhauer also agreed with Kant that music is a language different from any other, for it is a language without concepts. For Kant, this was a weakness. For Schopenhauer, it was a virtue. For it enabled music to express in an intuitive and pre-conceptual manner the very essence of the World as Will. Other art forms reveal the surface structures of the World, the phenomenal, the appearance and not the reality. Music reveals the metaphysical deep structure of the World as Will. 'Music', he wrote, 'is thus by no means like the other arts, the copy of Ideas, but the copy of the Will itself, whose objectivity the Ideas are. This is why the effect of music is so much more powerful and penetrating than that of the other arts, for they speak only of shadows, but it speaks of the thing itself' (Schopenhauer [1818] (1886), II, § 52).

Schopenhauer was therefore dismissive of attempts to use music in a mimetic or descriptive fashion. It should be independent of words and of the empirical structures of the physical world. He condemned Haydn's *The Seasons*, and his *Creation* oratorio, and any other music which tried to imitate the perceptible world or to engage in 'descriptions' of battle scenes. This was, he wrote, 'all stuff to be thrown away' (Schopenhauer [1818] (1886), II, § 52).

The metaphysical implications of Schopenhauer's aesthetics of music attracted the interest of Richard Wagner. The composer shared with the philosopher the conception of music as an art that reveals the substance and structure of reality. He also shared in Schopenhauer's tragic sense of human existence, although he did not go as far in the direction of pessimism and nihilism. He agreed furthermore that music was a language freed from the constrictions of conceptual thought. Finally, he shared the philosopher's belief in music as a liberation from the causal necessities of our worldly existence.

In other ways, however, Wagner was very different from Schopenhauer. For, although he believed in the primacy of music over the other arts, he simultaneously denied to music its self-sufficiency and autonomy. He wanted music to be used in the service of mythical and religious narratives. Music, he thought, should be fused with all of the other arts – poetry, dance, visual art – in order to achieve a *Gesamtkunstwerk*: a total work of art. Wagnerian drama was intended to be superior to music just on its own. Wagner thought that in this way he was returning to an allegedly original or archetypal symbiosis of poetry and music, as suggested by Vico, Rousseau and Herder. His compositions became intentionally mimetic and descriptive. He was not the only composer to take this direction at this time. Other musical genres of a similar kind were then developing: descriptive or programme music, symphonic poems, new kinds of musical theatre, new developments in opera. The compositions of Liszt and Berlioz, in particular, often had descriptive intentions. They strove, as they thought, to free music from its formal chains and to widen its expressive and semantic possibilities.

The story of the Romantic conceptions of music would not be complete without some reference to Friedrich Nietzsche. Influenced, in his youth, by Schopenhauer and Wagner, Nietzsche was in one sense the last of the Romantics. But he was also – along with Feuerbach, Marx and Kierkegaard – one of the first critics of Romanticism. He turned against Schopenhauer's nihilism, and his admiration of Wagner turned into vitriolic criticism of Wagner's nostalgic recourse to religious Christian themes, as in *Parsifal*. Nietzsche rejected Romanticism, Schopenhauer, and Wagner's music, as 'decadent'.

With Nietzsche, mainstream Romantic aesthetics came to an end, and with it the view that music was the privileged voice of the human spirit and a revelation of the essence of reality. The midwife to the birth of a new, postRomantic age had in fact started somewhat earlier than Nietzsche. This was Eduard Hanslick, in his *Vom Musikalisch-Schönen* (*The Beautiful in Music*), whose first edition appeared in 1854.

Hanslick was greatly influenced by the psychological and aesthetic theories of Johann Friedrich Herbart (successor to Kant in the chair of philosophy in Königsberg). He found Herbart's analytic methodology congenial, and approached the subject of music in an analytic and anti-literary way. But he also preserved some of the ideas of the Romantics, in particular that the language of music, which is without concepts, is asemantic; that it does not signify particular feelings or mental states; and that it is an autonomous form of art.

The prevailing belief of the time was that music had mimetic and descriptive power, and that the sort of meanings that it consequently communicated had the function of triggering powerful emotions in the listener. Against this, Hanslick argued that the value of music is quite autonomous, and that it arises exclusively and entirely from musical form. He held that music was quite distinct from the other arts, and has its own distinctive type of meaning.

> Music consists of tonal sequences, tonal forms; these have no other content than themselves. They remind us once again of architecture and dancing, which likewise bring us beautiful relationships without content. However each person may evaluate and name the effect of a piece of music according to its individuality, its content is nothing

but the audible tonal forms; since music speaks not merely by means of tones, it speaks only tones. (Hanslick [1854] (1986), p. 78)

The aesthetic value of music, therefore, resided in its formal structures, independently of emotive, descriptive or semantic force. Music is essentially form, not expression. The content of music is its form. Hanslick did not deny the emotive or expressive power of music. But he held that music does not depict feelings; rather it articulates, through its formal structures, the dynamics of feeling. Music 'can reproduce the motion of a physical process according to the prevailing momentum: fast, slow, strong, weak, rising, falling. Motion is just one attribute, however, one moment of feeling, not feeling itself' (Hanslick [1854] (1986), p. 11).

Contemporary Debate

After Hanslick, there emerged also a new kind of philosophical sensibility – anti-metaphysical and anti-systematic – that goes under the general name of 'Positivism'. This gave rise, in Germany and the Anglo-Saxon cultures, to a scientifically motivated approach to music known as *Musikwissenschaft*. But the evolutionary theories of Spencer and Darwin also promoted research into the origin and history of music, ethnomusicology, and the social and cultural dimensions of the art. Sociological theories of music had their beginnings in the seminal work of Weber and Durkheim, but they gained momentum and strength under the influence of Marx. These theories tended to emphasise the significance of music as expressive of particular social structures and ideologies.

Music and Society

In France, the most distinguished and erudite exponent of this approach was Jules Combarieu. He wrote both about the origin and history of music (*La musique et la magie*, 1909), and about the aesthetics of music (*La musique, ses lois et son évolution*, 1907). He combined Hanslick's kind of formalism with the view that music had evolved from its origins in magical rituals. Later it was absorbed into religious rituals and even theological discourse, and later still it developed its autonomy as an expression of nature.

In some respects more sophisticated than Combarieu, the Polish Marxist musicologist Zofia Lissa investigated musical structures throughout history in search of analogies and parallels with the social and cultural structures in which they were situated. Most Marxists consider music, like art in general, to be part of the superstructure, a result and mirror of socio-economic forces. Lissa is careful to argue that the link between society and music is mediated and indirect. It works by analogy, not by causal determination. Music, that is, has a degree of autonomy from the society which produces it.

Theodor Wiesengrund Adorno was a philosopher, sociologist, musician and musicologist, who made a very significant and complex contribution to debates on the musical avant-garde. Starting from Hegelian and Marxian presuppositions, he investigated the relations between musical structures and social systems and institutions. Human subjects, he noted, live in an alienated and repressed condition in the twentieth century. The two world wars, the holocaust, the power of impersonal institutions, the manipulation of people through propaganda and the culture industry are symptoms of a profound disorder masquerading as order. We therefore need a new music. The creative possibilities offered by the harmonic system are now exhausted. Music, in any case, has the vocation of denouncing the false appearances of order by revealing the true nature of society in our time.

In his *Philosophy of Modern Music* [1949] (1973) Adorno analysed the musical poetics, and the ideological implications, of Schönberg and Stravinsky. Schönberg, he said, was willing to abandon tonalism completely and was thus the champion of progress. Stravinsky was a neoclassicist who preserved the tonal conventions and who was therefore an uncritical reactionary. Schönberg gave voice to a suffering humanity; Stravinsky reinstated the old order and celebrated the demise of subjectivity. Adorno's thinking, which deeply influenced and inspired Thomas Mann's *Doktor Faustus*, is rich and profound, though impossible to do justice to here (see Santoro-Brienza 1993, pp. 55–77). In the end his pessimism gained the upper hand. He came to the view that even Schönberg had failed, and accused post-Schönbergian electronic music of being superficial. Perhaps he lost sight of music's fundamental autonomy, lost beneath his conviction that art is primarily a vehicle of ideological meaning.

If we look at the general condition of the philosophy of music now, we can divide its concerns into three kinds: acoustics and the psychology of musical perception; formalism; and linguistic-communicative theories. It is to these that, in conclusion, we now turn.

Acoustics and Psychoacoustics

The modern founder of acoustic studies was Hermann von Helmholtz. Helmholtz began this work with a re-examination of Zarlino's and Rameau's theories of harmony, in the course of which he experimented on the phenomenon of resonance, and succeeded in identifying the complex structure of wave bands. His experiments confirmed Zarlino's and Rameau's findings about the principles of harmony and the structure of intervals and of consonances. As a result, Helmholtz was convinced that harmony and consequently also the diatonic system constitute the ontological and natural order of sound and its properties. Thus, music could be practised only within the bounds of the harmonic diatonic system. It was a conclusion that many later musicians and theorists agreed with.

Helmholtz also discovered that each musical note contains, not only the principal and most obvious harmonic resonances – the fifth, the octave, the third, the fourth – but also more distant harmonics. In the end, when fully analysed, each note actually contains all twelve notes of the diatonic scale, even though not all may be perceivable by the listener. Thus it was that, ironically, a strenuous upholder of the 'natural' foundations of music provided scientific legitimation of twelve-tone or serial music, and of the avant-garde poetics sometimes accused of being 'unnatural'.

After Helmholtz, acoustic problems attracted the attention of others, and of psychologists in particular. Psychoacoustic studies of music are by now very plentiful. Not the least of their merits is the value of their analyses of musical perception, which shed light in turn on strictly aesthetic and philosophical issues. German theorists have made substantial contributions in this field. We must mention also the influential *Psychology of Music* (1967) by Carl Seashore, and *Information Theory and Esthetic Perception* (1966) by Abraham Moles.

Formalist Theories

One of the most radical expressions of the formalist theory of music was written by Igor Stravinsky: 'I consider that music is, by its very nature, powerless to express anything at all, whether a feeling, an attitude of mind, a psychological mood, a phenomenon of nature, etc . . . If, as is nearly always the case, music appears to express something, this is only an illusion, not a reality' (*Stravinsky* [1936] 1962, p. 53). His *Poetics of Music* (1947), and numerous other essays and interviews, make the same point. Expression, he asserts, has never been an immanent property of music. He was polemically critical of theories which claim that music has a meaning in the sense of an expressive or emotive content, or that it can give a mimetic description of natural phenomena. Stravinsky focused on the art of music, the actual process of making music, its poetics. The essence of music, he claims, is organised temporality. The act of composing is a cold and rational process of constructing temporal structures. Music is autonomous. It is not surprising, then, to observe that rhythm is the most elaborate and dominant element in Stravinsky's own compositions.

Stravinsky's formalism, his emphasis on temporality in music, his polemical anti-Expressionism, his implicit anti-Wagnerianism, were adopted by Gisèle Brelet, who must be regarded as one of the most significant figures in the aesthetics of music. She takes Stravinsky's music as the embodiment of her own view that music is pure temporality. 'Stravinsky's time', she writes, 'expresses consciousness in the purity of its fundamental activity, and not the world of empirical contents in which consciousness can be lost' (Brelet 1947, p. 158). In her seminal work, *Le Temps musical* (1949), she focused upon the formal aspects of music, on music as pure form, void of emotive or descriptive content or meanings. She rejected the view that it has anything to do with psychological diachrony or physical chronology. Instead, it pertains to inward duration, to lived time, to the unfolding of the consciousness. We see here the influence of Bergson's analysis of *la durée*, or *temps vécu*. We hear also echoes of Hegel's conception of music as organisation and articulation of time, and hence as an articulation of the structure and essence of the mind. For Brelet, the autonomy of music is grounded in the very nature of the development of musical discourse, which proceeds 'logically, according to immanent or internal rules, quite independently of the psychological temperament and character of the individual composers' (Brelet 1947, p. 7).

Linguistic-communicative Approaches

The study of language has occupied a central place in the philosophical and intellectual life of the twentieth century, and it was inevitable that theorists of music should begin to investigate the linguistic and communicative dimensions of music as well. This in turn reawakened the question of meaning in music.

Responses to the issue of musical meaning range between two poles: those which are close to formalism, and those which are closer to semantic expressionism. The former tend to emphasise the difference between music and natural language, and to study whatever is specific and unique to musical discourse and communication. The latter tend to assume that music communicates in a manner that is analogous, at the very least, to natural language; and to believe that music has a semantic content, whether it expresses emotions, denotes states of mind, or mirrors natural phenomena. Among the first set of positions we find Boris de Schloezer, Susanne Langer, Leonard Meyer, Leonard Bernstein, Ernst Bloch, Roman Ingarden, Jean-Jacques Nattiez, Gino Stefani and Eero Tarasti. Among the second set of positions we find the highly influential work by Deryck Cooke, *The Language of Music* (1959), and the musical ideas of Claude Lévi-Strauss. Here we will review just a few of these.

Boris de Schloezer states his formalist position quite clearly: 'In music, the signified resides immanently in the signifier. The content is in the form, to the extent that, speaking strictly, music does not *have* meaning, but it *is* meaning' (De Schloezer 1947, p. 44). His thinking here is similar to that of Roman Jakobson who, with the Russian Formalists and the Prague School, said that in aesthetic artefacts the level of content collapses into the level of form – producing, thus, self-referentiality and immanent autonomy. And music, perhaps more than any other kind of art, seems to be characterised by its immanent self-referentiality.

It follows that, if music is a kind of language, it is quite different from natural language. Its elements – its dictionary, so to speak – are signs of a very particular nature: signs that do not stand for anything beyond themselves, signs without reference. Musical discourse does not point to any meaning other than the contextual and structural organisation of the sounds themselves. (A somewhat similar semiotic can be found in Dufrenne 1973.)

Susanne Langer, in *Philosophy in a New Key* (1951), compares and contrasts musical symbols with the other sorts of symbols that we deploy in our mental and cultural lives. Music, she says, does express and communicate the structures of the life of feeling. But musical symbols are, at the same time, non-representational, non-referential. Unlike the symbols of natural language, which connote a conceptual content, and then point beyond themselves to something else, musical symbols have a meaning that is implicit, that emerges from the fact that they refer to themselves. As she puts it, 'Articulation is its life, but not assertion; expressiveness, not expression' (Langer 1951, p. 240).

It is worth referring here to the important semiological investigations of Umberto Eco. Eco has raised the question whether a semiotics of music is possible. He points out that music cannot be regarded as a 'language', if by this we mean a system wherein particular semantic contents belong to particular formal units in the system. There is, in this sense, no musical 'code' as a set of rules and conventions that allow us to identify or establish correlations between the level of form – or signifiers – and that of content, or signifieds. This poses serious problems for any attempt to speak of music as a communicative process. Langer and Eco thus question the very possibility of identifying elements of music to which we can ascribe specific meanings (see also Nöth 1990).

However, the search for meaning in music is a very ancient one, as we have seen, and its meaning is often believed to have something to do with its powerful effect upon the emotions. But all art forms affect the emotions. The empirical fact that music arouses emotion leads to no conclusion about whether it has a semantic content or not. If it is meaningful, that meaning must lie instead in the region of specific feelings, ideas or states of mind communicated by it, or by a power to depict or imitate natural phenomena.

One of the most powerful advocates of such a theory, in the recent past, has been Deryck Cooke. The central points of his thesis can be summarised as follows: (1) music is a language; (2) it is the language of feelings; (3) it expresses the composer's emotions; (4) it communicates those emotions to the listeners; (5) it succeeds in doing all of this because of a clearly identifiable correspondence between particular sonorous events and specific meanings.

If this is true, then there must be a kind of musical vocabulary, which ascribes specific and constant semantic values to specific sonorous events. And this is precisely what Cooke set out to supply, in *The Language of Music* (1959). Here he analysed a large number of musical quotations, in order to show 'that the conception of music as a language capable of expressing certain very definite things is not a romantic aberration, but has been the common unconscious assumption of composers for the past five-and-a-half centuries at least' (Cooke 1959, p. xi). His book, he continues,

> attempts to isolate the various means of expression available to the composer – the various procedures in the dimensions of pitch, time, and volume – and to discover what emotional effects these procedures can produce; but more specifically, it tries to pinpoint the inherent emotional characters of the various notes of the major, minor, and chromatic scales, and of certain basic melodic patterns which have been used persistently throughout our musical history. (Cooke 1959, pp. xi–xii)

Let us look at an example – by now very familiar because it has been widely debated – of how Cooke sets about this task: his discussion of the semantic values of the major and the minor chords. The major chord, according to Cooke, always signifies and so communicates joy, while the minor chord signifies and communicates sadness. It is a natural, and fixed, property of these chords that they should signify just these feelings.

This claim seems easy to rebut. First, Cooke implies that musical sounds and structures are natural phenomena: they 'naturally' connote sadness, or joy; we just find that this is so. But in fact the art of music is not a natural phenomenon, but a contrived organisation of sound. Secondly, feelings are quite subjective, and easy prey to the vicissitudes of circumstance. I may get a feeling of joy from something today, but fail to do so tomorrow.

We can think of numerous instances of compositions in minor keys which fill us with joy, and of compositions in major keys which, at the very least, induce a mood of pensiveness. We also know that, in ancient times, tunes in minor progressions were deemed suitable for battle songs, while tunes in major progressions were reserved for funerals. Interestingly, Cooke refrains from dealing with post-tonal music: the avant-garde, serial and electronic music, *musique concrète*. He writes:

> The investigation is further confined to tonal music, i.e. to music in a key, in the widest sense of the word, whether written by Dufay in 1440, Byrd in 1611, Mozart in 1782, or Stravinsky in 1953. It does not in any way attempt to deal with the entirely new musical language which has arisen out of the abrogation of tonality by some composers during the last half-century; since this new language clearly bears little or no relation to the long-established one based on the tonal system. (Cooke 1959, p. xiii)

It is in fact arguable that contemporary music is peculiarly resistant to semantic analysis, although it is hardly deniable that it is music all the same.

Claude Lévi-Strauss also attempted to formulate a semantic theory of music, but in so doing he compounded its difficulties (see Santoro-Brienza 1993, pp. 78–92). Lévi-Strauss wanted to criticise and reject the entire avant-garde movement, and to this end he argued that the structure of music is the same as the structure of natural language. Without going into detail, his position can be summarised as follows. Music, like myth and like articulate speech, is a language, because, as he put it, 'we understand it' (see Lévi-Strauss 1970, pp. 1–32). However, this amounts to no more than a vague and ambiguous assertion, unsupported by argument. His analogy between myth and music suggests that music can in some sense or other tell stories. But this claim, whatever its plausibility in a small number of cases, is hardly sustainable in the case of, for instance, Bach's *Goldberg Variations*.

Before concluding this summary, we should remember that the dream of a semantics of music is very old. It was connected with the myth of the natural and ontological status of music, and with the charming metaphor of the music of the spheres. This dream, furthermore, warranted a body of beliefs about the psychological and moral functions of music.

Interestingly, between Pythagoras and Lévi-Strauss we encounter a seventeenth-century figure, Athanasius Kircher. Kircher reinvented the concept of *musica pathetica*, with the suggestion that music can shape the human character and temperament. The variety of musical kinds and expressions, he held, is as vast as the variety of human temperaments

(Kircher 1650). The Baroque sensibility of the time also gave rise to a plethora of musical 'dictionaries', in which different feelings and mental states were ascribed to very specific musical features, such as styles, instruments, pitch, rhythmic figures, chords, melodic progressions, intervals and so on and so forth. At that time, music was still thought of as being inextricably linked with poetry. Vocal music was the predominant genre, and purely instrumental music was only beginning to appear. This may explain why such musical dictionaries seemed plausible.

There can be no doubt that the issue of a musical semantic emerges with particular force when we are considering vocal music, for here there is a kind of symbiosis between a verbal text and the musical discourse. This is very evident in plainchant, unaccompanied folksongs, choral music *a cappella*, oratorio, sacred music and opera. In these cases it is difficult to disentangle totally the music from the words. The musical 'diction' is inevitably charged with conceptual and imaginative representations mediated by the verbal text, and seems to be determined, in part, by the emotional character of that text. These are cases in which musical meanings live symbiotically with dramatic, descriptive, emotive, conceptual and religious meanings. It is not surprising, then, that we may be inclined to find extra-musical meanings in musical messages. Deryck Cooke's examples, in fact, come mainly from vocal musical genres.

In conclusion, we agree that music has the power to move us, but this is a different matter from saying that a particular musical event 'means' a particular mental state or 'describes' a particular natural phenomenon. Musical discourse, like language, has syntactic rules of articulation, and, like language, is conventional rather than natural. But when it comes to the question of semantic function, the analogy ceases.

10

The Visual and Plastic Arts

Where the spirit does not work with the hand there is no art.
(Leonardo da Vinci)

Introduction

This chapter will deal with the three major forms of visual art – architecture, sculpture and painting – also known as plastic and figurative arts. In all three cases, but particularly in the case of architecture, we run at once into the problem of the relation between aesthetic and functional values. A great deal of architecture is clearly practical and functional, but some is primarily monumental and aesthetic. Some is designed to satisfy the pragmatic demands of life and work; some is designed to convey ideological, expressive, formal and aesthetic values. There is also a subtler distinction, between spatial or volumetric architecture, which involves the construction of spatial masses and exploits the interactions between fullness and void; and, on the other hand, decorative architecture, which has as its goal the harmonisation and ornamentation of the internal and external surfaces that enclose the structured spaces.

These distinctions, however, do not imply that each type excludes the other. Architecture is functional and aesthetic simultaneously, and each value interacts with the other. Architecture is not alone in this. Music can be used for specific goals, such as relaxation or prayer, without losing its aesthetic character. Painting is not only decorative, but can be a financial investment or a status symbol. Painting, in any case, has very frequently been linked with ideological narratives, and with the dissemination of intellectual, political and religious messages. The same kind of thing could be said about all of the arts. Art is always located within a history and a culture. It exists within a context of technical, practical, financial, ideological and pedagogical aims and values (see Dewey 1934).

This may seem to undermine the autonomy of art, and the theory that it is self-referential. However, works of art are artefacts that are

189

intentionalised as *primarily* autonomous and self-referential, at least whenever we foreground their formal and aesthetic properties. Architecture may provide shelter, designate a sacred space, or signify the wealth and power of an individual or nation, but it is also artistic. Very often, indeed, its functions are fulfilled all the better when the aesthetic values are realised as well.

Theories of Architecture

The word 'architecture' comes from the Latin *architectura*, which denotes the art and craft of building. This in turn derives from the Greek *architékton*, which means a master designer and builder, the artist and craftsman who directs, with a creative and artistic ingenuity, the physical process of construction. In the classical world, architecture was the archetypal form of visual art. Sculpture and painting were in a sense dependent on it, first because they were physically located within architectural structures and contexts, and secondly because the art and craft of building included the knowledge and the disciplines of the other two arts as well as its own.

The concept of architecture combines the idea of the artistic/aesthetic with the idea of the practical/technical. These two ideas, of course, could easily be considered separately from one another, and this has given rise to three main approaches to the nature of the art: (1) holistic theories – that is, theories that stress the inseparable coexistence of aesthetic intention and scientific knowledge with practical techniques and methods; (2) formalist theories – that is, theories that emphasise the decorative properties and aesthetic values of architecture, architecture considered as art rather than as craft; (3) functionalist theories – that is, theories that emphasise the technical and functional aspects of architecture, architecture as engineering and craft rather than as art.

The Egyptian, Greek and Roman cultures, and later the civilisations of Byzantium and of medieval Christendom, produced extraordinary architectural works. But they produced remarkably little in the way of philosophical, critical or theoretical reflection upon the art. The forms of architecture have a geometrical and abstract character, and these cultures tended to consider architecture as being akin to music and mathematics. In addition, they did not distinguish as clearly as we do between art and craft, and so they were wont to focus upon the functional value of architecture. It might involve a great deal of scientific knowledge, but its products were seen as primarily useful artefacts. Even Plato, always ready to break a spear against the arts, had no quarrel with architecture; for what it produces are not copies, but the thing itself.

The first significant treatise on architecture was written by Vitruvius, in the first century AD. His *De Architectura* was to have a huge influence, which lasted well into the Renaissance, apart from a medieval parenthesis involving symbolic conceptions of architecture. At the very beginning of the work, Vitruvius defined architecture as a science: 'The science of architecture is adorned by many disciplines and forms of learning . . . It is born from building practice and theoretical reasoning' (Architecti est scientia pluribus disciplinis et variis eruditionibus ornata . . . Ea nascitur ex fabrica et ratiocinatione) *De Architectura*, I.1.1). As the definition suggests, Vitruvius understood the art to be a union of theory and praxis, of making and knowing. Its objects, he went on, were utility (*utilitas*), firmness or stability (*firmitas*), and charm or attractiveness (*venustas*). Despite this holistic view of architecture, Vitruvius concentrated in his treatise on technical problems and procedures. He did, however, list at one point what he took to be the six elements of architecture: numerical order (*ordinatio*), regular arrangement (*dispositio*), harmony (*eurhythmia*), symmetry (*symmetria*), gracefulness or beauty (*decorum*), and ordered or proportioned articulation (*distributio*). These concepts point to a perspective on architecture when seen from the outside, architecture as monumental rather than functional, an architecture in which the interior is seen less as a spatial arrangement than as a delimitation and enclosure of space.

De Architectura remained by far the most comprehensive and influential treatise on architecture for many centuries. When the Renaissance arrived, its influence increased if anything, in works by Palladio and later neoclassical schools and tendencies. It was only in the fifteenth century that we find what might be called the second general treatise on architecture, Leon Battista Alberti's *De re aedificatoria*. But Alberti himself, along with Palladio and all of the theorists in the following centuries, up to the nineteenth century, remained under the spell of Vitruvius. There were some changes in emphasis. Michelangelo, for instance, stressed the importance of Vitruvius' analogy between architecture and the human body. The conception of architecture as an art, not just the craft of building, was increasingly emphasised from the Renaissance onwards, although it was not spelled out clearly until Vincenzo Scamozzi's *L'idea della architettura universale* (*The Idea of Universal Architecture*), in 1615. This work was also the first historical and critical compendium of previous theories of architecture, and was to have a considerable influence on John Ruskin. Ruskin's focus on the decorative character of architecture was akin to nineteenth-century theories of 'pure visibility', articulated by Fiedler, von Hildebrand, Riegl, Schmarsow, among others. It also fed into the formalist theories of the twentieth century, of Wölfflin,

Panofsky, Brinkmann, Berenson, Bell, Fry, Stokes, Focillon, Longhi and Venturi. There has been, in short, a growing and seemingly prevalent tendency to privilege the aesthetic and formal values of architecture, and to foreground its visual and tactual properties rather than its kinetic and spatial properties. But, as we shall see, that tendency did not succeed in fully explaining the essence of architecture.

Several factors have contributed to the direction taken by theories of architecture in the twentieth century: a huge increase in urbanisation; the discovery and application of new materials; technological innovation and its architectural requirements; a new sort of technological sensibility in people in the developed world. Schelling and most of the Romantics thought of architecture as a fine art, in which utility and function were absorbed and metamorphosed into the beauty of form. The functionalists tend to identify aesthetic beauty with functional perfection, so that beauty is absorbed and metamorphosed into comfort and efficiency. What is useful is also, and for that reason, beautiful. Le Corbusier – seemingly espousing purely functionalist ideals – described architectural works as machines to be inhabited. Ironically, though not unexpectedly, many supposedly 'functionalist' architects have designed buildings of outstanding and lyrical beauty. Le Corbusier, in fact, rediscovered the merits – both aesthetic and constructive – of the Golden Section. The works by Sullivan, Mies van der Rohe, Frank Lloyd Wright, Rossi, Pen, Tallon, Dunne – to mention a few – illustrate, in different guises, the same ironic predicament.

Architectural functionalists, in fact, are not mere utilitarians. For they have emphasised that the distinctive nature of architecture resides in the visual, tactile, plastic and kinetic art of space. They have taught us in particular about internal architectural spaces, which are experienced and enjoyed by sight and touch, bodily movement, and the diachronic indwelling and using of the space and its various functions. Vitale, in his *Estetica dell'architettura* (see Zevi 1957), explored the ways by which architecture reveals space as itself a sense-perceptible reality, rather as music reveals the sensuous reality of time. Bruno Zevi (1957) described architectural volumes as limits, as interruptions of the space continuum. For this reason, every building creates and organises two types of space: internal and enclosed spaces, and external spaces connected with their urban and natural landscapes. By dwelling and moving within the internal spaces, and by experiencing both internal and external spaces from different points of view, we create for ourselves a kind of fourth dimension, and hence the full reality of this form of art.

The Art of Space

Architectural artefacts can be regarded as 'messages' addressed to our sight, to our tactile sense of mass and texture, and to our kinetic sense of movement in space. They are addressed, that is, to our conception and perception of ourselves – our image and *Gestalt* of ourselves – as seeing, sensing and moving bodies in space. Looked at in this way, architecture is the art that produces and organises space by means of mass and lines. Umberto Eco puts it as follows: 'Architecture consists of material, concrete, physical artefacts that delimit external and internal spaces of the architectural object, in respect of particular functions – ascending, descending, leaving, sheltering from the natural environment, gathering socially, sleeping, eating, praying, celebrating, having a sense of reverence' (Eco 1971, p. 159).

In an earlier book, Eco had already written a comprehensive semiological study of architecture (Eco 1968, pp. 189–250). There is no space here to go into this exhaustively, but in what follows we will refer to some of his main points.

We start by considering what we imagine may have been the beginnings of architecture. A stone age ancestor, let us say, is compelled by wind and rain, and perhaps copying the behaviour of animals, to seek refuge, for the very first time, in a cave. Here is Eco's account of the dramatic interior shift which might accompany the physical action.

Sheltered from the wind and the rain, in the light of day or of a fire (presuming that he has already invented it), our cavedweller observes the space of his shelter. He observes the surface of the vault, and sees it as the end limit of an external space, which is now, along with the wind and the rain, something distinct and separate. He sees it also as the beginning of an internal space, which perhaps confusedly evokes unconscious nostalgias for the maternal womb and induces a sense of security... After the storm, he leaves the cave, and observes it from the outside. He notices the cave entrance as a hole that allows access to the internal space, and the entrance also brings to mind an image of the space inside ... In the process, an 'idea-of-cave' takes shape. It serves at least as a mnemonic sign, so that on future occasions he can think of the cave as a possible destination and shelter from a storm. This 'idea-of-cave' also permits the recognition of another cave as 'possibility-of-shelter', just like the first cave. Thus the experience of the first cave and the idea of 'that' cave are replaced by the idea of caves in general. This idea is now a model and structure, a universal, something that does not concretely exist, in virtue of which he is able to recognise phenomena as caves ... After this, a drawing of a cave – no matter how partial and imprecise – or the sight of a distant cave, already communicate a possible function, even though the function may not be actually exercised and used. Something has happened, something that Roland Barthes has explained in these words: 'As soon as there is society, every function becomes the sign of that function'. (Eco 1968, p. 193)

Architecture, that is, both has useful functions and signifies the existence of those functions. A cave induces and promotes the act of seeking shelter, but also, simultaneously, *signifies the existence* of that function, even if it is not actually used. In the same way, the shape of a soup spoon has the function of inducing a certain way of eating, but simultaneously signifies that way of eating, even when we are not eating with it. Similarly, an architectural feature such as a staircase offers us the physical possibility of going up or down it, and also communicates to us that that is its function.

What is involved in the use of architectural artefacts – moving through, entering, pausing, climbing, looking out, leaning, handling, etc. – is not just their possible functions, but first and foremost the connected meanings which signify and lead me towards the functional uses. Consider how, when confronted with *trompe-l'oeil* phenomena, we feel ready to use them even though there is no possible function. (Eco 1968, pp. 194–5)

Thus, a frescoed wall representing an attractive garden disposes me to move into it. An illusionistic representation of an ascending staircase disposes me to ascend it.

This semiotic analysis of architecture shows how architectural functions are linked to the cultural and social experience of communication (see also Nöth 1990, pp. 435–9). We shall develop this point further, in 'Function, Style and Aesthetic Values' when considering the aesthetics of architecture. At this point, however, we turn briefly to the history of architecture in order to give an outline of its main styles and forms.

History: Models and Forms of Architecture

If caves were in fact the first human dwellings, they were natural phenomena transformed into cultural objects by human intentionality. But the first man-made buildings, or at least the first spatial constructions that we know of, were dolmens. These were simple constructions in which vertically placed rocks sustained a horizontal slab. The internal space was very limited, because of its design and the material involved: a very large slab of rock could easily crack at its weakest point, around the middle. Furthermore, the design did not allow for much elevation. There were no two-storey dolmens!

The simple principle of construction exemplified in the dolmen was adopted in ancient architecture, up to Roman times at any rate. Egyptian and Greek temples, for instance, were built as a series of vertical columns sustaining an architrave or main beam. The same principle was used for private dwellings. This structural model did not allow for much elevation, for the horizontal architrave could not support excessive weight. Temples were all one-storey buildings. Taller structures, such as the pyramids, had to be created by piling together large masses of stone, with very little in the way of internal space. For obvious reasons, this monumental sort of building was reserved for special functions, and its main purpose was to foreground symbolic values such as majesty, authority, power and religious awe.

A new and revolutionary model appeared in Roman times, brought about by the invention of the semicircular or round arch. The Romans preserved much of the right-angled, vertical-horizontal style, but because of the arch they could build more elevated structures, such as aqueducts, bridges and amphitheatres. The Colosseum is a well-known instance of these building methods. The Romans also began to construct buildings with a circular ground plan, such as the Pantheon, and, once again, the Colosseum. The Romans furthermore used bricks, whose lightness and resilience, when compared with marble or other kinds of stone, increased the strength and solidity of Roman constructions.

It was Byzantine architects, however, who made a further important discovery, which had to do with the problem of connecting a round dome with a square base. A circle drawn inside a square touches the square at only four points. Thus, if a round dome or cupola is erected on top of a square base, its entire weight falls on to only four points, and those the weakest points, of the base. A solution to this state of affairs, which greatly limited the size of such structures, was found by connecting all the points of the base of the circular dome with all the points of its square basis, by means of structural devices technically called 'pendentives' or 'squinches'. These are the connecting curved triangles, which are to be found at the four angles of the square upon which the dome is mounted. It was an ingenious feat of architectural engineering much used during the Renaissance.

In the Middle Ages a further novel architectural feature was devised, the ogival or Gothic arch. This arch, which needed supporting buttresses and rib vaults, allowed for greater elevation, though it limited the space enclosed in the arch. It allowed the possibility of constructing very tall buildings – such as the Strassburg Cathedral or the Milan Duomo – and, hence, enhanced the vertical dimensions of medieval cathedrals. At once, at the level of aesthetic experience, it imbued them with highly significant connotations: it enabled them to be regarded as symbols of transcendent values.

In our own times, round about the turn of the century, the invention of reinforced concrete, and the employment of lighter materials such as aluminium and glass, produced new developments in the history of architecture. Another invention was the cantilever. The cantilever started life as a bracket projecting from a wall to support a balcony. But it quickly developed into a form of design in which an extended horizontal structure rests, not on a co-extensive base, but on a much smaller base, almost a point in some cases, while it is anchored elsewhere at a terminal point. Modernist architects such as Frank Lloyd Wright have used this principle extensively, to produce buildings that seem to defy the laws of mass and gravity. Also, the extensive use of glass has tended to break down the barrier between internal and external spaces.

Postmodern architecture has adopted a syncretic approach to a variety of traditional styles, indulging in a kind of intertextual quotation. Contemporary architects have also returned to a traditional principle in taking account of the natural and urban contexts within which architecture is located (see Jencks 1986).

Function, Style and Aesthetic Values

So far we have considered the functional character and value of architecture, and we looked at Umberto Eco's explanation of how a building signifies or denotes its function. There are other meanings, however, as well functional meanings. Here is Eco again:

> When I look at a window on the façade of a building, generally I don't think about its function. I think of a window-meaning grounded in a function, but where the function has been absorbed so that I can easily forget it, and instead see the window, in relation to other windows, as elements of an architectural rhythm and disposition. Similarly, in reading poetry we can let the meaning of the individual words recede into the background, while fore-grounding the formal and textual interplay of the signifiers. (Eco 1968, p. 202)

This passage clearly refers to aesthetic experience. When architecture is considered as art, its aesthetic properties are foregrounded, together with its capacity to trigger within us the appropriate sensory and intellectual responses.

There are other architectural functions as well as those connected with its utility and its aesthetic character. For the design of a building obliges us to live in it, or interact with it, in a particular way. It guides us towards a particular register of communication. For instance, buildings can convey emotive values and experience. Romanesque churches induce a sense of quiet and pensive meditation. Gothic cathedrals make us feel both elevated and terrified. Greek temples induce a feeling of calm and luminosity. Baroque churches suggest a sense of drama and excitement. Buildings also exercise a phatic function, a function 'of contact'; that is, they are physical presences which guarantee a continuity within an urban network. They operate as points of reference: as points of orientation and landmarks.

Every architectural work, therefore, possesses some symbolic connotation in addition to its functional denotation. One set of connotations derives from the analogy between a building and the human body – an idea articulated by Vitruvius and echoed by Michelangelo. The underlying proposition here is that the internal relations among the parts of a building correspond in some way to the relations among the parts of the body.

This could be interpreted in at least three ways. First, it could mean that a building is an extension of the human body. For instance, we could think of it as an enveloping womb. Or we could think of it as a tool – also an extension and prothesis of the human body – adopting a functionalist interpretation of Le Corbusier's phrase 'a machine for living'. Secondly, it could mean that the size and proportions of buildings should be gauged with respect to the size of the human bodies which will dwell, work, or gather within it. Thirdly it could also be understood as a correspondence between the proportions obtaining among the parts of a building and those obtaining among the parts of the human body. This seems to have been the conception that held sway in classical Greece and in the Renaissance. In this case, a building could be on a very large scale and yet, in its internal proportions, reproduce the proportions of the human. The human body would thus provide a sort of canonical proportionality.

Other kinds of architectural connotations can be observed in the works of different periods and styles. Egyptian architecture is characterised by stylised and geometric forms which symbolise power, aloofness and impenetrability. Greek architecture, both religious and civic, is marked by its balanced proportions, which induce a sense of serenity, stability and luminosity. Roman architecture exhibits a solid style which is at once pragmatic and triumphalist. Byzantine cathedrals and palaces exploit the glittering power of mosaics to hide matter and convey the luminous symbolism of divine essence. Gothic cathedrals celebrate the transcendence of God and induce a sense of the disproportion between human creature and the Creator. In the Renaissance, as in ancient Greece, architecture pursues elegance of proportion and luminosity of space, attuned to the centrality of the human figure. The Baroque produced works of dramatic movement and theatrical spectacle. The eighteenth and nineteenth centuries built opulent and imperial neoclassical cities. The twentieth century has exploited unprecedented technical and material innovations to achieve the highest degree of agility, adaptability and functionality. It tends to celebrate industry, finance and technology, although in recent years it has also attempted to integrate new works within the existing frame of old cities, and in general to reintegrate itself with human presence.

Sculpture: Its Definition and Its Elements

Architecture, as we have seen, is pre-eminently an art of space. But the representation and exploitation of space is important also in sculpture and painting. These arts, however, are addressed primarily to sight and touch. Sculptural works induce us to move around them, both physically and imaginatively, rather as if we were encountering the external spaces of architecture. Conversely, some monumental architecture invites us to experience it as if it were sculpture. But sculpture is different none the less. For sculptures stand before us as physical objects, without any internal space, and without any primary functional purpose. We could also say that sculpture creates the illusion of space, rather than a real space.

Sculptures are visual, three-dimensional objects, placed in space and constituting a static mass or volume. Like architecture and painting, sculpture works with static, inorganic and relatively unchangeable materials. It is primarily a static art, an art of rest. As Alain has remarked, 'There is always a certain expression of madness in the statues that dance or smile. We could say that the search for movement makes even more evident the immobility of marble' (Alain 1926, p. 210). But paradoxically, this static art has nearly always represented living beings: plants, animals, humans. Prior to the avant-garde we do not find any sculpture – as autonomous work, and not just as ornamental adjunct – that is comparable to still-life painting.

Etymologically, the word 'sculpture' derives from the Latin *sculpere*, meaning 'to carve'. When we refer to sculpture as a 'plastic' art, we make implicit reference to the Greek verb *plésso*, which signifies the activity of moulding. Sculpture therefore comprises all types of production of figurative tridimensional works, whether in full relief (*tutto tondo*), or in partial relief (high and low relief, incision, stamping, graffito). When in partial relief, as if it were in two dimensions, sculpture comes closer to painting, and exploits some of the visual devices of painting: drawing and design, chiaroscuro, illusions of depth and space. The techniques of sculpture can be either carving or moulding of any kind of material: wood, stone, marble, bronze, clay, gold and silver, precious stones. The difference in the materials chosen is of enormous importance. Not only do they require different technical skills, but they can achieve different aesthetic effects and carry different expressive values.

Some Theoretical Considerations

A vast abundance of sculpture has been produced throughout history, but it is an art that has given rise to very little theoretical literature prior to the eighteenth century. Even technical literature has been thin on the ground, especially when compared with painting. In general, the aesthetic and poetic principles of antiquity were applied also to sculpture, which was regarded as an imitative, representational art ruled by mathematical laws of proportion.

Polyclitus, a sculptor of the fifth century BC, is said to have formalised these laws, in a treatise known as the *Canon*. This defined the canon or norm for the representation of a perfect, idealised, sculptured human body. His statue of the *Doriphoros* was deemed to illustrate these canonical principles. The influence of Polyclitus' canon was so long-lasting that, in the second century AD, Galenus could write:

> Chrysippus holds beauty to consist in the proportions, not of elements, but of parts. That is to say, of finger to finger and of all the fingers to the palm and wrist, to each other, as they are set out in the *Canon* of Polyclitus. For Polyclitus, when he had taught us all the proportions of the human figure by means of that treatise, confirmed his theory by a practical illustration and made a statue according to the dictates of the theory, and called the statue, like the treatise, his *Canon*. (Diels-Krantz, Frg. A3, quoted in Tatarkiewicz 1970, I, p. 77)

And, somewhat further on, Galenus added, 'After all, the statue by Polyclitus called Canon acquired that name because it possesses typical proportions in so far as the mutual relations of all parts of the body are concerned.' A second *Canon* was attributed to Lysippus, in the fourth century BC, whose concrete embodiment was said to be the sculptor's statue of the *Apoxiómenos*.

The canonical principles of classical Greek sculpture remained virtually unchallenged, even though they may have been elaborated and modified, until the emergence of the contemporary avant-garde.

Both Alberti and Michelangelo subscribed to them. The Baroque era dramatised and in a sense violated them, but none the less assumed them as the classical standard. Both Neoclassicism and nineteenth-century realism retrieved and reinstated them. Rodin and Maillol adopted them. Winckelmann, Lessing and Hegel saw in Greek statuary the apex and perfection of sculpture. Hegel, in fact, considered sculpture, and in particular Greek and Renaissance sculpture, to be the art most expressive of the classical harmony between what is said and how it is said.

Only with the avant-garde (futurism, constructivism, dadaism and surrealism, cubism and happenings, environmental sculpture, *arte povera* and so on) were the classical canons finally abandoned. It also abandoned the aspirations of representational sculpture. Nowadays, the sculptured work is conceived of as an autonomous object that interacts with external space. Abstract form, rather than the human form, is the goal. The traditional, fundamentally static nature of sculpture has been challenged and replaced in experiments with mobiles and other sorts of kinetic structures and effects.

History and Styles

The very first human artefacts, such as flints and utensils, could be considered the earliest attempts at sculpting, or at least at the skills of moulding and carving. The paleolithic age has left us a number of almond-shaped carvings of the female figure, the primitive 'Venuses' which can be called sculptures in the full sense. There also survive various decorated and carved objects, made from stone, bone or ivory, which have the character of sculpture. Sculpture, or sculpting, seems to have come before painting, possibly because a sculpted representation can be an independent object in its own right, not just an adornment of another object. Here, we shall confine ourselves to sculpting in the Western tradition, which includes neighbouring cultures in the pre-Hellenic period.

The Egyptians and the Assyrians, and other civilisations of the ancient Near East, achieved a high degree of perfection in their sculpture, which was closely linked to religious cults. The statue of a God was more than a representation, for it was also a symbolic substitute for the God's own presence. This is why food offerings were placed in front of statues. An animistic and symbolic conception of reality induced these cultures to believe that the gods represented by the statues actually inhabited the sculpted images.

Apart from their aesthetic merits, these works illustrate three points of interest. First, sculpture was understood to be part of architecture, for the statues were placed within architectural spaces and were related to the structure of those spaces. We are reminded here of the distinction between a sculpted monument and a statue. A monument, in this context, means a sculpted figure, or a group of statues or a group of reliefs, which are inserted into an architectural structure.

Secondly, Egyptian statues are carved in full relief, but they are visible from only three sides, and carved on only three sides. This is because in many cases they are carved in the side of a natural wall, such as a cliff face. Egyptian sculptures of the human figure were generally of a funerary or religious nature, and they convey a sense of eternity, sacredness and immobility. They thus manifest an almost universal aesthetic feature of all sculpture, in that it embodies ideal and supratemporal values.

Thirdly, ancient sculptures – especially statues rather than monumental sculptures – were adorned with paint, and so shared some of the visual properties of the art of painting. The Egyptians did this, and so did the classical Greeks. We can speculate that the paints were used to maximise the interaction of the volumes with light.

The art of sculpture reached its full maturity and perfection, both technically and aesthetically, in classical Greece. The Greeks liberated sculpted figures from their monumental, architectural, past. Even when employed as columns, as in the case of the *Chariátides* in the small temple on the Athenian Acropolis, the figures were treated as independent and individual units. Greek statues achieved a complete freedom of all their dimensions in space, yet combined this with the sacredness and dignity of the figures which, though human, symbolised mythical and divine beings.They combined textural variety and chiaroscuro on their surfaces with a stability and fullness of construction. Their idealised representations of the human body display a perfect proportion and a luminous visibility. They combined vitality with a restrained sense of movement.

This high degree of perfection in their statuary was matched by the perfection of their reliefs. The reliefs that once adorned the Parthenon, now in the British Museum, are cases in point. We must note, of course, the difference between a statue and a relief. The former represents a single and supratemporal figure, frozen in time regardless of its expressive vitality. The latter portrays groups of figures and articulates a narrative unfolding in time.

One final point. In classical Greece, sculptors were individually known and their names were famous, and each of them possessed a distinctive and individual style.

In the Middle Ages, up to the eleventh century at any rate, figurative artists returned to a condition of anonymity. Statuary was re-absorbed into architecture, and various subclasses of sculpture thrived, such as woodcutting, incision, relief, gold and silver smithery, jewellery. But with the emergence of Gothic in the High Middle Ages, sculpture re-emerged also in its independence and its character as the highest form of statuary. This was a culture that celebrated the dignity of a redeemed mankind, together with the divine order of the cosmos and the transcendence of God. Increasingly, however, Gothic sculpture became more naturalistic, and conveyed a sense of life, movement and expression. Its forms were increasingly humanised, and its surfaces were given textural qualities which enabled them to interact more effectively with their surroundings.

The Renaissance witnessed a prodigious triumph of the art of sculpture, as well, of course, as in all of the other arts. The classical Greek ideals were infused with a new energy, and a new sensibility attentive to the perfection of the human body. Portrait statuary flourished, and sculptural works were integrated into the surrounding spaces of the cities. In some cases sculptures actually determined and defined urban spaces.

Renaissance sculpture inevitably invokes the name of Michelangelo. This great genius subscribed to the traditional canons of proportion, but also achieved an energy and drama that conveyed powerfully expressive values. In a sense he disrupted the ideal balance and serenity of Greek sculpture by imbuing his works with a dramatic psychological pathos. He animated his works by means of complex arrangements of planes and elaborate manipulations of surfaces. Thus he was able to portray the heroic traits of human existence – struggle, suffering, pensiveness and triumph – in work after work: the statues in the Medici Chapel, his *David*, *Moses*, his various *Pietà*s. There is also his unfinished *Prigioni* or *Slaves*, in which we feel that the forms are actually emerging from the block of marble. It was Michelangelo who defined sculpture as the art of 'taking away'. He was expressing his Neoplatonic conception of a form locked, as it were, within the block of stone, awaiting the sculptor to liberate it from the enveloping matter. This was sculpture as a struggle against the inanimate stone, in order to conquer its resistance and make it docile to the artist and obedient to his intellect.

The age of Baroque emphasised even more the properties of vitality and drama. This new sensibility exercised inventiveness to the point of theatrical excess, and produced works of sinuous fluidity. Bernini, representative of this sensibility, used sculpture to express deep psychological experiences, as in his languid *Saint Teresa of Avila*, an ambiguous symbiosis of sensuality and spirituality. Baroque sculpture also was drawn to the monumental, as with the fountain in the Piazza Navona. It aimed at theatrical spectacle, not least in order to celebrate the triumphant Counter-Reformation. This spectacular character was abandoned in the succeeding centuries, and sculpture returned to its concern with the intrinsic value of the sculpted object. The last classical sculptors, we might say, were Rodin and Maillol.

In the twentieth century, sculpture also produced its avant-garde. It became common to disregard the traditional interest in the figurative, or the mimetic in any shape or form. Another impulse led to the exploration of movement, as if to defy the law of gravity. These impulses led to Boccioni's futurist works, and later to Calder's mobiles. Later again there were attempts to present movement as actual, real change, for instance by wrapping buildings with sheets of canvas or plastic, or by exhibiting real human or animal bodies. New developments in painting also spilled over into sculpture, so that the conceptions of space and volume were subverted. With Moore, Arp and Brancusi, volume is privileged so that the space surrounding it collapses into the totally autonomous mass. Another form of subversion was the introduction of readymades into a museum or gallery, in order to shock and estrange the viewer.

Despite recent excesses of experimentation (dead sheep, heaps of stone, grease, ordure, digging up a hole – with a JCB – in Central Park and filling it up again), sculpture has resisted attempts to reduce it entirely to abstract expression. Many sculptors still practise their art in some kind of continuity with the classical ideals. One example is Henry Moore, who, even with his relatively abstract works, has remained connected with representational statuary. Some others are – to mention a few – Marini, Sadkine and Manzù, who, rather than reject tradition, have renewed it by expanding its possibilities.

Painting: Its Definition and Its Elements

Painting can be defined as the art of colours. Colours are its primary, and its essential, materials. Painting addresses itself to our sense of sight, and is an exclusively visual art form. Tactile experiences – of texture, space or depth – are derivative from visual perception, and are, in a sense and in differing degrees, illusions. Painting creates visual messages on a two-dimensional surface. Because of the wide variety of these surfaces, it uses a wide variety of techniques and tools. Some of its sub-genres are: design, drawing, manuscript illumination, glass staining, engraving, woodcutting, etching.

Colours, and by implication light, are the primary materials of painting. But this does not exclude other elements, such as lines, volumes, mass, textures. These elements are corollaries of colour, and are produced by mainly chromatic methods. A line, for instance, is a chromatic trace on a two-dimensional surface. Lines are unable to convey the illusion of depth, unless they are supplemented by other symbolic and iconic devices. Thus, large lines and larger delineated objects are perceived as being closer to the viewer than thin lines and small drawings. We can see this effect even in naive and primitive drawings.

When lines and colours are employed with the technique of chiaroscuro, they produce the three-dimensional effect of volume, which fills in and gives body to the represented objects, and increases their individuality. Some striking examples of this are the drawings and preparatory sketches or *bozzetti* of architects, sculptors and painters, or the astonishing etchings of Dürer. When chromatic volumes are combined and interrelated in a pictorial composition, they produce mass of a kind that is more than the illusion of three-dimensional space and depth. Mass refers to a rich complexity of interactive spaces, depths and planes. It is to be found in elaborate landscapes, the spaces of architecture, sculpture, paintings and – a special case – paintings with mirrors and mirrored images within the painting.

Even though painting is essentially an art of light and colours, it has traditionally been representational as well. As a consequence, it has always been concerned with, and challenged by, the creation of spatiality. Visual objects, after all, exist in space and are experienced in space. We have mentioned some methods of achieving this; and painters have also used the laws of optics and perspective. But another element in painting is time. Lessing may have distinguished between spatial and temporal arts, but painting, even though it is primarily spatial, also implies diachrony. The experience of seeing is not instantaneous, but unfolds in time. And there are visual narratives – even in apparently atemporal landscapes and still-lifes – which carry with them references to imaginatively constructed time.

Some Theoretical Considerations

Theories of painting have focused on three main sets of issues: (1) technical problems of production and studies of materials; (2) problems relating to ways of creating the illusion of space; (3) pictorial representation or mimetic figuration, and consequent debates about figurative versus abstract painting.

Prior to the avant-garde revolution at the beginning of the twentieth century, painting was almost universally representational. It was thought of as being an art of representing figures and objects on a flat surface, in a manner that involved the illusion of space and volume. The different subject-matters of such painting produced three genres: paintings of human models; landscapes and paintings of animals and natural subjects; and finally, ornamental painting. The most striking advances in representational painting were made at the time of the Renaissance, when the study of perspective involved advanced scientific and mathematical skills. The Renaissance also perfected the medium of oil paint, which replaced the use of tempera and mainly organic-based pigments.

With the avant-garde, a new theory and poetics of painting appeared, which rejected representation in favour of more abstract, formal and autonomous treatments of pictorial elements. And at the same time, painters started to experiment with a large variety of materials other than oil paints.

Antiquity and the Middle Ages

The prehistoric cave paintings, which we considered above in Chapter 2, were two-dimensional only. The various figures, though they seem to be organised with some element of structural composition, are related to each other only as a contiguous series of separate images. The lines are, indeed, filled with colours – very few colours – but the colours are entirely contained within the contours of the drawings, with no chromatic relation to other figures on the same plane.

The same remarks can be made about pre-Greek and archaic Greek art: Cycladic, Minoan and Mycenean painting. Of course, most of our knowledge of early Greek painting is gleaned from their vases, where we find that the pictorial elements are two-dimensional, geometric and decorative.

With the birth of philosophical thought, and the attendant disposition to examine the world as an object of detached observation and scientific reflection, painting began to represent objects more realistically, and as three-dimensional. Chromatic values and differences were exploited in order to create volumes, and thus to produce the illusion of well-defined and individual objects. This illusionistic virtuosity of painters was greatly appreciated and valued (though not by Plato). The mimetic naturalism of classical Greek painting allowed them also to represent atemporal and ideal visual models. There appeared the beginnings of pictorial narrative, but a narrative outside or above time, a sort of synchronic narrative.

It was some centuries later, in Roman painting, that we find the pictorial articulation of diachronic narratives. Roman visual texts, more realistic and less idealistic than the Greek, are imbued with a sense of movement and time. Greek painting produced representations of volume, but Roman painting developed volumes into mass. It engaged in a sophisticated and complex articulation of spaces, depths and planes, gave a greater coherence to its visual narratives, and was thus able to fuse together all the elements and figures of their compositions. The connective tissue was provided by their exploitation of light and chromatic values. Light was used more realistically than in Greek painting. It articulated real variations in the environment: the light of day or night, of the seasons of the year, of internal or external spaces.

Byzantine painting was best expressed in mosaic. The prevailing religious sensibility sought to represent the atemporal, and, for this purpose, light was seen as the perfect medium. Light and chromatic effects were used to hide matter, to metamorphose matter into the ethereal element of light. Colours were employed in their chromatic purity. Mass and volume either disappeared or were absorbed into a two-dimensional space. A stylised geometric order ruled the composition.

The closed, linear, two-dimensional forms of medieval painting were eventually disrupted in the Gothic centuries, due in part to the influence of sculpture and architecture. Gothic art returned to a more realistic, more plastic and spatial, and more pictorial narrative. The first outstanding exponents of this new pictorial sensibility were Giotto and Cimabue. It is worth noting the sculptural character of Giotto's painting. Giotto also depicted figures seen from behind, and this helped to create a sense of depth and movement. It compels the viewer to move in imagination round the figure, seeking its face and its gaze.

The Renaissance

The Renaissance overflowed with technical, poetic and aesthetic theories of painting. One interesting debate concerned the question of supremacy in the visual arts. Some considered sculpture to be superior to painting because it was less illusionistic, more three-dimensional and realistic. Leonardo and others argued that painting was superior, because it was at once an art and a science. Painting embodied our scientific knowledge of nature, and represented spaces in linear perspective. It transformed natural space into an ideal space governed by the laws of optics and geometry.

Later in the Renaissance, the Venetian schools of painting began to break away from the geometric rigidity of linear perspective. They placed more emphasis on the role of chromatic values, which enabled them to construct free-flowing pictorial narratives. They exploited the tonal qualities of colours, both to organise the mass of the composition, and also to convey the vast range of intensities of light. Prior to this, colours signified light resting on the surfaces of volumes and figures, but in Venetian painting colour was used to produce light itself. Colour was light.

Giorgione was one of the pioneers of this pictorial and stylistic revolution. After it had taken place, painting was established in its full autonomy as the art of light and colour. After the Venetians, painting was set on the path that was to lead to Impressionism.

Modern Times and the Avant-garde

In modern times the greatest revolution in painting, before the avant-garde, was accomplished by the Impressionists. Prior to the Impressionists, painters tended to be academic and traditionalist, working in the artificial environment of their studios, and concerned with naturalistic modes of representation. The Impressionists abandoned the overriding concern for naturalism and, most importantly, took their canvases into the open air. Although the technique of oil-paint production and preservation had been quite sophisticated for some centuries before them, an apparently very simple invention particularly enabled them to do this – to go out and paint outdoors – with greater ease: namely, the collapsible tin or lead tube, which allowed painters to carry their paints around with them, without fear of either spoiling or wasting them. Certainly they had no need, instead, of laboriously having to grind pigments and mix their paints in a studio, as it had been done for many centuries before them.

The move away from figurative representation may have been due in part to the new art of photography, which seemed to be able to capture the shapes of things more accurately than painting. But more important was a new way of conceiving the art of painting itself – as an art returning to its essential elements of light and colour. Painting in the open air lent an extra impetus to this, and encouraged techniques of foregrounding chromatic values and light values, at the expense – one could say – of drawing, contours, chiaroscuro, tones and shading.

The Impressionist emphasis on purely visual elements of light and colour, and its relative indifference to mimetic realism, prepared the ground for avantgarde poetics. Another factor, although this is more debatable, was the emergence of new scientific theories which questioned the traditional understanding of space and time. In any case, the avant-garde completely abandoned the pursuit of a three-dimensional spatiality that was illusionistic and naturalistic, and even abandoned representationalism altogether. It foregrounded visual elements for their own sake, aiming at the pure interplay of simple colours. It purveyed no narratives, but created abstractions in two dimensions through lines and textures and cubistic planes, which merely hinted at volume and mass. Its intentional rejection of the past, in dadaism, surrealism, futurism, cubism, expressionism, constructivism, conceptual art, minimalism and the like, expressed a deep dissatisfaction with a pictorial language which had exhausted its expressive and technical possibilities.

The avant-garde, and experimental painting in general, has suffered its casualties and produced its peripheral aberrations. In the end it came to be seen that abstractivism and experimentation could not be carried any further. Postmodernism has, perhaps, come to the rescue, by revisiting and retrieving themes and techniques of past traditions. The figurative and the narrative have returned to the canvas, and with them have come a playful irony and various intertextual games. The viewer is less alienated by extreme novelty, and we can cheerfully return to exhibitions of paintings with renewed expectations.

Some Philosophic and Aesthetic Considerations

In classical antiquity, philosophical reflection on painting focused more or less exclusively on its mimetic character. This was also a pre-occupation in the Middle Ages and in the Renaissance, but there was an additional problem, connected with the use of painting to articulate and communicate biblical events and religious truths. Iconoclasm, and the debates that it provoked, revealed a tendency either to shower the highest praise upon painting, or to condemn it as an encouragement to idolatry. In the latter view we find the hidden presence of Platonic suspicions, and a manifestation of the prevailing theocentric conception of reality.

During the Renaissance, mimesis was understood in a manner more faithful and congenial to the original Aristotelian concept, signifying the ability to reproduce, in art, the inner workings of nature. Many of the treatises on painting, however, were either technical manuals or poetic programmes. Cennini's *Il libro dell'arte* is clearly of the first kind, while Alberti's *De pictura* and Leonardo's *Trattato della pittura* are of the second kind. There were some more lofty and abstract discussions of aesthetic ideas and questions in thinkers belonging to the Neoplatonist tradition.

The aesthetic theories of the seventeenth and eighteenth centuries did not contribute much to our understanding of painting. Kant, on the other hand, proclaimed that it was the most important of the figurative arts.

> Among the formative arts I would give the palm to painting: partly because it is the art of design and, as such, the groundwork of all the other formative arts; partly because it can penetrate much further into the region of ideas, and in conformity with them give a greater extension to the field of intuition than it is open to the others to do. (*Critique of Judgment*, [1790] (1952), Part One, § 53)

Hegel agreed with this assessment, and made use also of ideas taken from Herder, Humboldt and Schelling to argue that painting is superior to both sculpture and architecture. He considered painting to be a modern art, congenial to the Romantic sensibility, while sculpture was a classical art characterised by its perfect balance between content and form. Romantic art, in Hegel's view, refuses to portray God in external representations. Rather, it represents the Absolute as inwardness in outwardness, by means of light and colour, materials which are akin to the spirituality of the Absolute. Herder had said that sculpture is closer to truth, painting to dream. Humboldt thought that sculpture was the art of the external, painting the art of psychological inwardness. All of the Romantics, however, were concerned with problems of the narrative and ideological content of painting.

With Johann Friedrich Herbart we witness – as we have noted before – a shift of attention from the content of art to its form. Herbart's formalism heralded the psychological and empirical studies of the arts that were to follow. He was also ancestor to the theories of pure visibility and to the *Einfühlung* or empathy theory. Pure visibility theories argued that form should be completely detached from considerations of feeling. The Empathy theory, first formulated by Friedrich Theodor Vischer, in 1866 – later developed by his son Robert Vischer, by Theodor Lipps in the 1890s, and finally by Wilhelm Worringer (1908) – argued that there is a relationship between states of mind and elementary visual forms such as the vertical, the horizontal, up and down, straight and curved, continuous and discontinuous, unified and fragmented, and so on. Hence, a painting can be imbued with the imaginary and affective projections of our feelings, which we come to experience as if they were objective features of the painting.

Impressionism, with its immediate and diverse offspring – Van Gogh and Gauguin, Matisse and Monet, Cézanne and Picasso, still alien to radical rejection of the past and to gratuitous experimentation – and the radical avant-garde have produced a large variety of poetic programmes, projects and manifestos, and provoked a flurry of theoretical and critical reflections upon the nature of painting. More recently, also with reference to painting, as with all the other forms of art, there has been something of an increasing move away from aesthetic preoccupations with the beauty of the work, to poetic considerations concerning the ways of artistic production and the immanent or objective constitution of the individual work of art. Structuralism, formalism and semiotics have provided novel tools for the investigation of the arts, and have been proven to be – more so than other methods and approaches – particularly suited to the analysis of contemporary movements such as the avant-garde and postmodernism, and of contemporary culture in general (see Eco 1962 and 1989; Nöth 1990, pp. 456–9; Santoro-Brienza 1993, pp. 78–92).

Bibliography

Adorno, Theodor Wiesengrund [1949], *Philosophy of Modern Music*, trans. Anne G. Mitchell and Wesley V. Blomster, London: Sheed & Ward, 1973.

Alain (1926), *Système des beaux-arts*, Paris: Gallimard.

Alberti, Leon Battista [1452], *Ten Books on Architecture*, trans. James Leoni, facsimile of 1775 edition, London: Alec Tiranti, 1965.

Alberti, Leon Battista, *On Painting and on Sculpture* [*De pictura*, 1435; *De statua*, 1464], trans. C. Grayson, London, 1972.

Alperson, Philip (ed.) (1992), *The Philosophy of the Visual Arts*, New York and Oxford: Oxford University Press.

Alperson, Philip (ed.) (1994), *What is Music?*, University Park, Pennsylvania: Pennsylvania State University Press.

Alperson, Philip (ed.) (1998), *Musical Worlds: New Directions in the Philosophy of Music*, University Park, Pennsylvania: Pennsylvania State University Press.

Aquinas, Thomas (1980), *Opera Omnia*, ed. Roberto Busa, 7 vols, Stuttgart: Frommann-Holzboog.

Aristotle (1984), *The Complete Works of Aristotle*, ed. Jonathan Barnes, 2 vols, Princeton (New Jersey): Princeton University Press.

Arnheim, Rudolf [1956], *Art and Visual Perception*, new version, Berkeley and Los Angeles: University of California Press, 1974.

Arnheim, Rudolf (1958), *Film as Art*, London: Faber.

Arnheim, Rudolf (1969), *Visual Thinking*, Berkeley and Los Angeles: University of California Press.

Arnheim, Rudolf (1986), *New Essays on the Psychology of Art*, Berkeley and Los Angeles: University of California Press.

Arnheim, Rudolf (1992), *To the Rescue of Art*, Berkeley and Los Angeles: University of California Press.

Arnott, Peter D. (1989), *Public and Performance in the Greek Theatre*, London: Routledge.

Artusi, Giovanni Maria (1600–3), *L'Artusi, overo Delle imperfettioni della moderna musica ragionamenti dui*, Venice.

Auerbach, Erich (1953), *Mimesis*, trans. Willard Trask, Princeton (New Jersey): Princeton University Press.

Augustine, *De musica* [On Music], in Migne, *Patrologia Latina*, Vol. 32, cols 1082–1194.

Augustine (1947), *On Music*, in *Writings of St. Augustine*, in *The Fathers of the Church*, trans. R. C. Tagliaferro, Washington DC: Catholic University of America Press, Vol. 4, pp. 169–379.

Augustine (1951), *Letter 18*, in *Letters*, trans. Sister Wilfred Parsons,

Washington DC: Catholic University of America Press, Vol. I, pp. 43–4.

Augustine (1953), *De vera religione* [Of True Religion], in *Augustine: Earlier Writings*, ed. and trans. John H. S. Burleigh, London: SCM Press, pp. 225–323.

Augustine (1953), *Soliloquia* [The Soliloquies], in *Augustine: Earlier Writings*, ed. and trans. John H. S. Burleigh, London: SCM Press, pp. 26–63.

Augustine (1961), *Confessions*, trans. R. S. Pine-Coffin, Harmondsworth: Penguin.

Augustine (1970), *De ordine* [On Order], in *Corpus Christianorum, Series Latina*, ed. W. M. Green, Turnhoult: Brepols, Vol. 29, pp. 89–137.

Augustine (1972), *City of God*, trans. Henry Bettenson, Harmondsworth: Penguin.

Barnett, Dene (1987), *The Art of Gesture: The Practices and Principles of 18th Century Acting*, Heidelberg: Carl Winter.

Barrett, Cyril (1963), 'The Aesthetics of St. Thomas Re-examined', *Philosophical Studies*, 12, pp. 107–24.

Barthes, Roland (1977), 'The Death of the Author', in *Image–Music–Text*, trans. Stephen Heath, Glasgow: Fontana/Collins, pp. 142–8.

Barthes, Roland (1985), *The Fashion System*, trans. Matthew Ward and Richard Howard, London: Jonathan Cape.

Baxandall, Michael (1972), *Painting and Experience in Fifteenth-century Italy*, New York and Oxford: Oxford University Press.

Beacham, Richard C. (1991), *The Roman Theatre and Its Audience*, London: Routledge.

Beardsley, Monroe C. (1966), *Aesthetics from Classical Greece to the Present*, New York: Macmillan.

Beardsley, Monroe C. (1988), *Aesthetics: Problems in the Philosophy of Criticism*, 2nd edn, Indianapolis and Cambridge: Hackett.

Bell, Clive (1914), *Art*, London: Chatto & Windus (latest edn: Oxford University Press, 1987).

Berenson, Bernard (1950), *Aesthetics and History*, London: Constable.

Bernstein, Leonard (1976), *The Unanswered Question*, Cambridge (Mass.): Harvard University Press.

Bloch, Ernst (1985), *Essays on the Philosophy of Music*, trans. Peter Palmer, Cambridge: Cambridge University Press.

Blunt, Anthony (1940), *Artistic Theory in Italy 1450–1600*, London: Oxford University Press.

Boas, Franz [1927], *Primitive Art*, New York: Dover, 1955.

Boethius, *De institutione musicae*, in Migne, *Patrologia Latina*, Vol. 63, cols 1167–1300.

Bowie, Andrew (1990), *Aesthetics and Subjectivity: From Kant to Nietzsche*, Manchester and New York: Manchester University Press.

Bredin, Hugh (1977), 'The Theory of Beauty', in *Philosophy and Totality*, ed. J. McEvoy, Belfast: The Queen's University of Belfast.

Bredin, Hugh (1984), 'Sign and Value in Saussure', *Philosophy*, 59, pp. 67–77.

Bredin, Hugh (1986), 'I. A. Richards and the Philosophy of Practical Criticism', *Philosophy and Literature*, 10, pp. 26–37.

Bredin, Hugh (1996), 'Onomatopoeia as a Figure and a Linguistic Principle', *New Literary History*, 27, pp. 555–69.

Brelet, Gisèle (1946), 'Musique et silence', *La Revue Musicale*, pp. 169–81.

Brelet, Gisèle (1947), *Esthétique et création musicale*, Paris: PUF.

Brelet, Gisèle (1949), *Le Temps musical*, 2 vols, Paris: PUF.

Bremmer, Jan and Roodenburg, Herman (eds) (1991), *A Cultural History of Gesture: From Antiquity to the Present Day*, Cambridge: Polity Press.

Brook, Peter (1968), *The Empty Space*, London: McGibbon & Kee.

Budd, Malcolm (1995), *Values of Art*, Harmondsworth: Penguin.

Calbris, Geneviève (1990), *The Semiotics of French Gesture*, Bloomington: Indiana University Press.

Carlson, Marvin (1984), *Theories of the Theatre*, Ithaca and London: Cornell University Press.

Casetti, Francesco (1998), *Inside the Gaze: The Fiction Film and Its Spectator*, trans. Nell Andrew with Charles O'Brien, Bloomington: Indiana University Press.

Cennini, Cennino d'Andrea (1933), *The Craftsman's Handbook* [*Il libro dell'arte*], trans. Daniel V. Thompson, New Haven: Yale University Press (New York: Dover, 1960).

Chadwick, Henry (1981), *Boethius: The Consolations of Music, Logic, Theology, and Philosophy*, Oxford: Clarendon Press.

Chambers, E. K. (1903), *The Medieval Stage*, 2 vols, London: Oxford University Press.

Chomsky, Noam (1965), *Aspects of the Theory of Syntax*, Cambridge (Mass.): MIT Press.

Cicero (1942), *De oratore*, trans. E. W. Sutton and H. Rackham, London: Heinemann; Cambridge (Mass.): Harvard University Press.

Coggin, Philip A. (1956), *Drama and Education: An Historical Survey from Ancient Greece to the Present Day*, London: Thames & Hudson.

Collaer, Paul (1961), *A History of Modern Music*, trans. Sally Abeles, New York: Grosset & Dunlap.

Cooke, Deryck (1959), *The Language of Music*, London, Oxford and New York: Oxford University Press.

Cooper, David E. (1997), *Aesthetics: The Classic Readings*, Oxford: Blackwell.

Copland, Aaron (1961), *Copland on Music*, London: Deutsch.

Croce, Benedetto (1902), *Aesthetic*, trans. Douglas Ainslie, London: Macmillan.

Currie, Gregory (1989), *An Ontology of Art*, London: Macmillan; Cambridge (Mass.): Harvard University Press.

Dahlhaus, Carl (1982), *Esthetics of Music*, Cambridge and New York: Cambridge University Press.

Dante Alighieri (1924) *Opere di Dante Alighieri*, ed. E. Moore and P. Toynbee, 4th edn, Oxford: Nella Stamperia dell'Università.

Davies, Stephen (1991), *Definitions of Art*, Ithaca and New York: Cornell University Press.

De Bruyne, Edgar (1946), *Etudes d'esthétique médiévale*, 3 vols, Bruges: De Tempel.

Descartes, René [1631], *Letter to Balzac, 15th April 1630*, in *Oeuvre de Descartes*, ed. Charles Adam and Paul Tannery, 11 vols, Paris: Vrin, 1969, Vol. I, pp. 196–9.

Descartes, René [1630], *Letter to Mersenne, 18th March 1630*, in *Descartes:*

Philosophical Letters, ed. and trans. by Anthony Kenny, Oxford: Clarendon Press, 1970, pp. 7–8.

De Schloezer, Boris (1947), *Introduction à J. S. Bach: Essai d'esthétique musicale*, Paris: PUF.

Dewey, John (1934), *Art as Experience*, New York: Capricorn.

Dewey, John (1958), *Experience and Nature*, 2nd edn, New York: Dover.

Dialexeis (1952), in *Die Fragmente der Vorsokratiker*, ed. by Herman Diels, 6th ed. edited by Walther Kranz, 2 vols, Berlin: Weidmannsche, Vol. II, pp. 405–16.

Dickie, George (1969), 'Defining Art', *American Philosophical Quarterly*, pp. 252–8.

Dickie, George (1974), *Art and the Aesthetic*, Ithaca, New York and London: Cornell University Press.

Dickie, George (1988), *Evaluating Art*, Philadelphia: Temple University Press.

Diffey, Terry J. (1969), 'The Republic of Art', *The British Journal of Aesthetics*, 9, pp. 145–56.

Diffey, Terry J. (1973), 'Essentialism and the Definition of Art', *The British Journal of Aesthetics*, 13, pp. 103–20.

Diffey, Terry J. (1979), 'On Defining Art', *The British Journal of Aesthetics*, 19, pp. 15–23.

Diogenes Laertius (1925), *Lives of Eminent Philosophers*, trans. R. D. Hicks, 2 vols, London: Heinemann; Cambridge (Mass.): Harvard University Press.

Dufrenne, Mikel (1973), *The Phenomenology of Aesthetic Experience*, trans. Edward S. Casey and others, Evanston: Northwestern University Press.

Dufrenne, Mikel and Formaggio, Dino (eds) (1981), *Trattato di estetica*, 2 vols, Milan: Mondadori.

Durant, Albert (1984), *Conditions of Music*, London: Macmillan.

Dvorák, Max (1967), *Idealism and Naturalism in Gothic Art*, trans. Randolph J. Klawiter, Notre Dame (Ind.): University of Notre Dame Press.

Eagleton, Terry (1996), *Literary Theory: An Introduction*, 2nd edn, Oxford: Blackwell.

Eco, Umberto [1959], *Art and Beauty in the Middle Ages*, trans. Hugh Bredin, New Haven and London: Yale University Press, 1986.

Eco, Umberto (1962), *Opera aperta*, 4th edn, Milan: Bompiani.

Eco, Umberto (1968), *La struttura assente*, Milan: Bompiani.

Eco, Umberto (1971), *Le forme del contenuto*, 2nd edn, Milan: Bompiani.

Eco, Umberto (1976), *A Theory of Semiotics*, Bloomington: Indiana University Press.

Eco, Umberto (1979), *Lector in fabula*, Milan: Bompiani.

Eco, Umberto (1988), *The Aesthetics of Thomas Aquinas*, trans. Hugh Bredin, Cambridge (Mass.): Harvard University Press.

Eco, Umberto (1989), *The Open Work*, Cambridge (Mass.): Harvard University Press.

Eco, Umberto (1990), *The Limits of Interpretation*, Bloomington and Indiana: Indiana University Press.

Eco, Umberto (1994), *Six Walks in the Fictional Woods*, Cambridge (Mass.)

and London: Harvard University Press.

Fischer, Ernst (1963), *The Necessity of Art*, Harmondsworth: Penguin.

Foucault, Michel (1984), 'What is an Author?', in *The Foucault Reader*, ed. Paul Rabinow, New York: Pantheon, pp. 101–20.

Foucault, Michel (1990), *The History of Sexuality: An Introduction*, trans. Robert Hurley, London: Penguin.

Fowler, Alastair (1982), *Kinds of Literature*, Oxford: Clarendon Press.

Fubini, Enrico (1991), *The History of Music Esthetics*, London: Macmillan.

Gadamer, Hans-Georg [1960], *Truth and Method*, trans. edited by Garrett Barden and John Cumming, New York: Crossroad, 1984.

Gadamer, Hans-Georg (1986), *The Relevance of the Beautiful and Other Essays*, trans. Nicholas Walker, Cambridge and New York: Cambridge University Press.

Genette, Gérard (1972), *Narrative Discourse*, trans. Jane E. Lewin, Oxford: Blackwell.

Gerwen, Rob van (1996), *Art and Experience*, Utrecht: Utrecht University Press.

Gilbert, Katharine Everett and Kuhn, Helmut (1939), *A History of Aesthetics*, Bloomington: Indiana University Press (and 2nd edn, New York: Dover, 1972).

Gombrich, Ernst H. (1977), *Art and Illusion*, 5th edn, Oxford: Phaidon Press.

Gombrich, Ernst H. (1979), *The Sense of Order*, Oxford: Phaidon Press.

Gombrich, Ernst H. and Gregory, R. L. (eds) (1973), *Illusion in Nature and Art*, London: Duckworth.

Goodman, Nelson (1976), *Languages of Art*, Indianapolis: Hackett.

Graf, Fritz (1991), 'Gestures and Conventions: The Gestures of Roman Actors and Orators', in Bremmer and Roodenburg (1991), pp. 36–58.

Graham, Gordon (1997), *Philosophy of the Arts*, London and New York: Routledge.

Gray, Bennison (1975), *The Phenomenon of Literature*, The Hague and Paris: Mouton.

Green, Lucy (1988), *Music on Deaf Ears*, Manchester and New York: Manchester University Press.

Gropius, Walter (1955), *Scope of Total Architecture*, Cambridge (Mass.): Harvard University Press.

Hamburger, Käte (1973), *The Logic of Literature*, trans. Marilynn J. Rose, Bloomington: Indiana University Press.

Hanfling, Oswald (ed.) (1992), *Philosophical Aesthetics: An Introduction*, Oxford and Cambridge (Mass.): Blackwell.

Hanslick, Eduard [1854], *On the Musically Beautiful* [*Vom Musikalisch-Schönen*], trans. Geoffrey Payzant, Indianapolis: Hackett, 1986.

Hanslick, Eduard (1950), *Music Criticisms 1846–99*, Harmondsworth: Penguin.

Harrison, Charles and Wood, Paul (eds) (1992), *Art in Theory: 1900–1990: An Anthology of Changing Ideas*, Oxford: Blackwell.

Hegel, G. W. F. [1842], *Aesthetics: Lectures on Fine Art*, trans. T. M. Knox, 2 vols, Oxford: Clarendon Press, 1975.

Heidegger, Martin [1927], *Being and Time*, trans. John Macquarrie and Edward Robinson, Oxford: Blackwell, 1967.

Heidegger, Martin (1971), 'The Origin of the Work of Art', in *Poetry, Language, Thought*, ed. and trans. A. Hofstadter, New York: Harper & Row, pp. 32–48.

Helmholtz, Hermann L. F. von [1877], *On the Sensations of Tone as a Physiological Basis for the Theory of Music*, trans. A. J. Ellis, New York: Dover, 1954.

Heraclitus (1948), *Fragments*, in Kathleen Freeman, *Ancilla to the Pre-Socratic Philosophers*, Oxford: Blackwell.

Herbart, Johann F. (1964), *Sämtliche Werke*, ed. K. Kehrbach and O. Flügel, 2nd edn, Aalen: Scientia Verlag.

Hernadi, Paul (1972), *Beyond Genre: New Directions in Literary Classification*, Ithaca, New York and London: Cornell University Press.

Howard, John Tasker and Lyons, James (1957), *Modern Music*, New York: Mentor.

Hrotsvit of Gandersheim (1966), *The Plays of Roswita*, trans. C. St John, New York: Benjamin Blom (reissue of 1923 edn published by Catto & Windus).

Hutcheson, Francis [1753], *An inquiry into the origin of our ideas of beauty and virtue*, 5th edn, London; New York: Garland, 1971 (facsimile edn).

Ingarden, Roman (1986), *The Work of Music and the Problem of Its Identity*, trans. Adam Czerniawski, London: Macmillan.

Isocrates (1928–45), *Panegyricus*, in *Isocrates*, trans. George Norlin and Larue van Hook, 3 vols, London: Heinemann; New York: Putnam's Sons; Cambridge (Mass.): Harvard University Press, Vol. I, pp. 121–241.

Jakobson, Roman (1960), 'Concluding Statement: Linguistics and Poetics', in Thomas A. Sebeok (ed.), *Style in Language*, Cambridge (Mass.): MIT Press.

Jakobson, Roman (1987), *Language in Literature*, Cambridge (Mass.): Harvard University Press.

James, Jamie (1995), *The Music of the Spheres*, London: Abacus.

Jencks, Charles (1986), *Modern Movements in Architecture*, 2nd edn, Harmondsworth: Penguin.

Kahler, Erich (1959), 'What is Art?', in *Problems in Aesthetics*, ed. Morris Weitz, 1st edn, New York: Macmillan, pp. 157–71.

Kaminsky, Jack (1962), *Hegel on Art: An Interpretation of Hegel's Aesthetics*, Albany: State University of New York Press.

Kandinsky, Wassily and Marc, Franz (eds) [1914], *The Blaue Reiter Almanac*, ed. Klaus Lankheit, trans. H. Falkenstein with the assistance of M. Terzian and G. Hinderlie, London: Thames & Hudson, 1974.

Kant, Immanuel [1790], *The Critique of Judgement*, trans. James Creed Meredith, Oxford: Clarendon Press, 1952.

Kastelanetz, Richard (1989), *Esthetics Contemporary*, Buffalo (New York): Prometheus Books.

Kierkegaard, Soren [1843], *Either/Or*, 2 vols, trans. Howard V. Hong and Edna H. Hong, Princeton (New Jersey): Princeton University Press, 1987.

Kircher, Athanasius (1650), *Musurgia universalis, sive Ars magna consoni et dissoni*, Rome.

Kovach, Francis J. (1963), 'The Transcendentality of Beauty in Thomas Aquinas', in *Die Metaphysik im Mittelalter* ed. P. Wilpert (Miscellanea Mediaevalia, II), Berlin: De Gruyter, pp. 386–392.

Kovach, Francis J. (1974), *Philosophy of Beauty*, Norman: University of Oklahoma Press.

Kurzschenkel, Winfried (1971), *Die theologische Bestimmung der Musik*, Trier: Paulinus-Verlag.

Lalo, Charles (1951), 'Esquisse d'une classification structurale des beaux-arts', *Journal de Psychologie Normale et Pathologique*, 44, pp. 9–37.

Lamarque, Peter (1996), *Fictional Points of View*, Ithaca and London: Cornell University Press.

Lamarque, Peter and Olsen, Stein Haugom (1994), *Truth, Fiction, and Literature*, Oxford: Clarendon Press.

Langer, Susanne K. (1951), *Philosophy in a New Key*, 3rd edn, Cambridge (Mass.): Harvard University Press; New York: Mentor.

Langer, Susanne K. (1953), *Feeling and Form*, London: Routledge & Kegan Paul.

Leibniz, Gottfried [1714], *Monadology*, in *Philosophical Papers and Letters*, ed. and trans. by Leroy E. Loemker, Dordrecht: Reidel, 1969, pp. 643–53.

Leonardo da Vinci (1952), *Selections from the Notebooks of Leonardo da Vinci*, ed. Irma A. Richter, London: Oxford University Press.

Leppet, Richard (1988), *Music and Image*, Cambridge and New York: Cambridge University Press.

Lessing, Gotthold [1766], *Laocoön*, trans. W. A. Steel, London: Dent, 1930.

Lévi-Strauss, Claude (1970), *The Raw and the Cooked*, trans. John and Doreen Weightman, London: Jonathan Cape.

Lippman, Edward A. (ed.) (1990), *Musical Aesthetics: A Historical Reader*, New York: Pandragon Press.

Locke, John [1690], *An Essay Concerning Human Understanding*, Oxford: Clarendon Press, 1975.

Luere, Jeane (ed.) (1994), *Playwright versus Director: Authorial Intentions and Performance Interpretations*, Westport (Conn.) and London: Greenwood Press.

Lukács, Georg (1920), *The Theory of the Novel*, trans. Anna Bostock, London: Merlin, 1978.

Lyas, Colin (1997), *Aesthetics*, London: UCL Press.

Lynton, Norbert (1989), *The Story of Modern Art*, 2nd edn, Oxford: Phaidon Press.

Maconie, Robin (1990), *The Concept of Music*, Oxford: Clarendon Press.

Macquet, Jacques (1986), *The Aesthetic Experience*, New Haven and London: Yale University Press.

Malraux, André (1954), *The Voices of Silence*, trans. Stuart Gilbert, London: Secker & Warburg.

Malraux, André (1960), *The Metamorphosis of the Gods*, trans. Stuart Gilbert, London: Secker & Warburg.

Mann, James W. (1998), *Aesthetics*, New York and London: M. E. Sharpe.

Martin, Graham (1975), *Language, Truth and Poetry*, Edinburgh: Edinburgh University Press.

Matejka, Ladislav and Titunik, Irwin R. (eds) (1976), *Semiotics of Art: Prague School Contributions*, Cambridge (Mass.) and London: MIT Press.

Meyer, Leonard B. (1989), *Style and Music*, Philadelphia: Pennsylvania University Press.

Meyer, Leonard B. (1994), *Music, the Arts and Ideas*, Chicago: University of Chicago Press.

Minor, Jakob (1882), *Friedrich Schlegel 1794–1802. Seine prosaischen Jugendschriften*, Vienna: Konegen.

Mitry, Jean (1998), *The Aesthetics and Psychology of the Cinema*, London: Athlone Press.

Moles, Abraham (1966), *Information Theory and Esthetic Perception*, trans. Joel E. Cohen, Urbana and London: University of Illinois Press.

Montagu, Ivor (1964), *Film World*, Harmondsworth: Penguin.

Mukarovsky, Jan [1932], 'Standard Language and Poetic Language', in *A Prague School Reader on Esthetics, Literary Structure, and Style*, ed. Paul L. Garvey, Washington DC: Georgetown University Press, 1964.

Mukarovsky, Jan (1978), *Structure, Sign and Function*, trans. J. Burbank and P. Steiner, London: Yale University Press.

Munro, Thomas (1967), *The Arts and Their Interrelations*, Cleveland (Ohio) and London: Western Reserve University Press.

Nattiez, Jean-Jacques (1990), *Music and Discourse*, Princeton: Princeton University Press.

Nédoncelle, Maurice (1963), *Introduction à l'esthétique*, Paris: PUF.

Nicoll, Allardyce (1949), *World Drama from Aeschylus to Anouilh*, London: Harrap.

Nietzsche, Friedrich [1872], *The Birth of Tragedy*, trans. Francis Golffing, New York: Doubleday, 1956.

Nietzsche, Friedrich [1876–8], *Human all-too-human: A Book for Free Spirits*, trans. H. Zimmern, Vols 6–7 of *The Complete Works* of Friedrich Nietzsche, ed. O. Levy, 20 vols, Edinburgh and London: T. N. Foulis, 1910.

Nietzsche, Friedrich [1901], *The Will to Power*, trans. Walter Kaufmann and R. J. Hollingdale, New York: Vintage, 1967.

Ogden, C. K. and Richards, I. A. (1972), 'The Meaning of Beauty', in their *The Meaning of Meaning*, 10th edn, London: Routledge & Kegan Paul, pp. 139–59.

Osborne, Harold (ed.) (1972), *Aesthetics*, Oxford: Oxford University Press.

Nöth, Winfried (1990), *Handbook of Semiotics*, Bloomington and Indianapolis: Indiana University Press.

Panofsky, Erwin [1924], *Idea: A Concept in Art Theory*, London: Harper & Row, 1968.

Panofsky, Erwin (1951), *Gothic Architecture and Scholasticism*, Latrobe: Archabbey Press.

Panofsky, Erwin (1969), *Renaissance and Renascences in Western Art*, 2nd edn, New York, Evanston, San Francisco, London: Harper & Row.

Panofsky, Erwin (1975), *La Perspective comme forme symbolique*, Paris: Les Editions du Minuit.

Parsons, Michael J. (1987), *How We Understand Art*, Cambridge: Cambridge University Press.

Parsons, Terence (1975), 'A Meinongian Analysis of Fictional Objects', *Grazer Philosophische Studien*, 1, pp. 73–86.

Pevsner, Nikolaus (1943), *An Outline of European Architecture*, Harmondsworth: Penguin.

Pevsner, Nikolaus (1974), *Pioneers of Modern Design*, 3rd edn,

Harmondsworth: Penguin.

Pfeiffer, John E. (1972), *The Emergence of Man*, New York: Harper & Row.

Pfister, Manfred (1988), *The Theory and Analysis of Drama*, trans. John Halliday, Cambridge: Cambridge University Press.

Plato (1997), *Complete Works*, ed. John M. Cooper, Indianapolis: Hackett.

Plotinus (1966–88), *Enneads*, trans. A. H. Armstrong, 6 vols, London: Heinemann; Cambridge (Mass.): Harvard University Press.

Pratt, Carroll (1968), *The Meaning of Music*, New York: Johnson Reprint Corp.

Pseudo-Dionysius (1987), *Complete Works*, trans. Colm Luibheid, London: SPCK Press.

Quintilian (1920–1), *Institutio oratoria*, trans. H. E. Butler, 4 vols, London: Heinemann; Cambridge (Mass.): Harvard University Press.

Rameau, Jean Philippe [1722], *Treatise on Harmony*, New York: Dover, 1971.

Read, Herbert (1977), *The Meaning of Art*, 2nd edn, London: Faber & Faber (1st edn 1931).

Richards, I. A. (1926), *Principles of Literary Criticism*, London: Routledge & Kegan Paul.

Richardson, Tony and Stangos, Nikos (eds) (1974), *Concepts in Modern Art*, Harmondsworth: Penguin.

Robertson, Alec and Stevens, Denis (eds) (1960), *The Pelican History of Music*, Harmondsworth: Penguin.

Robinson, Jenifer (ed.) (1997), *Meaning and Music*, Ithaca: Cornell University Press.

Rookmaaker, H. R. (1973), *Modern Art and the End of a Culture*, 2nd edn, London: Inter-Varsity Press.

Rosenkranz, Karl (1853), *Aesthetik des Hässlichen*, Königsberg: Verlag der Gebrüder Bornträger.

Rousseau, Jean-Jacques [1781], *Essai sur l'origine des langues où il est parlé de la mélodie et de l'imitation musicale*, Bordeaux: Ducros, 1970 (English trans., with J. G. Herder [1772], *Essay on the Origins of Language*, trans. J. H. Moran and A. Gode, Chicago and London: University of Chicago Press, 1986).

Rousseau, Jean-Jacques [1743], *Project Concerning New Symbols in Music*, trans. B. Rainbow, Kilkenny: Boethius Press, 1982.

Ruskin, John (n.d.), *The Works of John Ruskin*, 26 vols, New York: United States Books Co.

Ruskin, John (1910), *The Seven Lamps of Architecture*, 2nd edn, London: Routledge & Kegan Paul.

Ruskin, John (1978), *Lectures on Architecture and Painting*, New York and London: Garland.

Sadie, Stanley (ed.) (1980), *The New Grove Dictionary of Music and Musicians*, 20 vols, London: Macmillan.

Saint-Martin, Fernand (1990), *Semiotics and Visual Language*, Bloomington and Indianapolis: Indiana University Press.

Santoro-Brienza, Liberato (1993), *The Tortoise and the Lyre*, Dublin: Irish Academic Press.

Santoro-Brienza, Liberato and Eco, Umberto (1998), *Talking of Joyce*, Dublin: UCD Press.

Sartre, Jean-Paul [1940], *The Psychology of Imagination*, London: Methuen, 1972.

Sartre, Jean-Paul (1950), *What is Literature?*, trans. Bernard Frechtman, London: Methuen.

Saussure, Ferdinand de [1916], *Course in General Linguistics*, ed. C. Bally and A. Sechehaye, in collaboration with A. Reidlinger, trans. Wade Baskin, Glasgow: Fontana/Collins, 1974.

Scamozzi, Vincenzo [1615], *L'idea della architettura universale*, facsimile ed, Ridgewood (New Jersey): Gregg Press, 1964.

Schaper, Eva (1968), *Prelude to Aesthetics*, London: Allen & Unwin.

Schaper, Eva (1979), *Studies in Kant's Aesthetics*, Edinburgh: Edinburgh University Press.

Scharf, Aaron (1974), *Art and Photography*, Harmondsworth: Penguin.

Schelling, Friedrich W. J. [1859], *Philosophie der Kunst*, Darmstadt: Wissenschaftliche Buchgesellschaft, 1966.

Schiller, Friedrich [1793–5], *On the Aesthetic Education of Man*, trans. Elizabeth M. Wilkinson and L. A. Willoughby, Oxford: Clarendon Press, 1967.

Schopenhauer, Arthur [1818], *The World as Will and Idea*, 3 vols, trans. R. B. Haldane and J. Kemp, London: Routledge & Kegan Paul, 1886.

Schopenhauer, Arthur [1851], *Parerga and Paralipomena*, 2 vols, trans. E. F. J. Payne, Oxford: Clarendon Press, 1974.

Scruton, Roger (1997), *The Aesthetics of Music*, Oxford: Oxford University Press.

Seashore, Carl (1967), *Psychology of Music*, New York: Dover.

Serlio Sebastiano [1537–47], *The Book of Architecture* [*L'Architettura*], facsimile of London edn of 1611, New York: Benjamin Blom, 1970.

Sextus Empiricus (1933–49), *Against the Logicians* [*Adversus Mathematicos*], in *Sextus Empiricus*, trans. R. G Bury, 4 vols, London: Heinemann; Cambridge (Mass.): Harvard University Press, Vol. 2 (reprinted 1939–61; Vol. 2, 1961).

Sheppard, Anne (1987), *Aesthetics: An Introduction to the Philosophy of Art*, Oxford: Oxford University Press.

Shklovsky, Viktor [1917], 'Art as Technique', in *Russian Formalist Criticism*, ed. Lee T. Lemon and Marion J. Rees, Lincoln (Nebraska): University of Nebraska Press, 1965.

Silverman, Hugh J. (ed.) (1990), *Postmodernism – Philosophy and the Arts*, New York and London: Routledge.

Sloboda, John (1985), *The Musical Mind*, Oxford: Clarendon Press.

Souriau, Etienne (1947), *La Correspondance des arts*, Paris: Flammarion.

Stravinsky, Igor (1936), *An Autobiography*, London: Calder & Boyars; New York: Norton, 1962.

Stravinsky, Igor [1947], *Poetics of Music*, trans. Arthur Knodel and Ingolf Dahl, Cambridge (Mass.): Harvard University Press.

Tarasti, Eero (1994), *A Theory of Music Semiotics*, Bloomington and Indianapolis: Indiana University Press.

Tatarkiewicz, Wladyslaw (1971), 'What is Art? The Problem of Definition Today', *The British Journal of Aesthetics*, 11, pp. 134–53.

Tatarkiewicz, Wladyslaw (1970–4), *History of Aesthetics*, 3 vols, The Hague and Paris: Mouton; Warsaw: Polish Scientific Publishers.

Tinctoris, Johannes [c. 1495], *Dictionary of Musical Terms* [*Terminorum musicae diffinitorium*], trans. C. Parrish, New York: Free Press of Glencoe, 1963.

Townsend, Dabney (1997), *An Introduction to Aesthetics*, Oxford: Blackwell.

Vasari [1568], *Lives of the Artists*, a selection trans. George Bull, Harmondsworth: Penguin, 1965.

Vattimo, Gianni (1988), *The End of Modernity*, London: Polity Press.

Venturi, Lionello (1964), *Storia della critica d'arte*, 4th edn, Torino: Einaudi.

Vico, Giambattista [1744], *The New Science*, rev. trans. of 3rd edn, T. C. Bergin and M. H. Fisch, Ithaca: Cornell University Press, 1968.

Vico, Giambattista (1982), *Selected Writings*, ed. and trans. Leon Pompa, Cambridge: Cambridge University Press.

Vitruvius (1931–4), *On Architecture* [*De Architectura*], trans. Frank Granger, 2 vols, London: Heinemann; New York: Putnams.

Wallis, Brian and Tucker, Marcia (eds) (1984), *Art After Modernism: Rethinking Representation*, New York: The New Museum of Contemporary Art; Boston: David R. Godine Publisher.

Webster, T. B. L. (1956), *Greek Theatre Production*, London: Methuen.

Wind, Edgar (1980), *Pagan Mysteries in the Renaissance*, 2nd edn, Oxford: Oxford University Press.

Wölfflin, Heinrich [1932], *Principles of Art History*, trans. M. D. Hottinger, New York: Dover, 1950.

Wollheim, Richard (1980), 'The Institutional Theory of Art', in his *Art and Its Objects*, 2nd edn, Cambridge: Cambridge University Press, pp. 157–66.

Wollheim, Richard (1987), *Painting as an Art*, Princeton: Princeton University Press; London: Thames & Hudson.

Worringer, Wilhelm [1908], *Abstraction and Empathy*, trans. Michael Bullock, London: Routledge & Kegan Paul, 1953.

Xenophon (1923), *Memorabilia and Oeconomicus*, trans. E. C. Marchant, London: Heinemann; Cambridge (Mass.): Harvard University Press.

Yanal, Robert J. (ed.) (1994), *Institutions of Art*, University Park, Pennsylvania: Pennsylvania State University Press.

Zarlino, Gioseffo [1558], *The Art of Counterpoint*, Part 3 of *Le istitutioni harmoniche*, trans. G. A. Marco and C. V. Palisca, New Haven and London: Yale University Press, 1968.

Zarlino, Gioseffo [1558], *On the Modes*, Part 4 of *Le istitutioni harmoniche*, trans. V. Cohen, New Haven and London: Yale University Press, 1983.

Zevi, Bruno (1957), *Architecture as Space: How to Look at Architecture*, trans. Milton Gendel, New York: Horizon Press.

Zima, Peter V. (1999), *The Philosophy of Modern Literary Theory*, London: Athlone Press.

Index

Absolute, 86, 88–9, 209
acoustics, music, 22, 182–3
acoustics for theatre, 156
acting, stage/film, 143–6, 156–7
Adorno, Theodor, 182
aesthetic experience, 56, 62–3, 83–4,
    95–6, 196–8
Alain, 111, 198
Alan of Lille, 58–9, 66
Alberti, Leon Battista, 70, 73, 191,
    200, 208
analogy principle, 57–9
anthropocentrism, 17–18
Apollonian impulse, 97–8
appetitus, 59, 60, 61–2
Appia, Adolphe, 150, 154
Aquinas, Thomas, 51, 57–66, 72
    aesthetic experience, 62–3
    art, 65–6
    beauty, 59–65
    Comm. Div. Nom., 59, 62, 63
    Comm. Nic. Eth., 61
    Comm. Phys., 65
    integrity, 63–4
    Summa Theologiae, 59, 60, 61,
        63, 64, 65, 66
architecture, 107, 189
    definition, 190, 193–4
    etymology, 190
    functionalism, 192
    history of, 194–6, 198
    and human body, 197
    postmodernism, 103–4, 196
    and sculpture, 200–1
    styles, 192, 194–8
    theories of, 73–4, 109, 190–8
    value of, 110, 196–8
    see also Vitruvius

d'Arezzo, Guido, 166–7, 174
Aristotle, 4, 33–44
    action, 39–40
    art/nature, 34–6, 38
    beauty, 33, 41
    diction, 43–4
    as influence, 45, 57, 65, 72
    Metaphysics, 22, 41
    mimesis, 36–42
    music, 173
    narrative, 159
    Nicomachean Ethics, 34, 36, 41
    Physics, 34–5, 36, 38
    poetic theory, 21, 33–44, 133–4
    Poetics, 4, 5, 36, 37, 38, 39, 40,
        41–2, 43, 75, 108, 114, 133–4,
        136
    Politics, 41–2
    Rhetoric, 4, 43–4, 75
    tragedy, 42–3
    truth, 133–4, 161
    verisimilitude, 38–42
Ars Nova, 167
art
    and Absolute, 86, 88–9, 209
    and artefacts, 9–13, 19–21, 105–6
    autonomy, xi–xii, 49–50, 67,
        71–2, 189–90
    and beauty, 5–8, 33
    classifications, 9–13, 111, 112
    context, 11–12, 189
    crisis, 89–92, 98, 103
    history of, 19–20, 23, 66, 88, 89,
        104, 107–8, 111, 205
    institutional theory, 7–8, 12
    language of, 106–7
    mimesis, 33
    minor arts, 9, 111, 112

nature, 29, 34–6, 38–9, 42, 65,
72–3, 105
philosophy, 84–5
and signs, 106–7, 108
spiritual contents, 41, 42, 87–8
subject, 75–80
truth, 57, 71–2, 87, 101–2
value of, 13
verisimilitude, 40–1, 75
art, works of, 6–8, 11, 189–90
artefacts, 9–13, 105, 106
epistemic metaphors, 90
plastic, 198–9
social/solitary, 111
spatial/temporal, 111, 112
static, 198
symbolic, 88, 109
artefacts, 3, 13, 19–20
artistic, 9–13, 19–21, 105–6
context, 11–12
arts, 71, 91, 94, 107–14, 163–4
see also fine arts; minor arts
Artusi, Giovanni Maria, 175–6
audience, 157–9
auditorium, 153, 155–6
Auerbach, Erich, 131
Augustine, Saint, 53–7, 140, 174
author, death of, 122–5
avant-garde, 103, 200, 203, 205,
207–8

Bach, Johann Sebastian, 169
Bacon, Francis, 14, 78, 135
Baroque era, 197, 202–3
Barthes, Roland, 122–3, 124, 147–8,
194
Baumgarten, Alexander, 3–4, 78
beauty, 5, 6, 56, 91, 93
Aquinas, 59–65
Aristotle, 33, 41
art, 5–6, 33
Augustine, Saint, 54, 56
Bacon, 14
Dante, 69
Herbart, 94
Leibniz, 77–8
Nietzsche, 96–7
objectivity, 27–8
Plato, 26–8
Plotinus, 47–51
Pseudo-Dionysius, 51–2

Pythagoreans, 23
relativism, 24–5
Renaissance, 67
Socrates, 25–6
Sophists, 24–5
transcendental, 51–2, 54–6, 57–9,
62–3
Vitruvius, 73
Beethoven, Ludwig van, 93, 94
Blake, William, 134
Boethius, 174
Boileau, Nicolas, xi, 77
Brelet, Gisèle, 184
Browne, Sir Thomas, 45
Bruno, Giordano, 71, 72
Burke, Edmund, 1, 5, 79, 80
Byzantines, 52, 53, 88, 195, 197, 206

Cage, John, 7, 173
Campanella, Tommaso, 71, 72, 78
cave paintings, 19–20
Cennino Cennini, 72, 74–5, 208
Chomsky, Noam, 118, 119–20
chords, 171–2, 184, 186–7
Christianity, 16–17, 45, 53–4, 174
cinema, 11, 114, 138
colour
clarity, 63, 64–5
music, 172
painting, 203–4
Combarieu, Jules, 181
Cooke, Deryck, 184, 186–7, 188
Le Corbusier, 192, 197
costume, 146–8, 156–7
craft/skill, 5, 20–1
see also téchne
creativity, 32–3
criticism, 4–5, 103, 115, 132
Croce, Benedetto, 5, 80, 110–11,
115, 117, 118

dance, 11, 107, 111, 138, 163
Dante Alighieri, 4, 67–70, 130
Descartes, René, 17, 67, 76, 77
design, 74–5
Dickie, George, 7–8, 12
diction, 43–4
Diffey, T. J., 8
Dionysiac impulse, tragedy, 97–8
drama
architecture for, 139, 155

conventions, 156, 157–8
elements, 107, 141–61
etymology, 159
history of, 97–8, 139–41, 149–50
human body, 142–3
language, 159
space/time, 158–9
theories of, 97–8, 114
tragedy, 42–3, 44, 97–8, 151
value of, 116, 139, 141
see also audience; auditorium;
    costume; gesture; lighting;
    scenery; theatres
Dufrenne, Mikel, 112
Dürer, Albrecht, 70, 204

Eco, Umberto, 44, 90, 185, 193–4,
    196
Egyptians, 195, 197, 200, 201
eídos, 36, 38
emotions, music, 185–6
empathy, 50–1, 209
empiricism, 76, 78–80
epochs, historical, 15, 16–18
Existentialism, 98–9, 100, 128–9
Expressionism, 150–1

feminist criticism, 132
Fichte, Johan Gottlieb, 84
Ficino, Marsilio, 71, 72, 75
fiction, 127–30
Fielding, Henry, 158
fine arts, 9, 29, 49–51, 107–14
Fischer, Ernst, 2
Flaubert, Gustav, 131–2
Formalism, 92–5, 103, 183–4, 185,
    190, 191–2
see also Russian Formalism
Forms, Theory of (Plato), 26–33
Forster, E. M., 161
Foucault, Michel, 122–3, 142
Freud, Sigmund, 18
functionalism, 25–6, 192
Futurists, 170

Galenus, Claudius, 199
Garlandia, Johannes de, 174
Genette, Gérard, 159
genres, 117–18
gesture, stage, 143–4
Giorgione, 206

Giotto di Bondone, 206
Glareanus, Henricus, 168, 175
God, 45–6, 57–8, 65, 66, 68, 200
Goethe, J. W. von, 67
goodness, 59, 60, 62
Gothic arts, 88, 195–6, 197–8, 202,
    206
Gray, Cecil, ix–x
Greeks, 16
architecture, 190, 195, 197
art, 23, 89, 107–8
drama, 97–8, 114, 139–40, 149,
    155
literature, 117
music, 164–6, 173
painting, 205
poetry, 21
sculpture, 199–200, 201
see also Aristotle; Plato

Hamburger, Käte, 126
Hanslick, Eduard, 94–5, 180–1
harmonic resonances, 176–7, 183
harmony, 2, 161–2, 167, 168–9,
    171–2
Augustine, Saint, 55
Kant, 82
Pythagoreans, 22–3
Hegel, G. W. F.
Aesthetics, 87–9
art, 3, 79, 86–7, 88, 89–92, 102–3,
    109, 208–9
human body, 142
Idealism, 67, 81, 86
music, 109, 178
Plato, 34
poetry, 109–10
on Romanticism, 90
on Schiller, 83
subjectivity, 76
truth, 86, 88–9
Volksgeist, 15, 88
Heidegger, Martin, 100, 101–2, 112
Helmholtz, Hermann von, 182–3
Heraclitus, 22, 24
Herbart, Johann Friedrich, 92–4,
    180–1, 209
Hesiod, 20, 117
Homer, 20, 21, 117, 130
Horace, 5, 108
Hroswitha, Abbess, 140

Hucbald of Saint Amand, 166
human body, 20, 138–9, 142–3, 144, 197
Humanism, 17–18, 67, 70, 71
Hume, David, 78–9
Hutcheson, Francis, 5, 6, 79, 80

Idealism, 67, 81, 86, 94, 109, 123–4
Impressionism, 207, 209
inspiration, 32–3
institutional theory of art, 7–8, 12
Intellect, 47

Joyce, James, 123, 125, 126, 130, 135

Kafka, Franz, 163
tó kalón, 5, 27
Kant, Immanuel, 80–5, 95, 177–8, 208
katharsis, 42–3
Keats, John, 126
Kierkegaard, Sören, 98–100
Kircher, Athanasius, 187–8
knowledge, 3–4, 61, 72

Lalo, Charles, 113
Langer, Susanne, 184, 185
Lawrence, D. H., 130
Leibniz, G. W., 77–8, 80
Leonardo da Vinci, 4, 72, 73, 189, 206, 208
Lessing, Gotthold, 93, 108–9, 110, 111–12, 204
Lévi-Strauss, Claude, 184, 187
light, painting, 52, 203–4
lighting, stage, 152–4
Lissa, Zofia, 181–2
literature
    definition of, 107, 116, 118–19, 120–5
    functions, 11, 120–1, 132
    history of, 72, 117–18
    and language, 118–20, 121–2
    theories of, 100–1, 103–4, 120–5
    truth, 119, 125–35
    value of, 125, 129–30, 135–7
    see also fiction; poetry
Locke, John, 78, 125
Logical Positivism, 121–2, 125
love, 69

Mallarmé, Stéphane, 116
Marxism, 181–2
meaning, 68–9
    artefactual, 105–6
    gesture, 144
    language, 101, 121–2
    music, 184–5
    speech, 146
medieval epoch see Middle Ages
Meinong, Alexius, 128
melodrama, 176–7
melody, 163, 171, 175
Mendelssohn, Moses, 80, 81
metaphysics, 27, 33, 34, 51–2, 93, 95
Michelangelo, 191, 197, 200, 202
Middle Ages
    architecture, 195–6
    art, 66
    arts classified, 71, 108
    beauty, 5
    music, 173–4
    sculpture, 201–2
    theocentrism, 16–17, 45–6, 57–8
mimesis, 33
    Aristotle, 36–40
    Plato, 27, 29–30, 36–7
    Platonists, 75
    Plotinus, 49–50
    Renaissance, 208
minor arts, 9, 111, 112
modernism, 91, 176–7, 196, 207
Monteverdi, Claudio, 168
Moore, Henry, 203
Mozart, Wolfgang Amadeus, 99
Munro, Thomas, 113–14
music
    aesthetics, 174, 175
    definition, 107, 109
    elements of, 163, 165–73, 175, 183, 188
    functions, 10–11, 165
    history of, 75, 163–70, 173–88
    language of, 107, 179, 184–8
    and melodrama, 176–7
    silence, 7, 170, 173
    theories of, 21–3, 54, 93, 94–5, 109, 177–88
    see also opera
musica artificiosa, 167

musica pathetica, 187–8
musical dictionaries, 188
musical instruments, 166, 167, 168
musical notation, 166
musical theory, 165, 168, 174
musique concrète, 170, 187
Mussorgsky, Modest, 172
myth, 179–80, 187

narrative, 159–61
nature, 1–2, 36, 38–9
    Aquinas, 65–6
    art, 29, 34–6, 38–9, 42, 65, 72–3,
      105
    God, 45–6
    music, 177
Nédoncelle, Maurice, 112–13
Neoplatonism, 46, 54, 72, 174, 202
Nietzsche, Friedrich, 96–8, 180
nominalism, 7, 103
Nous, 47

objectivity, 27–8, 54
onomatopoeia, 144, 145, 151
ontocentrism, 16
opera, 107, 110, 152, 168
oral storytelling, 159

painting
    definition of, 107, 108, 109,
      203–4
    elements of, 203–4
    function, 189
    history of, 205–8
    theories of, 52, 72, 74–5, 109,
      204–9
paleolithic art, 19–20
Palestrina, Giovanni, 167–8
perspective, 149, 150, 205
Peruzzi, Baldassare, 149
Pfeiffer, John E., 19–20
philosophy, ix–x, 84–5, 87, 92–3
pitch, 145, 163, 171
Plato, 45
    aesthetics, 4, 33–4
    architecture, 190
    art, 28–9, 30–3
    beauty, 26–8
    Forms theory, 26–33
    Hippias Major, 24, 27

Ion, 32
Laws, 30–1
metaphysics, 27, 33, 34
mimesis, 27, 29–30, 36–7
Phaedo, 165, 173
Phaedrus, 32, 33
Republic, 30, 31, 32, 133
Sophist, 28–9
Symposium, 28, 32
Timaeus, 28
Platonism, 72, 75, 174
Plotinus, 46–51, 174
poetics, 4, 21, 33, 39–40, 91
poetry, 21, 39–40, 84, 100, 117
    Dante, 69–70
    Hegel, 109–10
poíesis, 5, 37
Polyclitus, 4, 199
polyphony, 166, 167, 171–2, 175
Positivism, 181
    see also Logical Positivism
postmodernism, 18
    architecture, 103–4, 196
    art, 104, 111
    literature, 103–4, 125
    music, 170
    painting, 207–8
Prague Structuralists, 120
praxis, 38–40, 79–80
Prokofiev, Sergei, 172
proportion, 48, 63, 64
prosodic features, 145–6
Pseudo-Dionysius, 51–3, 59, 63
psychoacoustics, 183
Pythagoreans, 21–3, 64, 165, 173

Quintilian, 143–4

Rameau, Jean Philippe, 172, 176–7,
    182
rationalism, 77–8
realism, 130–3, 150
Reformation, 17, 167–8
relativism, 24–5, 77
Renaissance, 5, 17–18, 67, 70–2
    architecture, 198
    drama, 140–1, 149–50, 155
    human body, 142
    mimesis, 208
    music, 75, 163–4, 175–6

painting, 205, 206
sculpture, 202
subjectivity, 67, 70–1
representation, 131–3, 134, 159–61,
204–5
rhythm, 171, 183–4
Richards, I. A., 121–2, 125
Rilke, Rainer Maria, 134
Romans, 140, 190, 195, 197, 205–6
Romantics, 83, 86, 88, 90, 109,
177–80, 192
Rosenkranz, Karl, 91–2
Rousseau, Jean Jacques, 177
Ruskin, John, 191
Russian Formalists, 120

Sartre, Jean-Paul, 100, 128
Saussure, Ferdinand de, 118–19,
120
Scamozzi, Vincenzo, 191
scenery, stage, 149–52, 154, 156–7
Schelling, F. W. J. von, 84–5
Schiller, J. C. F. von, 83–4
Schlegel, Friedrich, 90–1
Schloezer, Boris de, 184, 185
Schönberg, Arnold, 169–70, 182
Schopenhauer, Arthur, 95–6, 110,
178–9
Scott, Walter, 130–1
sculpture
and architecture, 200–1
definition, 198–9
etymology, 198–9
Greek, 109, 199–200, 201, 202
history, 200–3
theories of, 199–200
value of, 201–3
self-referentiality, 124, 189–90
semiotics, 106, 123, 185
sense experience, 61, 78–9, 112–13
Serlio, Sebastiano, 140–1, 149
Sextus Empiricus, 23
Shakespeare, William, 70, 71, 126,
128, 134, 138
Shaw, Bernard, 160
signifiers/signified, 147–8, 152, 159
silence, 7, 170, 173
Socrates, 25–6
Sophists, 23–5

Soul, 47, 81
Souriau, Etienne, 111–12
spatiality, 111, 112, 158–9, 204
speech, 145, 146, 160
    see also diction
Stockhausen, Karl Heinz, 170
Stravinsky, Igor, 171, 172, 182,
183–4
structuralism, 103, 106, 125
subjectivity, 6, 75–80, 82
modern, 17–18
Renaissance, 67, 70–1
Schelling, 85
time, 112
Symbolism, 150

téchne, 5, 34, 37
teleology, 36, 38, 42, 65–6, 81, 83
temperament, musical, 169
texts and authors, 122–3
theatres, 139, 140–1, 155–7
theocentrism, 16–17, 45–6, 57–8
Theon of Smyrna, 22–3
timbre, 146, 172
time, 111, 112, 126, 127, 158–9
Tinctoris, Johannes, 175
Tolstoy, Leo, 128, 135
tragedy, 42–3, 44, 97–8, 151
Troyes, Chrétien de, 131

ugliness, 56, 91–2, 98

Venus, paleolithic, 19–20, 200
verisimilitude, 38–42, 75
Vico, Giambattista, 17, 79–80, 177
Vischer, Friedrich Theodor, 209
Vitale, A., 192
Vitruvius, 72, 73–4, 149, 151–2, 191,
197
Volksgeist, 15, 88

Wagner, Richard, 155, 169, 172,
179–80
Wordsworth, William, 125

Xenophon, 25

Zarlino, Gioseffo, 175–6, 182
Zevi, Bruno, 192